# Food Cultures of Japan

**Recent Titles in
The Global Kitchen**

Food Cultures of the United States: Recipes, Customs, and Issues
*Bruce Kraig*

Food Cultures of Israel: Recipes, Customs, and Issues
*Michael Ashkenazi*

Food Cultures of France: Recipes, Customs, and Issues
*Maryann Tebben*

Food Cultures of Mexico: Recipes, Customs, and Issues
*R. Hernandez-Rodriguez*

# FOOD CULTURES OF JAPAN

## Recipes, Customs, and Issues

Jeanne Jacob

The Global Kitchen

An Imprint of ABC-CLIO, LLC
Santa Barbara, California • Denver, Colorado

Copyright © 2022 by ABC-CLIO, LLC

All rights reserved. No part of this publication may be reproduced, stored in a retrieval system, or transmitted, in any form or by any means, electronic, mechanical, photocopying, recording, or otherwise, except for the inclusion of brief quotations in a review, without prior permission in writing from the publisher.

The publisher has done its best to make sure the instructions and/or recipes in this book are correct. However, users should apply judgment and experience when preparing recipes, especially parents and teachers working with young people. The publisher accepts no responsibility for the outcome of any recipe included in this volume and assumes no liability for, and is released by readers from, any injury or damage resulting from the strict adherence to, or deviation from, the directions and/or recipes herein. The publisher is not responsible for any reader's specific health or allergy needs that may require medical supervision, nor for any adverse reactions to the recipes contained in this book. All yields are approximations.

**Library of Congress Cataloging-in-Publication Data**

Names: Jacob, Jeanne, author.
Title: Food cultures of Japan : recipes, customs, and issues / Jeanne Jacob.
Description: Santa Barbara, California : Greenwood, an imprint of ABC-CLIO, LLC, [2022] | Series: The global kitchen | Includes bibliographical references and index.
Identifiers: LCCN 2021012448 (print) | LCCN 2021012449 (ebook) | ISBN 9781440866838 (hardcover) | ISBN 9781440866845 (ebook)
Subjects: LCSH: Food habits—Japan. | Cooking, Japanese. | Japan—Social life and customs.
Classification: LCC GT2853.J3 J33 2021 (print) | LCC GT2853.J3 (ebook) | DDC 394.1/20952—dc23
LC record available at https://lccn.loc.gov/2021012448
LC ebook record available at https://lccn.loc.gov/2021012449

ISBN: 978-1-4408-6683-8 (print)
        978-1-4408-6684-5 (ebook)

26 25 24 23 22    1 2 3 4 5

This book is also available as an eBook.

Greenwood
An Imprint of ABC-CLIO, LLC

ABC-CLIO, LLC
147 Castilian Drive
Santa Barbara, California 93117
www.abc-clio.com

This book is printed on acid-free paper ∞

Manufactured in the United States of America.

# Contents

*Series Foreword* — vii
*Preface* — ix
*Introduction* — xi
*Chronology* — xvii

**Chapter One**   Food History — 1
**Chapter Two**   Influential Ingredients — 25
**Chapter Three**  Appetizers and Side Dishes — 57
**Chapter Four**   Main Dishes — 75
**Chapter Five**   Desserts — 95
**Chapter Six**    Beverages — 111
**Chapter Seven**  Holidays and Special Occasions — 129
**Chapter Eight**  Street Food and Snacks — 147
**Chapter Nine**   Dining Out — 165
**Chapter Ten**    Food Issues and Dietary Concerns — 183

*Glossary* — 201
*Bibliography* — 215
*Index* — 223

# Series Foreword

Imagine a typical American breakfast: bacon, eggs, toast, and home fries from the local diner. Or maybe a protein-packed smoothie, sipped on the go to class or work. In some countries in Europe, breakfast might just be a small cookie and a strong coffee, if anything at all. A South African breakfast might consist of a bowl of corn porridge with milk. In Japan, breakfast might look more like dinner, complete with rice, vegetables, and fish. What we eat varies from country to country, and even region to region. The *Global Kitchen* series explores the cuisines of different cultures around the world, from the history of food and food staples to main dishes and contemporary issues. Teeming with recipes to try at home, these volumes will delight readers by discovering other cultures through the lens of a treasured topic: food.

Each volume focuses on the culinary heritage of one country or one small group of countries, covering history and contemporary culture. Volumes begin with a chronology of major food-related milestones and events in the area, from prehistory to present. Chapters explore the key foods and meals in the country, covering the following topics:

- Food History;
- Influential Ingredients;
- Appetizers and Side Dishes;
- Main Dishes;
- Desserts;
- Beverages;
- Holidays and Special Occasions;
- Street Foods and Snacks;
- Dining Out; and
- Food Issues and Dietary Concerns.

Chapters are textual, and each chapter is accompanied by numerous recipes, adding a hands-on component to the series. Sidebars, a glossary of important terms, and a selected bibliography round out each volume, providing readers with additional information and resources for their personal and scholarly research needs.

Whether readers are looking for recipes to use for classes or at home, or to explore the histories and traditions of world cuisines, the *Global Kitchen* series will allow readers to fully immerse themselves in other cultures, giving a taste of typical daily life and tradition.

# Preface

What is food like in Japan today? It is certainly not all raw fish, despite sushi and sashimi topping the list of Japanese diners' favorites. Nor is it always tempura or steaks on a *teppan*, the offerings of pioneering Japanese restaurants outside Japan. Meals vary widely and—perhaps unsurprisingly in our global age—happily mix local and international dishes, especially in major urban areas. A weekday family breakfast of toast with butter and jam, and eggs with sausages, is not unusual. Lunch for an office worker in a major city such as Tokyo or Osaka could be Vietnamese pho, or Chinese-style fried rice, or Central Asian-flavored noodles. Supper for a young family is likely to be the children's choice of hamburger, eaten with rice, at a family restaurant. In contrast, young working adults prefer to drink and eat at an *izakaya*, where specialty seafoods, such as grilled giant shrimp and crab coral (*kani miso*), are paired with regional craft *sake*, as crisp and dry as white wine. A cold day may be perfect for a nostalgic sweet red bean "soup" with tiny dumplings, and for the evening, a hot-pot (*nabe*) of meat and vegetables, cooked on a tabletop stove. Foods familiar to Americans and some not so familiar, such as *Baumkuchen* and *choux à la crème* (*shū kurīmu*), are widely available. Neighborhood convenience stores (*kombini*) have these and cooked foods too—a hodge-podge stew called *oden* simmering away, grilled skewered chicken (*yakitori*), and meat-filled buns (*nikuman*) piping hot. *Mukokuseki* ("without a nationality") is how many Japanese describe this eclectic, gastronomic landscape common to urban areas.

Since the 1960s, once Japan's economy had recovered from the war, the ideal meal of white rice, miso soup, and pickled vegetables plus two or more side dishes of fresh (*not* salted or preserved) fish and seafood or meat and cooked vegetables had become attainable for the majority. Less than half a century later, however, many are too busy to prepare such a meal other than on weekends. Fifty years ago, every component of a traditional meal would have been prepared from scratch. Each household had its unique way of fermenting miso and vegetable pickles, imbuing them with what is fondly known as *ofukuro no aji* ("the taste of mom's cooking").

Today's lifestyles make the daily re-creation of such meals unfeasible for working people. The variety of cooked dishes readily bought at reasonable prices from supermarkets, department store food sections, and convenience stores makes it too easy not to cook from scratch. Japanese meals today tend to focus less on rice and fish, and more on chicken, pork, beef, and dairy products. With the sheer diversity of ingredients imported from all over the world, nontraditional vegetables, herbs, and other condiments (and ways of cooking and eating them) have become commonplace, not only in specialist kitchens and gourmet restaurants, but in the average home kitchen, too.

# Introduction

## Geography and Climate

Japan is a small country in East Asia comprising 6,852 islands, of which 430 are inhabited. To provide a perspective, it lies on the same latitude as California, with an area slightly smaller. The five major islands from north to south are Hokkaido, Honshu, Shikoku, Kyushu, and Okinawa. Honshu, the main island, is where Tokyo, Osaka, and Kyoto are located, and where the majority live. Japan's position on the Western Pacific's Ring of Fire, at the junction of four active tectonic plates, gives rise to frequent earthquakes (around 1,500 annually) and volcanic activity. Its long, narrow stretch of territory from the Sea of Okhotsk to the Philippine Sea traverses several climate zones, so that northernmost Hokkaido is subarctic, northern Honshu is temperate, and southern Honshu, Kyushu, and Shikoku enjoy a Mediterranean-like subtropical climate, while Okinawa is quite tropical. This broad climatic range provides four seasons that support the production of diverse food crops and livestock. The surrounding seas, with their warm and cold currents, offer a diversity of fish, seafood, and edible seaweeds.

Mountains, including 80 active volcanoes, comprise three-quarters of the land, leaving few level areas for agriculture: the Kanto plain around Tokyo, the Kinki plain in the Osaka-Kyoto region, the Sendai plain in northern Honshu, and the Ishikari plain in Hokkaido. Generous rainfall from seasonal monsoons produces lush vegetation, and this, combined with forested mountains and multiple water features, makes for a landscape of striking beauty. The Japanese attribute their aesthetic sensitivity to their naturally beautiful surroundings. The ever-present threat of disasters from earthquakes, typhoons, volcanic eruptions, and tsunami, combined with the romanticism of its classical art and literature, have produced a cultural awareness of the brevity and preciousness of life, a concept known as *mono no aware* (the fleeting nature of things). Perhaps this may explain the Japanese penchant for creating aesthetic experiences in all aspects of everyday life—above all in the preparation, serving, and partaking of food.

Japan's position 124 miles from the Asian mainland (the Korean peninsula) has shaped its development as a nation, influenced by Korean and Chinese cultures. Nevertheless, despite a shared cultural history, Japan, China, and Korea have developed as distinct nations with distinctive food and food cultures. Despite some shared preparation methods and ingredients, the individual taste principles, manner of serving, and sociocultural contexts of the cuisines of China, Korea, and Japan make them unique and completely different from each other.

## Food Culture

Japanese traditional cuisine comprises seven styles: *honzen ryōri* (formal banquet cuisine), *cha kaiseki* (tea ceremony formal cuisine), *kaiseki* (haute cuisine), *shōjin ryōri* (Buddhist vegetarian cuisine), *kyōdo ryōri* (regional cuisine), *gyōji ryōri* (celebratory and festival dishes), and *katei ryōri* (home cooking). Additionally, Western-style cooking (*yōshoku*) and Chinese-style cooking (*chūka ryōri*) are now so thoroughly assimilated that they are accepted as Japanese. However, they are distinct from authentic cuisines, referred to by country, such as *itaria ryōri* (Italian), *furansu ryōri* (French), *chūgoku ryōri* (Chinese), or *taiwan ryōri* (Taiwanese).

A characteristic common to the formal traditional cuisines is their aesthetic quality. A formal Japanese table arrangement is a visual feast. In contrast to the homogeneity of Western tableware, Japanese formal table settings combine vessels made of different materials that display food in the most complementary manner. Shallow plates (whether rectangles, triangles, or other polygons) and small deep bowls of porcelain, wood, lacquer, glass, or rough-glazed stoneware share space with tiny baskets, aspidistra leaves, or hollowed-out bamboo culms. Leaves, flowers, stalks, and other parts of edible, cultivated and wild plants adorn dishes to denote the seasons, simultaneously contributing their flavors, scents, and colors. Even the simplest home meal is presented with a nod to aesthetics and the season—for example, a *shisō* (perilla) or maple leaf, quickly picked from the garden, to adorn the main dish.

This aestheticism extends to the host's or hostess's demeanor and the quality of welcome toward a guest, a cultural construct called *omotenashi*. *Omotenashi* encompasses not only the way that food and the dining space

*Introduction* xiii

are prepared and presented, but also the attention to and consideration for a diner's comfort, and it is as important to both host and guest as the quality and flavor of the meal. It is this rather intangible aspect of Japanese food culture—encountered equally in the author's experience in specialist restaurants, humble diners, and people's homes—that distinguishes it among the world's food cultures.

## Regional Cooking

The cooking in Japan's 47 prefectures reflects the unique ingredients of their geographic and climate zones. Although modern infrastructure, more efficient distribution, telecommunications, and social media are blurring geographical separation, regional taste preferences nevertheless remain. Hokkaido's food combines the food culture of the original Ainu inhabitants with foods and cooking traditions brought over by migrants from all over Japan when Hokkaido was opened up for settlement in the late 19th century. Once considered too cold for rice growing and more noted for its dairy products, Hokkaido now produces excellent rice, with its newest cultivar Yumepirika rivaling Koshihikari, heretofore considered the tastiest. Its wheat crop is showcased in *rāmen* dishes topped with top-quality crab, sea urchin, and salmon from surrounding seas. Stocks for these noodle broths owe their fine flavor to another local specialty: seaweed, the best in the country.

At the other extreme is Okinawa, the seat of the ancient Ryukyu Kingdom, once a protectorate of China, and annexed to Japan in 1879. Its food culture reflects influences from Chinese culinary tradition, especially its pork dishes. Its iconic vegetable, the bitter melon (*gōya*), is credited with conferring longevity to Okinawa's centenarians. The American military base established there after World War II introduced American dishes to Okinawa much earlier than the rest of the country.

Historically isolated and snowbound regions, such as the Japan Alps and northern Honshu, have a rich repertoire of preserved foods. These include the elaborate pickles of Akita Prefecture, where gourds are stuffed with eggplants, carrots, and chrysanthemum flower petals and packed into *sake* lees (the residue from pressing *sake*) or miso for a year, and which, when sliced crosswise, reveal a striking pattern. Locusts, silkworm larvae, and other aquatic larvae braised in salty-sweet *tsukudani* sauce were once important foods for mountain-locked regions, such as Nagano Prefecture. Although modern transportation has made other protein sources available, these foodstuffs represent local food culture, though now produced solely as tourist souvenirs. Wild ingredients from mountain forests—fungi, fern fronds, tubers, and berries—continue to be relished in rural areas. A few have been propagated, leading to domesticated varieties of wild yams and mushrooms.

Regional variation in foodstuffs is most pronounced in dishes for the New Year and local festivals. In the former whaling communities of Hokkaido and Aomori, the New Year stew (*zōni*) was once enriched with salted back fat from minke whales. Another Hokkaido New Year dish is *izushi* (rice sushi), prepared from salmon, herring, and other fish, with cabbage, giant radish, carrots, ginger, and cooked rice. The same dish is made in northern Honshu combined with mountain fruits, such as akebi berries and wild grapes. *Izushi* is only made in regions with sub-zero temperatures over several months.

However, the most marked distinction in Japan's food cultures is between that of the Kanto region (around Tokyo) and that of the Kansai region (around Kyoto and Osaka). Tokyo's food culture, in particular its style of preparing sushi—*nigirizushi* (hand-shaped sushi) or *Edomaezushi* (Edo-style sushi)—is the one most widely known outside Japan. Kansai-style sushi, called *batterazushi*, in contrast, is formed in a mold. Kanto cooking is robustly flavored with dark miso; Kansai cooking favors sweet, milder flavors with pale miso. As the capital, Tokyo is the modern trendsetter, but historically it was the Kansai region's food culture and artistic sensibility, based on Kyoto's aristocratic and Buddhist tastes and preferences, as well as Osaka's merchant culture, that set their imprint on traditional Japanese cuisine. Japanese meals owe their structure, most cooking methods, presentation on dishes of varying pattern and materials, the use of plant materials as garnishes to denote the seasons, and the formal order of service to Kyoto food culture. This is unsurprising, because the Imperial Court, based in Kyoto, was the arbiter of good taste until 1600, when the Tokugawa family assumed power and established their administrative center in Edo (modern-day Tokyo).

Kyoto cooking is regarded as the finest of Japan's regional food cultures. Being distant from the sea and thus historically dependent on salt-preserved and dried marine ingredients, Kyoto cooks developed ingenious ways of making these ingredients attractive and palatable. They encouraged local farmers to improve the flavor and quality of plant crops. Kyoto vegetables are renowned today for sweetness and depth of flavor, and are responsible for the reputation of Kyoto home-style dishes (*obanzai*) and pickles among Japanese gourmets. Kyoto-bred varieties of winter squash, eggplant, giant radish, and leafy greens are branded vegetables. Whether feeding the imperial court or other aristocrats, Kyoto cooks learned to distract diners' attention from the meager ingredients at their disposal by presenting food in an elaborate and sophisticated manner. First feed the eye, then the belly, is attributed to Kyoto cooks. This luxurious manner of presentation survives in the formal cuisine called *honzen ryōri*.

Similar ingenuity and creativity are evident in the vegetarian meals prepared in Buddhist monasteries and nunneries. At the heart of Buddhist vegetarian food culture (*shōjin ryōri*) is an incredible array of products derived from the soybean—not only as seasonings in the form of miso, soy sauce, and tamari, but also as its curd, tofu, morphed into such diverse and interesting forms, textures, and flavors that no vegetarian could ever feel they were deprived of the pleasures of eating animal-sourced protein.

## Japanese Food in a Global Context

In 2013, *washoku*—the traditional food cultures of the Japanese people—was registered in UNESCO's list of the world's intangible cultural heritage. Outside Japan in 2017, there were more than 117,000 Japanese restaurants, not all serving authentic Japanese food. Innovative restaurants in the Spanish province of Valencia, where the author lives, are adopting Japanese food preparation techniques, although their *bacalao* (cod) tempura and salmon *tataki* bear no resemblance to their authentic counterparts. Japanese ingredients such as *panko*, tempura flour mix, shiitake and enoki mushrooms, *wasabi*, *nori*, soy sauce, frozen *mochi* cakes, and sushi kits are commonplace in supermarkets in Spain, Germany, UK, and elsewhere in Europe. Joint ventures of Japanese and Spanish companies are producing fresh tuna and bonito flakes for distribution throughout Europe. Japanese-style angular plates, motifs, food presentation using flowers and micro-greens as garnishes, and minuscule portions have been adopted worldwide, and not only for Japanese-style foods. Back in the 1960s, French chefs invited to Japan to teach their cuisine discovered *washoku*, and traditional French cuisine has not been the same since.

The application to UNESCO was an intentional display of authentic Japanese traditional food culture, increasingly at risk of misrepresentation through its global dissemination. The application was also an attempt to preserve its integrity at home. Is traditional Japanese food in danger of disappearing altogether, as many food observers in Japan fear? The fear is justly sparked by the spread of "hyphenated" Japanese food worldwide, in part due to the phenomenal success of Nobu Matsuhisa's fusion Japanese-Peruvian food, where sushi and sashimi meet fiery Peruvian *aji* (chili pepper), and David Chang's fusion Japanese-Chinese food focusing on *rāmen*.

An optimistic future for traditional Japanese food culture is provided by the novel dining experience and setting embodied in the new Tokyo restaurant-cum-theater, Suigian. Suigian offers a Noh performance with dinner, its separate courses created by different chefs, in contrast to the traditional *kaiseki* (formal dinner) where all the courses bear the imprint of one chef alone. There is a surging market in regional craft *sake*, each brewery promoting not only the rice and water that distinguish its product, but also providing an appropriate pairing for local gastronomic specialties as well. Home cooks are deepening their interest in regional varieties of *dashi* and pickles, in search of alternatives to industrialized, chemical-laden foods. There is a widespread interest in eating and cooking well, made more extensively accessible to all thanks to social media, specialized food and cooking publications (in print and online), foodie blogs and forums, in addition to television shows, documentaries, videos on YouTube, and films.

With the cross-fertilizing influences of international cuisines on Japanese cuisine and vice versa, diners in Japan are spoiled for choice. One does not have to search far for examples of successful adoption and adaptation of non-Japanese dishes into the Japanese kitchen and table. *Rāmen* is now a typical Japanese noodle dish, and each region has its own distinctive version. More than a century since its introduction, *rāmen* has become as genuinely Japanese as soy sauce and miso, similarly introduced from China and Korea; after centuries of adaptation to local taste, these ingredients have become totally distinct from the Chinese and Korean originals. Tempura, a dish adapted from the Portuguese, is nowadays distinctly Japanese in its combination of seafood and vegetables accompanied by a sauce of freshly grated radish and ginger. However, throughout Japan, the assembly of acceptable ingredients in tempura is rarely the same, owing to regional preferences and tastes. Not all regions offer grated ginger in their tempura dip, for instance. However, a slice of tender ginger may appear, duly dipped in batter, as a tempura ingredient in Matsue city, the capital of Shimane Prefecture. Even in Tokyo, a long-established tempura restaurant only offers fish and seafood—no vegetables—having kept to the original Portuguese recipe as it was introduced and maintained over several generations.

It is this respect for tradition among certain restaurateurs and chefs, and concurrently a spirit of innovation among other restaurateurs and chefs, which ensure that Japanese food and food culture will continue to preserve its identity, and to evolve and develop by adapting novel cooking techniques and global trends to local taste, eventually infusing them with a distinct Japanese character that can only further enrich Japanese food culture.

# Chronology

This chronology is based on dates from recent archaeological research. With new results from ongoing excavations, scientific analyses, and paleobotanical research, certain prehistoric dates are likely to change (the earliest date for Yayoi, for example is 1000 BC or 300 BC). Contemporary technology and methods—flotation, scanning electron micrography, and accelerator mass spectrometry—for analyzing plant and animal remains and artifacts are bound to result in revised (and academically contested) dates.

**35,000–~30,000 BC**
Paleolithic people from mainland Asia reach Japan over land bridges. They hunt or scavenge Naumann's elephant, elk, boar, and fallow deer with stone axes and spears. They broil, smoke, or dry the meat for storage. Wild berries, nuts, bulbs, and roots are foraged.

**~13,500 BC–1000 BC/300 BC**
Earthenware pottery called *jōmon*, referring to their decorative cord marking, appears. Round-bottomed pots are used for boiling, cone-bottomed pots for storage. Lavishly decorated pots may have contained ritual food offerings.

Jōmon people settle in large villages, gather and hunt food communally, undertake rudimentary nurturing of edible trees (chestnut, walnut, hazelnut) and small-scale home cultivation of plants (foxtail millet, broomcorn millet) for additional food.

Inland dwellers eat wild boar, deer, bear, rabbit, fox. Coastal dwellers eat fish—tuna, sea bream, sea bass, whale, and dolphin (sliced, dried, and smoked for storage), clams, and sea snails. Dry cultivation of rice develops. Rice is stored unhusked. Just before cooking, rice grains are pounded to remove the husk, resulting in brown rice porridge.

Buckwheat (*Fagopyrum esculentum*), foxtail millet, broomcorn millet, barnyard millet, and barley are cultivated in areas unsuited for growing rice.

The plant foods foraged and eaten are:

- mulberry, elderberry, wild grapes, silver vine fruits (*Actinidia* species, related to modern-day kiwiberries).
- wild vegetables—gourds (*Lagenaria* species), beans (*Vigna* species), soybeans, goosefoot (*Chenopodium* species), rapes (*Brassica* species).
- wild roots and tubers—lilies (*yuri*), burdock (*Arctium* species), true yams (*Dioscorea* species, e.g., *mizu imo, yama imo*), taro, water chestnuts (*kuro kuwai*), water caltrops (*hishi*).
- roots of *kuzu* vine and bracken (these are pounded for starch).
- chestnuts, horse chestnuts, walnuts, ginkgo nuts, various acorns (*konara, mizunara, kunugi, arakashi, ichiigashi, shii*).
- wild plant seeds, e.g., sesame (*goma*), hemp (*Cannabis* species), and yew (*kaya*), are eaten and pressed for oil.
- Japanese pepper (*sanshō, Zanthoxylum piperitum*), beefsteak plant (*shisō, Perilla frutescens*), ginger, and leek (*Allium* species) for seasoning.

Seawater is boiled down to produce salt by 2000 BC.

### 1000 BC or 300 BC–300 AD, Yayoi Period
Rice cultivation in irrigated paddies develops, brought by two waves of migration from northern China via Korea.

Beans (soybean, *azuki*) and fruits (apricot, peach, pear, plum, melon, watermelon) are brought from the Asian continent, including cultivation methods. Yayoi immigrants also bring bronze and iron-working skills for crafting agricultural tools and weapons (swords, spears).

### 300–538, Kofun Period
Greater food availability from rice cultivation increases the population. Rice becomes the staple of the elite. Commoners pay taxes with rice, but subsist on chestnut, millet, and buckwheat.

A militaristic aristocracy arises, and the country is unified under Yamato imperial rule.

Close contact with the Korean kingdom of Baekje brings Chinese writing, kiln technology for firing ceramics, metallurgy, Korean and Chinese literature, architectural styles, and silkworm breeding.

### 538–710, Asuka Period
In 552 Buddhism is introduced to the aristocracy, through the King of Baekje, and competes with Shinto for imperial favor. The new religion creates political, social, and cultural changes, and rivalry among the aristocracy. Japan's name changes from Wa to Nihon.

### 607
The first Japanese embassy journeys to China to gain knowledge of Chinese ways. Seeds for cultivating tea and new forms of food and porcelain ceramic ware are brought back.

*Chronology*

**675**
Emperor Tenmu bans the eating of wild animals (horse, cattle, birds, monkeys, dogs, except for deer and wild boar) between the fourth and ninth months. Buddhist monasteries develop a vegetable-based cuisine (*shōjin ryōri*).

**710–794, Nara Period**
A permanent imperial capital is established in Nara.

Aristocratic food and commoners' food become highly differentiated. Elite diets become meatless, due to acceptance of Buddhist practices. Among commoners, Buddhism has not spread, and meat of wild deer and boar continues as food.

Chopsticks, metal spoons, footed trays called *zen*, bronze vessels, porcelain and lacquer ware, and glass are tableware for the elite. Common folk use trays called *shiki* and fingers for eating and earthenware bowls and cups.

Chinese fermented soybean paste and brown sugar are adopted for imperial court and Buddhist meals.

Kōbō Daishi, also known as Kūkai, founder of the Shingon sect of Japanese Buddhism, codifies Japanese aesthetic ideals.

**794–1185, Heian Period**
The imperial capital is moved to Heian (modern Kyoto). Court life is luxurious and refined, recorded in diaries, poetry, novels, and paintings. Ceremonies and rituals are lavish, celebrated with elaborate feasts.

**815**
First mention of tea drinking in the Late Japan Chronicles (*Nihon Koki*). Tea becomes an exclusive drink for the elite and Buddhist monks.

**838**
A last embassy is sent to China. From here onward, Japan develops its own identity.

**1185–1333, Kamakura Period**
Factional rivalry in the imperial court brings in the provincial warrior clans Taira and Minamoto, leading to the Gempei War and the end of aristocratic rule. The Minamoto family triumphs and establishes a samurai government in Kamakura, near modern Tokyo. A restrained aesthetic develops in art and food.

**1338–1573, Muromachi/Ashikaga Period**
Portuguese arrive at Tanegashima in 1542, and introduce European firearms, European styles of cooking, and Christianity. Wine, bread, milk, white sugar, and confections made of wheat flour and sugar [*konfeito, alfeito* (Portuguese)]; deep frying (tempura); and baking (*kasutera*, Castella cake) are introduced. Oda Nobunaga is recorded as the first to eat bread.

**1568–1600, Azuchi-Momoyama Period**
Sen no Rikyū establishes principles for the tea ceremony in 1585. *Cha kaiseki* cuisine develops, based on Buddhist temple cooking styles.

## 1600–1868, Edo Period

The Tokugawa clan comes into power and administers the country from Edo (now Tokyo), beginning 300 years of peace and political stability.

Japan is closed to foreigners, and Japanese are not allowed to leave the country. Only Dutch and Chinese traders are permitted in Dejima island, Nagasaki.

Japanese food culture fully develops, with the rise of a moneyed, urban merchant class.

Restaurants serving Western cuisine appear in Nagasaki at Edo period's end.

Tempura becomes a popular street food. Shogun Tokugawa Ieyasu is rumored to have died of overeating red grouper tempura. Restaurants are established in Edo.

### 1643
An anonymous author publishes Japan's first cookbook for the public: *Ryōri Monogatari* (The Story of Cooking), the ancestor of today's cookbooks.

### 1715
Japan's first cookbook specializing in sweets is published: *Kokon Meibutsu Gozengashi Hidenshō* (Secrets of Ancient and Contemporary Famous Confectionery).

### 1785
*Manpo Ryōri Himitsu Bako* (Secret Chest of Myriad Cooking Treasures) is published; it is also known as *Tamago Hyakuchin* (Eggs—A Hundred Wonders), for its 100 egg recipes.

### 1848
A guide to Edo's best specialty restaurants is published, *Edo Meibutsu Shuhan Tebikigusa*.

### 1853
Commodore Perry arrives in Japan and forces the opening of five Japanese ports to foreign trade and settlement, ending the government's national seclusion policy.

### 1859
Foreign traders settle in Yokohama.

### 1868
Fugetsudo becomes the first bakery to cater to Japanese customers. Bread is supplied to the Satsuma clan during its war against the Tokugawa shogunate.

## 1868–1912, Meiji Period

The Tokugawa shogunate ends. The emperor is restored as ruler, and the capital is moved from Kyoto to Edo (now Tokyo). Japan's modernization begins, changing it from a feudal to an industrial state.

### 1871
Tokyo's first Western-style restaurant opens in a hotel in Tsukiji, frequented by Japanese elite. Prices are too high for common folk.

Chronology

**1872**
The first curry rice recipes are published in two Japanese cookbooks featuring Western cooking: *Seiyō Ryōritsu* and *Seiyō Ryōrishinan*.

**1873**
Emperor Meiji lifts the ban on eating beef. *Gyūnabe* (literally, "beef pot," precursor of *sukiyaki*) becomes popular. The domestic beef industry is established in Kobe, Aizu, Tsugaru, Izumo, and Izu.

**1875–1885**
Talented Japanese youth are sent abroad to the United States, UK, Germany, and France to study Western sciences, engineering, and law, and bring back their expertise. Foreign instructors are employed to teach Western subjects (e.g., sciences, technology, law, literature, and philosophy) at Japanese universities.

**1875–1883**
Bakeries making Western-style bread and pastries take off. Fugetsudo bakery makes Western-style biscuits and pastries. Kimuraya creates fusion bread: *anpan* with sweet bean filling. In 1883, Tokyo Western-style bakeries total 116.

**1877**
The Dainippon Yamanashi Budōshū Kaisha starts industrial wine production; it closes down after 10 years.

**1904–1905**
Strawberry jam is introduced after the Russo-Japanese War. Japan sinks the Russian Far-East Fleet in Tsushima Straits, the first victory of a non-European country over a major European one.

**1905**
Magazines for women promote new cooking methods, menus, and recipes.

**1907**
Thirty-six Western-style restaurants are established in the newer parts of Tokyo, popularizing *hayashi raisu* (beef hash and rice), *karē raisu* (curry rice), croquettes, and deep-fried pork cutlets.

**1912–1926, Taisho Period**
*Karē raisu*, Friday fare for the Japanese navy, is introduced to home kitchens by crews on home leave.

*Karē raisu*, *tonkatsu* (pork cutlet), and *korokke* (croquettes) appear in home meals.

Western vegetables are introduced, cultivated, and sold commercially: cabbage, potatoes, tomatoes, carrots, onions.

Coffee drinking and coffee shops spread beyond Nagasaki, Kobe, and Yokohama to the general population.

Western-style sweets—ice cream, lemonade, chocolate, candy—already introduced during the previous era, become affordable to common folk. The Morinaga

Confectionery Company introduces milk caramel in 1913, milk chocolate and wafers in 1923.

**1919**
First sweetened fermented milk drink, Calpis, is introduced.

**1924**
Yamazaki, Japan's first Western-style distillery, produces whisky.

**1926–1989, Showa Period**
Ministry of Education launches school lunch programs in 1932 to improve child nutrition.

Food models by Takichi Iwasaki are used in department-store dining rooms.

**1937**
Second Sino-Japanese war starts. *Hinomaru bentō* ("rising sun lunch box") is a way of displaying patriotism and supporting the war effort.

**1940**
Government restricts distribution of food and other goods. Rationing of rice, other major foods, clothing, and fuel is underway in Tokyo, Osaka, Yokohama, Nagoya, Kyoto, and Kobe. The black market offers food and restricted goods at inflated prices.

**1941**
The Japanese attack on Pearl Harbor initiates the Pacific theater of World War II. Rice shortages lead to sweet potatoes becoming a staple, grown in backyards. Wild plants are foraged and added to rice gruel. Food items on the black market are exchanged for valuable items (silk kimonos, antiques).

**1945**
Japan surrenders to the Allied Powers after the atomic bombing of Hiroshima and Nagasaki.

**1946–1956**
Postwar food aid brings wheat flour, canned meat, and powdered milk into the national school nutrition program.

**1960s**
Japan's economy recovers and food production is restored. Fresh fish and seafood become available daily.

**1970**
American fast-food companies establish branches, popularizing hamburgers and fried chicken. Japanese food companies set up rival chains with similar offerings adapted to local taste.

**1975**
Cheesecake becomes a fad food. Demand increases for cheese and other dairy products.

## 1979
Health- and weight-consciousness popularize low-calorie foods, such as *konnyaku* (devil's tongue jelly).

## 1980
The concept of functional foods—products with health and nutritional benefits—gives rise to a list of approved foods for specified health use (FOSHU).

## 1983
The Post Office delivers gift packages of regional foods throughout the country.

## 1989, Heisei Period
The Showa era ends with the death of Emperor Hirohito. Hirohito's son, Akihito, is enthroned as Emperor Heisei.

## 1991
Demand for organic, locally grown, and artisanal foods increases.

## 2000
*Panko* (Japanese bread crumbs) becomes popular outside Japan.

## 2003
The list of functional foods expands to include 330 foods, beverages, and processed capsules and tablets.

*Yuzu* (*Citrus junos*), an aromatic citrus fruit, becomes popular among American and European chefs.

Traditional Japanese restaurants establish branches in Paris to present authentic food prepared by Japanese chefs.

## 2013
No Food Loss Project is set up by the Ministry of Agriculture, Fisheries and Food and six other ministries to address 18 million tons of food waste annually.

## 2013
UNESCO includes *washoku* in its list of the world's intangible cultural heritage.

## 2014
Japanese eel (*unagi*) is declared an endangered species.

## 2015
The Geographical Indication Act guarantees the provenance of regional quality food products.

## 2016
The Saezeriya restaurant chain discovers melamine contamination of China-sourced milk.

## 2017
Japanese restaurants outside Japan total 117,568.

**2019, Reiwa Period**
Emperor Naruhito, son of Emperor Emeritus Akihito, is enthroned.

**2020**
January 15: first case of novel coronavirus is detected in Japan.

April 7–May 23: Nationwide state of emergency is declared. Food service businesses are heavy affected. Cooking and eating at home increase as people work from home and self-isolate, and schools are closed. Food ingredients are bought in larger quantities to limit frequency of shopping trips.

Tokyo Olympic and Paralympic Games 2020 are postponed to 2021.

**2021**
January: Second state of emergency for greater Tokyo area and other major cities. Restaurants and other dining venues close at 8:00 p.m. Business bankruptcies are filed, mostly in the food service sector.

April–May: Third state of emergency is declared for Tokyo and other major cities, quasi-emergency restrictions for certain prefectures. Alcohol is forbidden at restaurants, bars, and other eating places. Department stores and eating establishments are required to close at 8:00 p.m.

CHAPTER ONE

# Food History

## Introduction

The food eaten in Japan today reflects several millennia of historical, sociocultural, and economic development: the results of selecting, adapting, growing, hunting, and gathering endemic wild, field-grown, globally sourced ingredients; preparing them using local and introduced methods; and adapting them to local preferences and tastes. It may undoubtedly surprise many, including the Japanese themselves, to know that rice—so central to Japanese food culture—is an introduced crop. Brought by waves of migrants from the Asian continent, directly or via Korea, rice grown in the flooded fields called paddies was an important factor in shaping Japan. So deeply ingrained in the Japanese consciousness is the emotional and aesthetic significance of rice in flooded fields that the poetic name for Japan is *mizuho no kuni*, the land where reeds and grains flourish forever (*toyoashihara no mizuho no kuni*). Indeed, rice is so culturally important that the emperor undertakes ritual rice planting in the imperial palace grounds in spring, with another ritual, the *Niinamesai*, in the fall as thanksgiving for the harvest and to ensure the coming year's prosperity.

The increased food production resulting from irrigated rice cultivation and related agricultural knowledge enabled the original population to expand and develop into self-governing groups, which led to Yamato, the first Japanese nation-state in central Japan. Later, Buddhism and social, cultural, artistic, political, and philosophical knowledge from China, including ways of cooking and eating, brought further changes to the original lifestyle and diet. The imperial court and the aristocracy adhered to a Buddhist meatless diet for five months of the year, with vegetables supplemented by fish, seafood, and poultry (not classified as meat). Until Buddhism filtered down to common folk, their omnivorous diet included domestic and wild vegetables and other plant foods, fish, seafood, poultry, wild boar, deer, and other game. Purely vegetarian diets became the norm in Buddhist monasteries.

Centuries later, trade with European countries and the United States took the Japanese back to an omnivorous diet by imperial decree. Western-style foods were adopted and adapted to local taste, until World War II, when nationalism and rationing limited people's choices. The immediate postwar period brought food aid from the United States, Australia, and other countries to allay famine until food production and distribution could be restarted. From the 1960s onward, the country's economic recovery enabled importation of food ingredients from all over the world, resulting in diminished food self-sufficiency—at 37% to 39%, the lowest among developed countries. The foodstuffs and cooking methods from various countries incorporated and assimilated into Japanese food culture and adapted to Japanese taste were eventually transformed thereby, so that they have become "Japanized." Curiously, some are now, in this global 21st century, making their way back to their countries of origin as "authentic" Japanese food.

## Prehistory

Archaeologists and historians posit that Japan was settled 30,000–35,000 years ago. The settlers ate meat, evidenced by excavated bones of Naumann's elephant, Yabe's elk, wild boar, and deer, whose meat was likely broiled, smoked, and dried. They ate plant foods, such as wild berries, nuts (horse chestnuts, acorns), lily bulbs, and tubers, some of which are still eaten today. Between 15,000 BC and 1000 BC, an extraordinary, elaborately incised pottery with cord markings (*jōmon*) developed and enabled cooking and food storage. This distinctive pottery gave the era and its creators the name Jōmon. Jōmon people seasoned their foods with *sanshō* (*Zanthoxylum piperitum*) and *shisō* (*Perilla frutescens* and *Perilla ocimoides*), herbs that provide a distinctive signature to Japanese food today. The earliest foods were hunted and gathered from the mountains and fished from the sea: a combination that still denotes the ideal Japanese menu: *yama no sachi, umi no sachi* (the delights of the mountains and the seas).

Jōmon people hunted, trapped, fished, and foraged for food. Food inland consisted of wild boar, deer, bear, rabbit, macaque monkey, hare, fox, otter, wolf, and lynx. Wild birds included pheasant, duck, pigeon, goose, and crow. Trout, salmon, and carp were trapped or fished with hooks and spears. Jōmon coastal dwellers collected shellfish and fished in shallow bays for bream, horse mackerel, and sardine. They also used dugout canoes and harpoons to catch tuna, whale, seal, sea lion, and dolphin in deeper waters. Shell mounds attest to their extensive marine diet.

# Food History

Food plants included chestnuts, walnuts, horse chestnuts, and acorns—the latter two required leaching in water to remove bitterness. Plant tubers and roots included Dioscorea yams (*yama imo*), lily (*yuri*) bulbs, burdock (*Arctium lappa*), and taro tubers (these are still ingredients of Japanese meals today). Wild fungi and tender shoots of ferns and bracken may have been eaten too, as they still are. Bracken and *kuzu* roots were pounded for starch. (*Kuzu* root's jelly-like quality is appreciated to this day as an ingredient in fine Japanese confectionery and to thicken sauces.)

> Jōmon people prepared two dishes similar to modern foods. One was patties from wild boar or deer meat and blood mixed with chopped nuts, wild birds' eggs, and starch from bracken roots. Japanese archaeologists called these Jōmon "burgers." The other was finely chopped horse chestnuts, walnuts, and acorns with birds' eggs and bracken root starch shaped into disks. Archaeologists dubbed these Jōmon "cookies," and assume that the burgers and cookies had been cooked on flat stones heated over a coal fire. Archaeologists have found evidence that the acorns were leached in water to remove their bitterness before being used for food.

Other food plants that have left identifiable remains are bottle gourd (*Lagenaria siceraria*), beans (*Vigna* species), goosefoot (*Chenopodium* species), rape (*Brassica* species), and hemp (*Cannabis sativa*). Fruits such as grape (*Vitis*), silvervine (*Actinidia*, related to kiwifruit), elderberry (*Sambucus*), and blackberry (*Rubus*) were also eaten.

Jōmon people ate three kinds of millet (foxtail millet, *Setaria italica*; broomcorn or common millet, *Panicum miliaceum*; barnyard millet, *Echinochloa esculenta*), barley, and buckwheat. Millet and barley continued to be eaten on their own or mixed with rice until modern times. [Buckwheat in noodle form (*soba*) is still commonly eaten today.]

Jōmon clay vessels were used to boil food and store nuts and grains, and elaborately incised ones were made for ceremonial or ritual use. Prehistoric processed foods that have been discovered include "bread" from root starch, Jōmon cookies from ground nuts and acorns mixed with boar or deer blood and birds' eggs, and patties called Jōmon burgers from wild meats. These were cooked over flat stones laid over a fire or coals. By the end of this period, small-scale dry-land rice cultivation was underway, including back-garden cultivation of millets, buckwheat, and other food crops. Toward the latter part of the Jōmon period, 2000 BC, salt was being produced by boiling down seawater.

## Jōmon Burgers, *Jōmon Bāgā*

Carbonized (burnt) cookies and patties were among the remains unearthed by Japanese archaeologists in Jōmon archaeological sites. When analyzed, the patties were found to contain wild boar and deer meat and blood. Japanese archaeologists fancifully dubbed them "Jōmon burgers."

*Yield:* 4–6 servings

**Ingredients**
1 pound venison (deer meat) or wild boar meat, coarsely chopped
1 pound taro roots, peeled, boiled until tender, then mashed (taro roots are available from Asian food shops)
1 pound chestnuts, boiled until tender, peeled, and finely chopped (alternatives are unsweetened chestnut puree or unsweetened roasted or boiled chestnuts)
salt to taste
8 green *shisō* leaves (available from Asian food shops), chopped
2 tablespoons cooking oil, or more

**Procedure**
1. In a bowl, thoroughly mix the venison, mashed taro, chestnuts, salt, and chopped *shisō*.
2. Form into 3-inch patties.
3. Heat a frying pan over medium heat. Add 2 tablespoons cooking oil; when oil is hot, add the patties, leaving space in between each.
4. Cook until brown, about 3 minutes.
5. Turn down the heat, cover, and cook the other side until brown, about 2 minutes.

## Chestnut Rice, *Kuri Gohan*

Chestnuts are among the nuts gathered in the fall. One way of enjoying this seasonal crop is to cook it with rice, a method called *takikomi gohan* (mixed rice). See Chapter 2 for a *konbu dashi* recipe.

*Yield:* 4 servings

**Ingredients**
2 cups short-grain rice
1 ½ cups raw peeled chestnuts, quartered

> 7 cups *konbu dashi*
> 1 teaspoon salt
> 3 tablespoons *sake*
>
> **Procedure**
> 1. Wash and rinse the rice well, until the rinse water is no longer cloudy.
> 2. Place rice in a heavy-bottomed pot with cover. Alternatively, use an automatic rice cooker and follow instructions for use.
> 3. Stir in the chestnuts, *konbu dashi*, and salt.
> 4. Bring to a boil, covered, over medium heat.
> 5. Reduce heat to low and continue cooking for another 10–15 minutes, or until all liquid has been absorbed.
> 6. Turn off heat and sprinkle *sake* over the rice.
> 7. Let rice rest, covered, for 10 minutes before serving.

## Chinese and Korean Migrants Introduce Changes

The subsequent Yayoi period, 300 BC to 300 AD, marked the beginning of links with China and Korea that brought wide-ranging changes to the Jōmon way of life. (Recent research pushes the beginning of this period to 1000 BC.) The most significant was agriculture—growing rice in irrigated fields and cultivating fruits and other food crops. The second significant change was metallurgy—the forging of iron and bronze agricultural tools, weapons, and ceremonial objects. These two technologies, brought by migrants from Korea and China, paved the way for the first Japanese nation-state, called Yamato. Metal tools increased efficiency and agricultural yields, and the increased crop production could support a greater population. The larger population enabled cooperative work on common irrigation systems for growing rice. Greater productivity resulted in social stratification and unequal distribution of crops and material goods. In contrast to the (presumed) egalitarian communities of the Jōmon, agricultural development led to social, economic, and political hierarchies.

Hunting wild animals, freshwater and sea fishing, and gathering wild food plants, as in the previous Jōmon period, continued alongside organized farming. The new settlers' cultivated crops from the Asian mainland included peaches, plums, apricots, pears, melons, watermelons, *azuki* beans, and soybeans. (These latter two beans continue to be important foods today. *Azuki* bean was and still is a constant in sweet foods and at rituals and celebrations. The soybean's versatility lent itself to fermented seasonings and other protein-rich products.) The three types of millet and barley from the previous era were cooked into porridge or gruel, often mixed with rice and *azuki* beans, or were steamed and eaten with wooden spoons or with the hands.

Further developments in food elaboration and sophistication occurred, resulting from these introductions and the influence of the Japanese imperial court in Yamato (in present-day Nara Prefecture). The most significant development was soybean-based seasoning, offshoots of fermented, salted soybean balls from Korea and similar soybean-based seasonings from China. Salt production in the previous Jōmon period had enabled pickling and preserving of foodstuffs. The earliest seasonings in Japan were based on marine animals, such as small fish, squid, and their entrails, pickled in salt. These seasonings are still in use today—*shottsuru* (fish sauce) in Akita Prefecture, *shiokara* (salted squid) from the Kanto region, and *konowata* (preserved fish and seafood entrails). Besides marine ingredients, vegetables and animal flesh (wild boar, deer) were transformed through lactic acid fermentation with salt into liquid seasonings known as *hishio*.

Buddhism was introduced to the Yamato court around the mid-6th century AD (538–552) from the Korean kingdom of Baekje. Because Buddhism prohibited animal-sourced (both land and marine) foods, soybeans replaced these ingredients, and the resulting product was also called *hishio*. Eventually soybean *hishio* evolved into the modern seasonings soy sauce, miso, and tamari.

## Chinese Script and Buddhism

Chinese script introduced from Korea made it possible to keep records, exchange information, read Korean and Chinese literature, and learn about various aspects of Korean and Chinese cultures. Previously, the Japanese language had no written form. The introduction of Buddhism in 552 caused a further evolution in Japanese culture and food. Buddhism's cultural and aesthetic aspects had so impressed the Yamato Imperial Court that in 607, the first Japanese embassy was sent to China to gain deeper knowledge of Chinese ways. The returning embassy brought back new forms of food, new ways of food preparation and dining, and porcelain tableware. Among the food-related knowledge was the preparation of edible temple offerings for Buddhist festivals. These pastries, called *gūzen gashi*, were flavored with brown sugar and Chinese spices and fried in sesame oil—unusual ingredients and an unknown cooking method in Japan, and these influenced the development of Japanese sweet pastries (*okashi*). These Buddhist festival sweets are still made today in Kyoto's temples.

In 675, Emperor Temmu banned the use of wild animals (horses, cattle, birds, monkeys, dogs) for food between the fourth and ninth months.

White rice, vegetables, fish, seafood, and poultry became the foundation of aristocratic daily meals. Buddhist monasteries developed a vegetable-based cuisine (*shōjin ryōri*). However, wherever Buddhism had not yet taken hold, people continued to hunt and eat wild boar and deer, calling these mountain whale (*yama kujira*) and maple leaf (*momiji*).

Administrative reform by the Emperor Monmu through the Taiho Law Code in 702 created paid court appointments for the aristocracy. The new capital, completed in 710 in Nara, became the center of lavish rituals and feasts with music, dancing, and other forms of entertainment. The aristocracy adopted Chinese and Korean eating customs, using metal chopsticks and spoons, bronze, porcelain, lacquer ware, and glassware for dining on low-footed trays called *zen*. (By the ninth century AD, spoons were no longer used for eating in Japan.) Common folk used their fingers to eat from trays called *shiki*, earthenware bowls, and cups. Two meals a day were the norm. (Three meals a day became common only during the Kamakura period, 1190–1333.)

> As previously mentioned, rice is not an endemic Japanese food plant. It was brought over by immigrants from the Asian mainland through Korea between the Yayoi Period (1000 BC to 300 AD) and the succeeding Kofun Period (300 to 538 AD). These immigrants also brought a method for cultivating their rice in irrigated fields called *paddies*. The immigrants also brought fruits, such as pears, persimmons, peaches, and vegetables. They introduced the forging of iron and bronze, and began producing tools such as chisels, saws, axes, spades, hoes, and plows; weapons such as arrowheads, swords, and daggers; and bronze bells and mirrors for rituals.

The staple food became rice, prepared by steaming and boiling. The aristocracy only ate white rice. Steamed rice was called *kowa ii* (strong rice), or *okowa*, made with glutinous (sticky) rice, or a mixture of glutinous and regular rice. *Okowa* was reserved for special occasions, as it still is today, often mixed with *azuki* beans. Nonsticky rice was boiled and called *hime ii* (maiden rice), or *hime*. Breakfast for the aristocracy could include gruel (*kayu*) of white nonsticky rice boiled with red *azuki* beans or chestnuts. A favorite was *imo kayu*, a gruel of taro corms. For common folk, white rice was a rarity.

As gleaned from written records, side dishes for the aristocracy and wealthy included dried meat from wild animals and birds, fresh and preserved seafood, and vegetables. Among these were pressed and salted sweetfish (*ayu*) and abalone preserved in *hishio* seasoning; salted fish and seafood included bonito, sea bream, octopus, squid, and cuttlefish.

Preserved or pickled fish included *narezushi* (fish packed in cooked rice, the precursor of modern sushi); *konowata* (seafood entrails in *sake* and salt); and mackerel pickled in a mixture of vinegar and *hishio* seasoning.

By the end of the Nara period (8th century AD), *hishio* had diversified into more than 15 kinds of seasoning. Vegetables such as eggplant, turnip, radish, and fruits such as Japanese apricot (*ume*) were pickled in salt, and collectively called *kusa bishio*—the forerunners of the salted pickles (*tsukemono*) that come with the traditional Japanese meal today. Fish, seafood, eggs, fowl, and wild game (deer, wild boar) were pickled in salt, sake, and water for meat-based *shishi bishio*. Soybeans with grain, such as rice, barley, or wheat, were fermented with salt and called *koku bishio*; these would later evolve into soy sauce, tamari, and miso.

## Sophisticated Dining in the Heian Period (794–1160)

The transfer of the capital from Nara to Heian (modern Kyoto), which was built to mirror the Chinese capital at Chang-an, continued the sophisticated lifestyle of the aristocracy. Details of court life come from the diaries and other writings of the nobility, including the world's first novel—*The Tale of Genji*, by Murasaki Shikibu—and essays by Sei Shonagon, both imperial ladies-in-waiting. An aristocratic banquet featured the following menu:

- Steamed glutinous rice—shaped as a tall cylinder placed on a footed stand
- Soup—bonito cooked in broth (*katsuo irori*)
- Eight side dishes on individual footed trays called *kubotsuki*—cooked fish, seafood, or fowl with vegetables, with broth (*dashi*) or miso dressing
- Four kinds of shellfish—abalone (*awabi*), turbo clam (*sazae*), surf clam (*ou*), and *kase* clam
- Four raw dishes—carp, grouper, trout, sweetfish (*ayu*) marinated in vinegar
- Four dried dishes—salted, sun-dried sweetfish (*ayu*), salted and dried pheasant, dried cuttlefish, and dried octopus
- Eight sweets (*kudamono*)—pears, jujube, small citrus fruits, wild pear (*yabu nashi*), and "Chinese sweets" (*kara kashi*, also *tōgashi*), molded wheat pastries (*kakko, tensei*), fried in sesame oil and flavored with cinnamon (*keishin*)
- Four seasonings—sake, salt, vinegar, and *hishio* in small dishes (raw fish and shellfish were dipped in vinegar or *hishio*)
- Four unusual foodstuffs (*oitsu mono*), such as roasted pheasant or the first buds of a wild herb

Most court dishes were pickled in salt or *hishio* and dried for storage. Some were marinated in *sake* or vinegar. Kyoto was far from the coast, and ingredients used to prepare court meals included tributes from distant farms that had to be preserved to survive the journey. Nevertheless, the court also enjoyed freshwater fish from nearby Lake Biwa. Dishes at these banquets were served cold and unflavored by the cook: hence the condiments salt, sake, vinegar, and *hishio* for each diner to season each dish to his or her taste.

The knife ritual (*shiki bōchō*) began as entertainment for court banquets during this period. It introduced an elegant manner of cutting up a large carp or crane, using only chopsticks and a knife, without the fingers touching the object. This ritual's influence on contemporary Japanese food slicing and presentation is immense, and includes the ergonomics of body stance, the slicing angles that enhance the texture and appearance of ingredients, and food styling (in modern parlance, *plating*). The Heian court's refinement would greatly influence Kyoto cuisine, to this day noted for subtle flavors, restrained seasoning, and elegant settings and tableware.

In 815, tea became *the* drink of the elite. Sesame oil, cinnamon, tofu, and other soybean-based foodstuffs (such as *yuba*, fried tofu, freeze-dried tofu) were introduced from China. Snack foods (from Chinese *tenshin*, today's *dim sum*) and sweets were developed with the introduction of brown (unrefined) sugar (the method of extracting it from sugar cane had come to China from India).

## Assimilation and Adaptation, 9th–12th Centuries

The end of the 9th century to the 12th century marked the maturation of Japan as a nation. The regular official exchanges between the Japanese and Chinese imperial courts between 607 and 838 ceased because of chaotic political conditions in China that led to the collapse of the Tang dynasty in 907. The cessation of official contact with the Chinese imperial court enabled Japan to assess and evaluate the knowledge acquired and adapt it to local circumstances. Unofficial travel by monks, scholars, and traders continued, however, and books, art objects, perfume, incense, and luxuries flowed from China to Japan's upper classes and monasteries. The next centuries continued the development of Japanese politics, religion, philosophy, and literature, and the evolution of Japanese taste in food, eating, and cooking.

## Warrior Taste and Buddhist Cuisine, Kamakura Period (1185–1333) and Muromachi Period (1336–1538)

Civil unrest due to famine, natural disasters, and conflicts between the imperial court and Buddhist establishments led to the aristocracy's use of the Taira and Minamoto warrior clans to restore order and normalcy. A civil war ensued, with the Minamoto emerging victorious and relocating the seat of government to Kamakura, away from the influence of the imperial court in Kyoto. At first, a shift toward simpler meals developed, as befitted the samurai ideals of simple living. New Buddhist sects established themselves in Kamakura, distancing themselves from the established sects patronized by the imperial court.

This period's most important development was the elaboration of soybean-based seasonings to suit Japanese taste. From the strong-flavored Chinese *jiang* and Korean fermented soybean balls, Japanese miso evolved into a milder product using various proportions of salt, grains (rice, wheat, barley), and soybeans. By 901, miso had become a local product, written with different ideographs (*kanji*) from the imported products to emphasize the distinction. By the middle of the 10th century, miso making had spread from the capital and distinctive regional miso types appeared. By the end of the 10th century, miso had become a common seasoning for salads, stews, and soups. Interestingly, although miso owes its provenance to China and Korea, it is only in Japan that miso evolved into a staple soup eaten daily. Miso soup, pickled vegetables, and rice established the basic format of a traditional Japanese meal. This standard format begins (in abbreviated fashion) and ends a formal tea ceremony banquet (*cha kaiseki*). Likewise, it signals the culmination of a formal dinner (*kaiseki*) and the finale of any drinking party.

Tea in leaf form, unlike its previous introduction as a brick (which was not widely accepted), was brought to Japan by the Buddhist Zen monk Eisai to prevent sleep during meditation. It became the centerpiece of a new way of eating and drinking as embodied in the tea ceremony (*chanoyu* or *sado*). Another Buddhist Zen monk, Dōgen, founder of the Sōtō Zen sect, wrote the *Tenzo Kyōkun* (Instructions for the Cook) in 1237. In this guide can be traced the attention to detail in every step of cooking that remains the hallmark of quality Japanese cooking to this day.

Buddhist temple cuisine, which eschewed animal-based food, including beef, pork, poultry, eggs, fish and seafood, developed many products from vegetables, in particular soybeans, ranging from the condiments miso, soy sauce, and tamari to diverse forms of tofu—fresh, freeze-dried, fresh and dry sheets, and fried. Due to the efforts of Buddhist monasteries in Kamakura, miso evolved during the Muromachi period (1336–1538) from a luxury condiment to an everyday seasoning for all. The energy-giving and health-fostering qualities of miso were duly acknowledged, and miso became a cornerstone of daily meals, especially when mixed with protein- and mineral-rich *dashi* for miso soup. As long as they had miso (*miso sae areba*), a household felt protected from starvation and ill

*Food History*

health. Takeda Shingen, the samurai lord of Shinshu province (today's Nagano Prefecture), saw miso's potential as a quickly made, nutritious meal for soldiers in the battlefield, and encouraged the cultivation of soybeans and manufacture of miso (to this day Nagano is a major miso producer). The flavorsome liquid at the bottom of the miso-fermenting barrel became a separate seasoning called tamari.

## Tea Ceremony and *Ichijū Sansai*

The change from aristocratic to warrior rule and the move from Kyoto to Kamakura resulted at first in a more restrained way of eating, as befitted the frugal warrior lifestyle. Following the Minamoto rulers' support of Buddhism, tea drinking and the tea ceremony became popular. Conceived at first as cultural events for tea-tasting and poetry, the tea ceremony had degenerated into drunken, rowdy parties. The monk Sen no Rikyū reformed the tea ceremony into relaxed gatherings for enjoying tea and simple food prepared well with seasonal ingredients. These took place in a humble hut in a peaceful setting. Rikyū called this reformed tea ceremony *wabi cha*. (Among *wabi*'s elusive meanings and connotations are "impoverished" and "imperfect," mirroring Rikyū's penchant for the simple and humble; *cha* is tea.) Rikyū preferred everyday tableware from local kilns over imported Chinese porcelain, and set a standard meal format—one soup, three side dishes (*ichijūsansai*) that remains a basic format for traditional meals. Rikyū's meals are acknowledged as the beginning of genuine Japanese cuisine: serving food that is delicious, seasoned to taste by an attentive cook (rather than by each diner), and considerate of the diner: hot foods served hot, cold foods served cold. To ensure this, dishes are served in the order they are to be eaten. No further courses are served until the previous one has been eaten; hence, there is less waste as well.

---

### Rikyū-Style Konjac, *Konyakku Rikyū Yaki*

Sen no Rikyū was apparently extremely fond of sesame seeds. To this day, dishes with sesame seeds bear his name. *Konnyaku* is a jelly-like substance made from the corm of the devil's tongue plant, *Amorphophallus konjac*. It has no calories, and is therefore popular as a diet food. In noodle form, it is called *shirataki*, a sukiyaki ingredient. When konjac is frozen and thawed, its texture becomes meatlike, so it is used in vegetarian and vegan dishes. *Konnyaku* and other ingredients are available in Japanese and Korean food shops and health food stores.

*Yield:* 4 servings

**Ingredients**
¾ pound *konjac* slab (*konnyaku*)
Oil for cooking
2 tablespoons sesame paste (*neri goma* or *tahini*)
2 tablespoons water, or more as needed
1 egg yolk (optional)
1 tablespoon *sake*
2 tablespoons mirin
1 tablespoon soy sauce
2 tablespoons black or white sesame seeds

**Procedure**
1. Parboil *konnyaku* in plenty of water, at least to cover. Drain and let cool.
2. Use a spoon to tear out bite-size pieces (*konnyaku* is difficult to slice with a knife). Dry the pieces thoroughly with paper towels.
3. In a frying pan over medium heat, add 3 tablespoons oil and stir-fry the *konnyaku*. Set aside.
4. Make the sesame sauce: in a saucepan, whisk sesame paste with water until it starts to loosen.
5. Whisk in the egg yolk, *sake*, mirin, and soy sauce.
6. Place saucepan with sesame mixture over low heat, whisking continuously until the sauce is hot.
7. If too thick, add water, a teaspoon at a time. The consistency should be like pourable cream.
8. Taste and add more soy sauce or mirin as desired.
9. Once the sauce is hot, about 5–10 minutes, turn off the heat.
10. Add the fried *konnyaku* to the sauce, stirring well to combine.
11. Place a frying pan over low heat and dry-roast the black or white sesame seeds until they start to give off their characteristic aroma, about 1–2 minutes. Turn off heat.

*To serve: Distribute* konnyaku *and sauce into 4 small deep bowls. Sprinkle with the toasted sesame seeds. Serve as a side dish for a traditional meal.*

## Edo Period (1600–1896)

Civil war during the Warring States period ensued until Tokugawa Ieyasu and allies emerged victorious, and initiated three centuries of peace in their new administrative center, Edo (now Tokyo). The relocation of

# Food History

regional *daimyos* (lords) and their retainers to Edo increased the city's male population, and as they were mostly bachelors or away from their families (left in their home provinces) they needed regular meals. This presented an opportunity for mobile food carts (*yatai*) to serve quickly prepared and conveniently eaten dishes—the first fast foods: tempura on skewers, sushi (using local fresh fish and seafood), *kabayaki* eel, *udon* (wheat noodles), and *soba* (buckwheat noodles). These Edo specialties were prepared and eaten with soy sauce; without it, these foods might not have been created. By 1811, Edo boasted more than 7,500 eating places, perhaps the most in any world city at the time, and by 1848 a guide to Edo's famous restaurants was published (*Edo Meibutsu Shuhan Tebikigusa*), predating France's Michelin Guide by more than a century. Disposable chopsticks were invented at this time, and though used initially at high-end restaurants, by 1877 (the tenth year of Meiji) they were commonly used at all eating places for hygienic reasons.

## Introductions from Traders' Cuisines

The 16th century brought further changes. Portuguese traders in Tanegashima introduced deep-frying and baking, white sugar, eggs, and dishes such as tempura, Castella cake, bread, and other wheat- and sugar-based foods. Dutch traders introduced a way of braising by initial frying, a style of cooking called *orandani* (Dutch stew). Chinese traders also influenced the cooking, eating, and dining styles of southern Japan, specifically Nagasaki's *shippoku* (red-lacquered table) cuisine. This style of dining antedates today's eclectic, *mukokuseki*-style (no nationality) by serving Japanese, Chinese, and European dishes on large platters on a red-lacquered table—its round shape conferring equal status to all diners, regardless of social station.

---

### Squash-Filled Hand Pies, *Kesaina Mochi*

This sweet pastry from the Edo period was mentioned in the first book on Japanese sweets, *Kokon Meibutsu Gozen Kashi Hidenshō* (Secrets of Past and Present Famous Sweets), published in 1715. *Kesaina* is the Edo-period Japanese pronunciation of the Portuguese word *queijada*, the original Portuguese tartlet on which this pastry is based. The filling is pureed squash (*kabocha*), known as *bōbura* in old Edo, from the original Portuguese word, *abóbora*, "squash." Contemporary *queijadas* in Portugal are tartlets made with cheese. Some regions use quince paste. The following recipe is an adaptation by the author. Unflavored pumpkin purée may be substituted for the cooked squash.

*Yield:* 10–12 pieces

**Ingredients**

*Pastry*
5 cups all-purpose flour, plus extra for rolling out dough
2 tablespoons sugar
½ teaspoon salt
2 cups cold butter, diced, or 1 cup cold butter, diced plus 1 cup cold vegetable shortening, diced
1 cup ice-cold water

*Squash filling*
1 pound squash (acorn, kabocha, or butternut type) or pumpkin purée
2 tablespoons water
¼ cup sugar, or to taste
2 tablespoons butter, optional
Grated zest of 1 *yuzu* citrus or ½ lemon
1 tablespoon lemon juice

*Egg wash*
1 egg yolk, beaten
1 tablespoon milk
Sugar for sprinkling

**Procedure**
1. In a food processor, pulse flour, sugar, and salt until well mixed.
2. Add butter until well combined.
3. Add water, and process just until the mixture comes together into a dough. Take care not to overprocess, or the pastry will be tough.
4. With lightly floured hands, remove dough, and smooth into a ball. Wrap in plastic film and chill for 30 minutes to 1 hour.
5. While dough is chilling, prepare the filling. Wash squash well and cut into quarters. (It is not necessary to peel or remove seeds at this point.)
6. Place in a microwaveable container with 2 tablespoons water. Cover with plastic film, but leave a slight gap for steam to escape.
7. Microwave on full power for 5 minutes. Check that the squash is soft enough to mash. If not, repeat microwaving for 1 minute each time, until the squash is sufficiently soft.

*Food History*

8. Take care when removing the container from the microwave, as the container and contents will be extremely hot. Also be careful of hot steam rising when releasing the plastic film from the container.
9. Scoop out the flesh and place in a bowl. Discard seeds and skin.
10. There should be about 2 cups flesh. Stir in sugar, and adjust the sweetness to your taste.
11. Stir in butter and *yuzu* zest. Set aside.
12. Preheat oven to 385°F.
13. Prepare the pastry crust: Cut dough into two pieces. Leave one piece, still wrapped in cling film, in the refrigerator while you work with the first one.
14. On a lightly floured surface, roll the dough to ⅛-inch thickness.
15. With a floured 3.5-inch cookie cutter, cut out 10 disks. Place these on a parchment-covered cookie sheet. Repeat with the second piece of dough.
16. Leave the second group of pastry disks on the floured working surface and cover with a damp (not wet), clean kitchen towel, to prevent them from drying out.
17. Fill 10 pastry disks, placing 1 tablespoon of squash filling in the center.
18. Top with remaining disks. Crimp edges of filled pastries firmly with a fork, and make three or four tiny slits on the top pastry (if you wish, make a pattern) to enable steam to escape during baking.
19. In a small bowl, whisk the yolk and milk for the egg wash.
20. With a pastry brush, apply the wash to the top pastry disks. Sprinkle with sugar.
21. Bake in the center rack of the preheated 385°F oven for 15–20 minutes, or until golden.
22. Transfer pastries to a wire rack.

*Serve the pastries while still warm with green or regular tea, coffee, milk, or a cold beverage.*

## Quince Sweet, *Kaseita*

A confectioner in Kumamoto, Okashi no Kōbai, has revived an ancient sweet whose original recipe was given by a Portuguese priest. The sweet is *kaseita*, and was one of the Hosokawa clan's regular gifts to the Tokugawa shogunate during the 18th century. The name derives from the Portuguese *caixa de marmelos*, meaning "box of quinces." The revived, modern *kaseita* is composed of two rectangular wafers that enclose a red filling of Japanese quince. The wafers are white, which suggest that they are made of rice flour, and decorated with the family crest of the Hosokawa clan.

Another Portuguese sweet, called *queijada de marmelos*, is mentioned in the book *Creating Edo Cuisine* (*Edo Ryōri o Tsukuru*). The Portuguese word *queijada* becomes *kaseita* in 18th-century Japanese. The following recipe is typical of Portuguese sweets made with lots of eggs, cream, and milk. The quinces used are true quinces, *Cydonia oblonga*, rather than the Japanese quinces called *karin*, which are *Chaenomeles japonica*, used in the revived commercial pastry.

*Yield:* about 30 pieces

**Ingredients**
3 tablespoons softened butter
2 quinces
4 eggs
1 cup whole milk
Zest and juice of 1 lemon
¾ cup sweetened condensed milk
Icing sugar (optional, for dusting)

**Procedure**
1. Lightly butter 12 custard cups or tart molds.
2. Preheat the oven to 385°F.
3. Wash and peel the quinces, core them, and slice into small cubes.
4. Put the quinces with water to cover in a pan over medium heat. Bring to a boil, then allow to simmer for 45 minutes, or until the quinces are soft enough for a toothpick to pierce through them easily.
5. Take out the quinces, drain them, and let them cool. Once cold, mash them and set them aside.
6. In the bowl of a mixer, beat the eggs until well combined and frothy. Mix in the milk, lemon zest, lemon juice, and condensed milk.
7. Pour the mixture into the custard cups, and bake for 25 minutes, or until the tops are golden brown.
8. Transfer the custard cups to a rack and let them cool to room temperature.
9. Refrigerate overnight.

*To serve:* Unmold onto a dessert plate. Dust with icing sugar (if desired).

## Dutch-Style Braised Eggplant, *Nasu no Orandani*

The Dutch style of stewing or braising vegetables and other ingredients, known as *orandani*, is a legacy of the Dutch trading presence in Nagasaki throughout the Tokugawa period (*oranda* is Holland, *ni* is stew). Originally confined to Nagasaki regional cuisine, *orandani* became disseminated throughout the country. The ingredients are initially deep-fried or seared in oil, then hot water is poured over the fried ingredients to remove excess oil. The ingredients are then gently and slowly braised until tender in a mixture of *dashi*, soy sauce, and mirin or *sake* or both. The initial searing in oil works best for eggplant, as it helps to keep the eggplant's vibrant color. Tender, medium Japanese or Chinese eggplants work best for this recipe (the large, oval American or Italian eggplants would absorb too much oil and are not recommended). Japanese or Chinese eggplants are also not as bitter and have a finer texture than the large American or Italian types. In Tokyo today, *orandani* is more commonly called *agedashi*.

*Yield:* 4 servings

**Ingredients**
4 Japanese or Chinese eggplants, about 5–6 inches long
3 ½ cups *dashi*
6 tablespoons soy sauce
3 tablespoons mirin
3 tablespoons *sake*
¼ teaspoon salt (optional)
oil for deep frying
12 small green beans or sugar pea pods, trimmed
2-inch piece fresh ginger
1 cup fine (thread-type) *katsuobushi*

**Procedure**
1. Cut off and discard the stalks of the eggplant, but leave the calyx (the frilled cap that covers the upper end of the eggplant). Leaving the calyx intact keeps the eggplants from falling apart during cooking.
2. Slice the eggplants in half lengthwise. Insert the tip of the knife in the middle of the eggplants and make 4–5 shallow slashes lengthwise. Take care not to cut all the way through. These cuts allow the eggplant to absorb the seasoning and cook evenly.
3. In a frying pan over medium-high heat, deep-fry the eggplants for 1 minute. Place eggplants in a colander and pour hot water over them to remove excess oil. Set aside until needed.
4. Put the *dashi*, soy sauce, and mirin in a stewing pan wide enough for the eggplants to lie in one layer, and bring to a boil. Add the eggplants and let them cook for no more than 10 seconds.
5. Remove the eggplants from the pan and fan them to cool them quickly. This will make them retain their vibrant color.

> 6. Cool the *dashi* mixture quickly by pouring it into a bowl sitting in a larger bowl of ice-cold water.
> 7. Once the eggplants and *dashi* mixture are cool, combine them and chill for 2–3 hours or overnight in the refrigerator.
> 8. Meanwhile, prepare the garnishes. Parboil the green beans or sugar pea pods until tender, but still crisp. Immediately plunge the beans or pods into ice-cold water to stop them cooking further and to retain their fresh green color. Leave the green beans whole. If using sugar pea pods, slice them into very fine julienne strips. Set aside and refrigerate, covered, until needed.
> 9. Peel the ginger and slice into very fine julienne strips.
>
> *To serve: Place two eggplant halves per serving in a shallow bowl, preferably one with a light-colored glaze to contrast with the eggplants' color. Spoon* dashi *mixture over them, and garnish with beans or finely julienned sugar pea pods and ginger. Carefully place the* katsuobushi *alongside.*
>
> *Serve as a side dish for a traditional Japanese meal.*

## Meiji Period and Westernization

The Edo period ended with Emperor Meiji restored as ruler of Japan. Japan was forced to open its ports to American, British, and other nations' traders, bringing further changes to Japanese food culture. The Meiji period also ushered in Westernization in other aspects of Japanese life, as Japan began upgrading its armed forces and improving infrastructure and education. In the realm of food, Western-style restaurants and food shops initially catered exclusively to foreigners, and ingredients such as beef and Western vegetables were shipped in. However, in 1871, the first Western-style restaurant for Japanese elite and intelligentsia opened in a hotel in Tsukiji, Tokyo.

Curry rice, made with beef, became popular enough to be featured in two cookbooks on Western-style cooking: *Seiyō Ryōritsu* and *Seiyō Ryōrishinan*, published in 1872. In 1873, Emperor Meiji lifted the ban on eating meat, and set an example by eating beef and granting permission to all citizens to eat meat. From 1905 onward, women's magazines featured recipes for Western-style dishes with accompanying menus. By 1907, 36 Western-style restaurants for Japanese diners had opened in Tokyo. The most popular dishes were *hayashi raisu* (hashed beef and rice), *karē raisu* (curry rice), *korokke* (croquettes), and *tonkatsu* (deep-fried pork cutlets). *Gyūnabe* ("beef pot," precursor of today's *sukiyaki*) was popular, as beef became locally available from cattle breeders in Kobe, Aizu, Tsugaru, Izumo, and Izu by 1873.

In 1875, the Fugetsudo bakery began to produce Western-style biscuits and pastries, and Kimuraya created the first fusion pastry, *anpan* (wheat buns filled with sweet red bean paste). By 1883, Tokyo had 116 Western-style bakeries. Strawberry jam began to be industrially produced from 1905. Wine was produced in Yamanashi Prefecture at the state-owned Dainippon Yamanashi Budōshū Kaisha in 1877 (although it ceased operation in 1887).

Throughout the Meiji period, eating Western-style foods (*yōshoku*) was confined to the upper classes, but by the Taisho period (1912–1926), such dishes became accessible to the average Japanese diner. The Japanese navy's menus included curry and rice (*karē raisu*, mirroring the British navy's menu), eventually introduced to their families by navy crews on home leave. *Tonkatsu* (pork cutlet) and *korokke* (croquettes) were also introduced to home meals at this time. Coffee drinking was no longer exclusively for Nagasaki, Kobe, and Yokohama's resident foreigners, as coffee shops opened elsewhere, making coffee and Western cakes and sweets accessible to the wider public.

Western vegetables—cabbage, potatoes, tomatoes, carrots, onions—began to be grown nationwide and used in Japanese dishes. Western-style sweets—ice cream, lemonade (*ramune*), chocolate, candy—though introduced earlier, became more widely available as local manufacturer Morinaga began to produce milk caramel candies in 1913, and milk chocolate and wafers in 1923. Caramels became hugely popular. In 1919, the first sweetened fermented milk drink, Calpis, was introduced, and remains a popular summer drink to this day. In 1925, butter began to be produced locally. Japan's first Western-style distillery, Yamazaki, began producing whisky in 1924.

## Rationing and Postwar Period

Japanese militarism during the early Showa period caused the colonization of Taiwan, Korea, and Manchuria, war against China, and the attack on Pearl Harbor in 1941, which precipitated the Pacific Theater of World War II. From 1941 to 1945, Southeast Asia—comprising the Philippines, Vietnam, Malaya, Singapore, Indonesia, Burma—was under Japanese control. At home, the meager meal of *hinomaru bentō* ("rising sun lunch box")—white rice topped with a red pickled plum—symbolized patriotism.

In 1940, rationing began as domestic food stocks were diverted to support Japan's military activities. After the attack on Pearl Harbor, insufficient rice stocks made sweet potatoes the staple. Desperate people foraged wild plants and used empty lots, including near railway tracks, to grow food. After Japan's surrender in 1945, food shortages continued until agriculture could be revived. From 1946 on, wheat flour, chocolate bars, powdered eggs, canned meat, canned salmon, and other canned foods arrived as food aid from the United States, Australia, UNICEF, and other international organizations. Whale meat disguised as bacon and sausages became a regular ingredient of school lunch programs.

## Economic Boom (1956–1990)

By 1956, full food production was underway, and Japan's economy had fully recovered. Rice and other food items became freely available for purchase, though rice ration cards were only revoked in 1981. The 1960s ushered in the "traditional" Japanese diet as we know it today, made possible by two of the three "sacred treasures"—refrigerator, television, washing machine. A refrigerator enabled perishable ingredients to be kept fresh, so that daily shopping was no longer required. Previously, highly perishable ingredients, such as fish, had had to be salted to preserve them. Eating fresh rather than salt-preserved ingredients changed Japanese diners' perceptions of food and how food should taste. (The decreased salt consumption also made a difference in health.) Cooking shows on television promoted changes to daily menus and acceptance of novel ingredients. The introduction of piped-in gas, more reliable than propane gas, made fuel-intensive cooking methods, such as frying and stir-frying, possible at home. Consumption of chicken, pork, beef, and dairy products (milk, cheese, cream) increased, while that of rice decreased, a trend ascribed to the new custom of eating out as family restaurants and fast-food restaurants boomed in the 1970s. By the end of the 1980s, rice consumed per capita decreased to half a pound per day—half of that eaten previously. By this time, half of all households had microwaves to thaw frozen foods. Innovations in food manufacturing created instant and retort-packed foods, and more efficient chilling technology enabled more fish (including whale) and seafood to be imported from all over the world to be served as sashimi and sushi.

## Contemporary Period

The period from 1990 to the present is characterized by a greater awareness of health, food safety, and food security, as evidenced by a widespread demand for certifiable, traceable, locally grown, organic, and artisanal foods. Health issues prompted the Ministry of Health, Labor, and Welfare to draw up a list of functional foods (foods that have the added function of enhancing health). The high-calorie intake of meat and dairy products has resulted in an increase in average height and freedom from nutritional diseases, such as rickets, but also a rising incidence of metabolic diseases. Japan's low rate of food self-sufficiency and contaminated food imports from China have also become causes for concern. The Fukushima nuclear meltdown and widespread destruction from typhoons, tsunamis, and earthquakes have highlighted the need for emergency food stocks.

In 2007, Tokyo became the city with the most Michelin-starred restaurants (more than Paris) and continues to hold the record. One Japanese gourmand boasts that there is no food that cannot be eaten in Tokyo, and the Japanese have been characterized as food-obsessed. The Japanese themselves are beginning to question the ethics of importing so much of the world's food to feed just 2% of the world's population, at the same time wasting a good deal of it.

Japanese cuisine is increasingly popular worldwide, with Japanese restaurants overseas totaling more than 115,000 as of 2017, and international gastronomes cite it among their favorite cuisines. Nevertheless, this worldwide popularity comes at a price—following the globalization of sushi and sashimi, blue-fin tuna and eel have become endangered species.

In January 2020, the first case of the novel coronavirus in Japan was detected, and from April 7 to May 23, a nationwide state of emergency was declared to try and contain the spread of infection. Two further states of emergency were declared in Tokyo and major cities in January and April 2021. Closure of schools, department stores, stadiums, libraries, and theaters; working from home; restraints on the number of diners and closing time at 8 p.m. for eating places; and staying at home have had a negative impact on the food service business, with many eating establishments declaring bankruptcies. The pandemic is profoundly affecting contemporary food culture: cooking and baking at home are on the rise. Food ingredients are purchased in bulk to minimize shopping trips. In contrast to dine-in establishments, take-out, drive-through, and food delivery businesses are booming, thanks to online ordering. An innovative alternative to dining out is to book a chef through an agency to cook at one's home. This has the added benefit of providing employment to chefs who have become unemployed due to restaurant closures. Other alternatives for unemployed chefs are food trucks and virtual kitchens. Virtual kitchens, also called ghost or cloud kitchens, are professional cooking facilities that can accommodate several chefs, each preparing different types of cuisine.

This type of food business depends on an online ordering and delivery service. Although virtual kitchens had been introduced before 2020, they have become more common with the pandemic's closure of restaurants and restrictions on dining out. In a survey of 10,000 respondents aged over 20 on changes in dietary lifestyles and food perceptions, those who had reported an increase in preparing food from scratch at home said they would continue to do so even after the pandemic restrictions are relaxed. Additionally, the pandemic has engendered greater awareness of the role of food, such as the fermented soybean product called *nattō*, in maintaining health.

---

### Soufflé Cheesecake, *Sufure Chīzu Kēki*

Cheesecake has become a regular offering in confectionery shops and coffee shops throughout the country since the 1970s. This is a soufflé-type, baked cheesecake.

*Yield:* 10–12 servings

**Ingredients**
1 cup cream cheese
2 ounces butter plus extra for greasing
½ cup whipping cream
¼ cup cake flour mixed with 1 tablespoon cornstarch
6 eggs, separated
¼ teaspoon salt
1 tablespoon lemon juice
1 teaspoon lemon rind, grated
¼ teaspoon cream of tartar
½ cup granulated sugar
Powdered (confectioner's) sugar for garnish

**Procedure**
1. Line the bottom and sides of an 8-inch cake pan with parchment paper to extend 1½ inches above the pan. Lightly butter the parchment paper.
2. Preheat the oven to 300°F.
3. Melt the cream cheese, butter, and cream in the top pan of a double boiler over—not in—hot water.
4. Remove and quickly cool the mixture by placing the top pan in a basin of ice-cold water, stirring well while it cools.

5. Mix in thoroughly the flour, egg yolks, salt, lemon juice, and grated lemon rind.
6. Using an electric mixer, gently beat the egg whites with cream of tartar.
7. Gradually add sugar and beat to soft peaks.
8. Fold in gently ⅓ of the beaten egg white into the cream cheese and flour mixture.
9. Fold in gently the remaining beaten egg white until completely incorporated. Take care not to overmix.
10. Spoon into the prepared pan, and smooth the surface.
11. Place the cake pan inside a bain-marie or a deep roasting tray.
12. Pour boiling water halfway up the tray.
13. Bake in the preheated oven for 1½ hours, or until golden.
14. Turn off the oven but leave the cake inside with the door ajar for an hour until the cake cools.
15. Remove from the oven, refrigerate for at least 4 hours or overnight, and unmold.
16. Place a tablespoon or more of powdered sugar in a fine sieve, and gently tap over the unmolded cake.

*Serve cold with Japanese or English tea, coffee, or milk.*

CHAPTER TWO

# Influential Ingredients

## Rice and Other Grains

Rice is the focus of traditional Japanese meals. Without plain white rice, a meal was not considered a "proper" meal. Even multi-course banquets conclude with rice. Rice grains are called *kome* or, politely, *okome*. When cooked, rice becomes *gohan*. Rice comes in two types: ordinary rice (*uruchimai* or *uruchigome*) for daily meals, and glutinous rice (*mochi gome*) for special occasions, sweets, and snacks. Pounded glutinous rice (*mochi*) is eaten as a festive dish for New Year and other celebrations. Ordinary rice cooks to a slightly sticky texture with a subtle sweet aftertaste. This minimal stickiness enables cooked rice to cohere for eating with chopsticks. More than 500 rice varieties are grown throughout Japan; of these, 104 are the most widely grown. Rice is ranked by the Japan Grain Testing Association into five grades, with Special A the highest, based on sensory tests for external appearance, flavor, aroma, stickiness, and hardness. The variety Koshihikari, developed in 1956, has long been the sole awardee of Special A rank, and comprises 40% of rice grown nationwide. Since 1991, California, Australia, Taiwan, and China have grown Koshihikari for export to Japan. A newly developed variety from Hokkaido, called Yumepirika, and 15 other newly developed cultivars have now been awarded Special A rank.

Historically, rice was mixed with millet or barley for common folks' meals. Rice unmixed with other grains was called "white rice" and reserved for the elite. These days, contrary to negative perceptions in the past and also because of contemporary diners' awareness of the healthful qualities of fiber, eating mixed grains with rice has become popular, especially among the younger generation. From three, five, and up to 16 kinds of grains are conveniently pre-mixed and packed, often in ready-to-cook pouches. These mixtures typically include barley, red rice, green rice, sprouted brown rice, glutinous white rice, red beans, amaranth, sesame seed, and several varieties of millet. Rice is most commonly sold as brown rice (*genmai*, the rice grain complete with germ and bran), white rice (*hakumai*), completely polished rice without germ and bran, and semi-polished in varying percentages of polish—30%, 50%, and 70%. The 30% polished rice retains the germ and 30% of the nutrient-rich bran, while the 50% and 70% have the germ and bran removed in ascending order, with the 70% retaining less germ and having all the bran removed. In taste, 70% polished rice approaches the sweetness and whiteness of completely polished rice, while benefiting from greater nutrients.

Japan's annual rice production is just over 10 million tons; when milled, this yields about 8 million tons. Japan imports another 1 million tons, not all for direct consumption. The yearly consumption of rice per capita is at 60 kilos (132 pounds), half that consumed in 1963. In 2011, households in Japan spent more on bread than rice for the first time. This reversal is ascribed to Western-style breakfasts and other meals eaten with bread.

Rice is also used to produce rice wine (*sake*), miso (fermented soybean paste), processed snacks (rice crackers, confectionery), noodles, and vinegar. No part of the rice is wasted. The bran (*nuka*, the external coat removed during rice milling) is used to prepare vegetable pickles, called *nukazuke*.

## Buckwheat, Wheat, and Other Grains

Buckwheat (*Fagopyrum esculentum*), neither cereal grain nor wheat, is mostly prepared (with wheat flour added) into noodles called *soba*. Buckwheat grows in areas with cold winters, such as Hokkaido, Nagano, and Fukushima. Due to increased demand, buckwheat is also imported from China, Canada, and Africa. Other cereals produced and eaten are wheat, barnyard millet, foxtail millet, proso millet (*kibi*), and barley. Proso millet was eaten historically by country folk, traditionally mixed with rice (1%–2% rice to total proso millet). Wheat is widely used for bread and confectionery, as well as noodles such as *udon*, *sōmen* (the thinnest wheat noodle), *kishimen* (flat wide noodles), and "Chinese-style" noodles served in soup called *rāmen*. Nowadays 90% of the wheat used in Japan is imported from Canada, Australia, and other countries, with the rest grown in Hokkaido. Wheat is also used in the processing of soy sauce and miso.

*Influential Ingredients* 27

## Basic Rice

The automatic rice cooker makes cooking rice practically effortless. Follow the manufacturer's directions for its use. However, it is not difficult to cook rice without one. The quantity of water given depends on the variety and how old the rice is (newly harvested rice takes less water to cook). In general, the proportion of short-grain rice to water is 1:1 ¼, that is 1 cup of rice to 1 ¼ cups of water. However, check the packet of rice for the appropriate amount of water for that particular variety.

*Yield:* 4 servings

**Ingredients**
2 cups short-grain rice
2 ½ cups water

**Procedure**
1. Wash the rice well in 2 changes of water, or as soon as the rinse water is no longer cloudy. Drain using a sieve. If you have time, air-dry the rice, still in the sieve, for 30–60 minutes (this step is optional).
2. Transfer rice to a heavy-bottomed pot with cover, and add water. Cover the pot and, over high heat, let the rice come to a rolling boil.
3. Turn heat down to medium, and let rice simmer for 10 minutes. Keep the pot covered throughout cooking.
4. Turn heat down to lowest setting, and let rice simmer for another 5 minutes, or until all the water is absorbed. Turn off heat and let the rice rest, still covered, for 10 minutes before serving.

## Shiitake and Carrot Rice, *Shiitake to Ninjin no Takikomi Gohan*

This dish is one of many versions of *takikomi gohan* (rice cooked with other ingredients)—here, shiitake mushrooms, carrots, and fried tofu (*aburaage*). One could fancifully call it the Japanese version of paella or risotto, only that *takikomi gohan* is not cooked with oil or butter. Other popular *takikomi gohan* variants include chicken pieces with burdock root and carrot. Others may showcase a vegetable representative of the season, such as the earliest bamboo shoot or wild mountain fiddleheads in spring, or aromatic and prized *matsutake* (pine mushrooms in autumn). You may substitute another kind of mushroom, such as *shimeji*, an autumn mushroom, for the shiitake. Failing that, use the freshest mushrooms available in your local shop, such as small Portobello mushrooms. This recipe is suitable for vegetarians and vegans if the *dashi* powder used is not based on *katsuobushi* (dried bonito flakes). Its use is optional, as the shiitake mushrooms provide enough *umami* flavor on their own. Choose firm, thick-fleshed shiitake (called *donko*) for best quality, flavor, and aroma. *Aburaage* are pre-fried, thin-walled tofu pieces that are often used to make stuffed dishes. *Takikomi gohan*, of whatever variety, makes a light lunch with a vegetable salad. This recipe can also be prepared in an automatic rice cooker.

*Yield:* 4–5 servings

**Ingredients**
2 cups rice
10 fresh shiitake mushrooms
1 large carrot, peeled and sliced into fine julienne strips, 1 ½ inches long
2 pieces *aburaage*
2 ½ cups water
1 4-inch-square piece *konbu*
3 tablespoons mirin
5 tablespoons *sake*
2 teaspoons soy sauce
½ teaspoon salt
1 teaspoon *dashi* powder (optional)
*Mitsuba* (trefoil) leaves for garnish

**Procedure**
1. Wash rice well in 2 changes of water, or until rinse water is no longer cloudy. Drain with a sieve. If you have the time, air-dry the rice, still in the sieve, for 1 hour before cooking.
2. Trim the bottom end of the shiitake stalks. Slice stalks and caps into fine strips.
3. Peel the carrot, and slice it into fine julienne strips, 1 ½ inches long.
4. Place the *aburaage* in a sieve or colander, and pour boiling water over them to remove excess oil. Pat dry with paper towels, and dice or slice into fine julienne strips.
5. Place rice, shiitake mushrooms, carrots, *aburaage*, water, mirin, *sake*, soy sauce, salt, and *dashi* powder in a heavy-bottomed pan with a tight-fitting cover.
6. Place the *konbu* over the rice and vegetable mixture.
7. Cover the pan, place over medium heat, and bring to a boil.
8. Once pot is boiling briskly, turn down the heat and let mixture simmer for 15 minutes, or until all liquid has been absorbed.

9. Turn off heat and allow rice mixture to rest, covered, for 10 minutes.
10. Discard the *konbu*. Gently mix the rice, bringing up rice and vegetables from the bottom, so that all the ingredients are equally distributed.

*To serve:* Mound into individual bowls. Garnish each bowl with mitsuba.

## Stock, *Dashi*

The basis of traditional Japanese food is a stock called *dashi*. *Dashi* is at the heart of virtually all Japanese stews, soups, braised dishes, and dipping sauces. It is to the Japanese kitchen what *fond* is to the French kitchen. Although commonly called "stock," *dashi* is technically not one, as stock is made from long-simmered ingredients, whereas *dashi*, in particular *ichiban dashi*, is more of an infusion. The first ingredient of *dashi* is dried giant kelp or sea tangle (*konbu*, *Laminaria* species). The best *konbu* are harvested from the cold waters off Hokkaido. There are approximately 13 edible species of konbu, and of these the most commonly used in the Japanese kitchen for *dashi* are *makonbu* (true or genuine kelp), *rausu konbu, rishiri konbu,* and *hidaka konbu*. The kelp's leaf blades, which grow to 2–6 meters and 8–12 inches wide, are harvested at 2–3 years. *Konbu* quality is determined by its thickness and aroma. The thicker the blade, the more pronounced the aroma and taste, and the higher the price. *Makonbu,* also known as Matsumae *konbu* or Yamadashi *konbu,* can be as thick as $1/10$ inch and 10–12 inches wide. It is considered the best quality for *dashi* making, as well as for other processed *konbu* products. For all-around *dashi* making, the next favored konbu is *rishiri konbu*. It grows almost as long as *makonbu*, but is slightly narrower, at 8 inches maximum width. *Rausu konbu* is noted for its distinctive flavor and scent. *Konbu* by itself is enough to make *dashi*, and *konbu*-based *dashi* is used to prepare vegetarian dishes.

The second ingredient used for *dashi* is a fermented, dried, and aged fillet of *katsuo* (bonito or skipjack, *Katsuwonus pelamis*). The rock-hard fillet, which resembles petrified wood, is called *katsuobushi*, and is shaved into fine flakes using a tool called *katsuobushi kezuriki* that looks like a woodworker's plane.

Dried anchovies or baby sardines, called *niboshi* or *iriko*, as well as dried baby flying fish (*ago*) are also used to make *dashi* instead of or in addition to bonito flakes, especially in southern Honshu and Kyushu. These are used without the head and belly, and are soaked overnight in cold water. They are then added to *konbu*-infused stock. Nowadays, instant, ready-prepared *dashi* is more commonly used at home, to spare the modern Japanese cook time and effort. Instant *dashi* comes in the form of granules and is sold in packets. *Katsuo* flakes are also available in packets. However, there is no comparison to the flavor of fresh shavings directly from the rock-hard *katsuobushi* using the time-honored *katsuobushi kezuriki* shaving tool, not only because of the chemical additives in instant *dashi*, such as monosodium glutamate (a flavor enhancer that incidentally is present in its natural state on the surface of dried kelp), but also because of the quickly discernible difference in flavors obtained from freshly prepared ingredients.

---

### Konbu Stock, *Konbu Dashi*

There is no need to wash kelp. The whitish powder on its surface is naturally occurring glutamine, which led to the scientific discovery of monosodium glutamate. Any surface dirt can be lightly brushed with a clean kitchen cloth.

*Yield:* 4 cups

**Ingredients**
1 ounce *konbu* (giant kelp)
4 cups water

**Procedure**

*Slow method*
1. Soak *konbu* in water overnight.
2. Remove konbu, but do not discard (use for *niban dashi* or other dish). The water in which the *konbu* was soaked is now *konbu dashi* (konbu stock), and can be used for vegetarian and vegan dishes.

*Rapid method*
1. Over medium heat, place a pan with water and *konbu*.
2. Let it come almost to a boil, then immediately turn off the heat. Prolonged cooking makes kelp viscous and its flavor too prominent. [However, for *dashi* intended for long-simmered dishes, such as *oden*, or one-pot dishes (*nabemono*), the kelp is allowed to remain longer or throughout cooking.]
3. Remove the kelp but do not discard (use for *niban dashi* or other dish).
4. The *konbu dashi* is ready to be used for vegetarian and vegan dishes, or to be added to *katsuo*-based stock for *ichiban dashi*.

*Influential Ingredients*

---

## Primary *Dashi* (Mixed *Konbu* and *Katsuobushi Dashi*), *Ichiban Dashi*

*Yield:* 4 cups

**Ingredients**
4 cups *konbu dashi* (from preceding recipe)
1 ounce *katsuobushi* (bonito flakes)

**Procedure**
1. Put *konbu dashi* into a pan, and over medium heat, bring it close to a boil (just until small bubbles form at the walls of the pan).
2. Turn off the heat and add the bonito flakes.
3. Leave it to infuse for 1–2 minutes, or until the bonito flakes settle at the bottom of the pan. Then pass the liquid through a fine sieve, preferably through cheesecloth or a paper coffee filter.

*This* ichiban dashi *is now ready for use. The bonito flakes and* konbu *can be reused for* niban dashi.

---

## Secondary *Dashi*, *Niban Dashi*

*Yield:* 4 cups

**Ingredients**
4 cups water
Used *konbu* and *katsuobushi* from *ichiban dashi*
½ ounce *katsuobushi*

**Procedure**
1. In a pan over medium heat, place 4 cups of water and the used *konbu* and *katsuobushi*.
2. Bring to just under boiling point, then lower the heat; allow to simmer gently for about 15 minutes.
3. Add the *katsuobushi* and turn off heat.
4. Let the *katsuobushi* settle to the bottom of the pan.
5. Pass the liquid through a fine sieve lined with cheesecloth or a paper filter.

---

## Seasonings

Besides sea salt, soy sauce and miso are the main seasonings. Soy sauce comes in two types: dark *koikuchi shōyu* (literally, "thick mouth soy sauce") and light *usukuchi shōyu* ("thin mouth soy sauce"). *Koikuchi shōyu* is the most common, and constitutes 80% of all soy sauce made in Japan. It has a dark color, but contrary to what one expects, it is not very salty, containing only about 14%–18% salt. In contrast, *usukuchi shōyu,* which constitutes 18% of the soy sauce made in Japan, has a light color. but its salt content is actually greater at 20%–21%. The longer soy sauce is fermented, the more flavorful it becomes, and its color becomes darker, too. The pale color of light soy sauce results from a shorter fermentation period because of its higher salt content. Dark soy sauce is preferred over light soy sauce as a dipping sauce because of its more robust flavor. Light soy sauce is often finished with a light syrup or sweet *sake* to balance its high salt content. Because of its gentler aroma, it is mainly used for vegetable dishes. In general, the Kansai region (areas around Osaka and Kyoto) prefers light soy sauce for cooking, and the Kanto region (area around Tokyo and further north) prefers dark soy sauce.

There are three additional types of soy sauce—tamari, *saishikomi* (double-fermented), and *shiro* (white). Tamari is the highly flavored liquid produced during the fermentation of soy sauce. It constitutes about 2% of all soy sauce manufactured in Japan. It is highly prized (and priced) for dipping sashimi and sushi. Double-fermented soy sauce, *saishikomi shōyu*, was originally made in Yamaguchi Prefecture, but is now being made nationwide. Instead of using brine to ferment the soybean paste, dark soy sauce is used, thus resulting in a stronger-tasting, thicker sauce. Because of its rich flavor as a result of its longer processing period (often as long as three years), *saishikomi shōyu* commands a high price, and is the most sought-after sauce by gourmets for dipping sashimi and sushi. Double-fermented soy sauce represents about 1% of all soy sauce manufactured in Japan. White soy sauce is paler than light soy sauce, almost the color of beer, and has a salt content of 18%. Fastidious cooks use it to keep the color of a dish's ingredients unspoiled by dark soy sauce.

Each region in Japan has its own preferred type of miso (fermented soybean paste). The main types are white, red, and dark miso. The Kansai region prefers "white" (light-colored) miso with a high salt content, pronounced sweetness, and a sophisticated aroma. Northern Japan (Sendai, Tsugaru, Akita, Echigo, and Sado areas) prefers to cook with red miso, with a marked saltiness and intense flavor. The well-known and highly valued *hatchō miso* is a dark miso—full-flavored with a characteristic robust aroma—that keeps for a long time because it is made with pure soybeans.

*Sake* and mirin are used individually or together to balance the saltiness of soy sauce. Much as wine is used in French cuisine, *sake* and mirin impart their intrinsic flavors and enhance those of other ingredients.

## Spices and Herbs

Spices and herbs are seldom used to flavor traditional Japanese dishes during cooking; rather, they are added before serving or as edible garnishes that release their aroma at the point of eating. The exceptions are the Japanese Western-style dish called curry rice, which at home is usually made with cubes of industrially manufactured curry roux; and the broth for the Japanese Chinese-style *rāmen* which benefits from garlic, ginger, leeks, green onions, and in some cases bay leaf. Contemporary cooks use foreign herbs (cilantro, Thai basil, lemon grass, mint, dill, flat and curly-leafed parsley, etc.), and spices such as cumin and coriander to give an innovative spin to Japanese dishes.

Some herbs and spices used in traditional Japanese dishes are described below.

> *Sanshō* (*Zanthoxylum piperitum*) is a spice customarily sprinkled over roasted or grilled foods, such as *unagi no kabayaki* (grilled eel) and *yakitori* (grilled chicken on bamboo skewers). It is also one of the spices in the seven-spice mixture called *shichimi tōgarashi*. The young leaves of *sanshō* are valued as a garnish and for their aroma. *Shisō* (*Perilla frutescens*) is an herb whose leaves and flower buds are used both as garnish and as flavoring. The red-leafed variety of *shisō* provides color and flavor to preserved salted plums *umeboshi*. The use of *sanshō* and *shisō* dates back to prehistoric Jōmon times.

The spice *sanshō* is sprinkled on roasted or grilled foods just before serving. *Sanshō* are the ground, roasted berries of Japanese pepper, *Zanthoxylum piperitum*, a relative of Sichuan pepper. Its young leaves, called *kinome*, and flowers (*hanazanshō*) are used as aromatic edible garnishes. Its bark is made into an appetizer called *kara kawa* in Hyogo Prefecture.

Ginger (*shōga, Zingiber officinale*) is most often seen in its pickled form, *gari*, which accompanies sushi or sashimi. Fresh finely grated ginger is paired with finely grated fresh giant radish (*daikon*) to add to tempura dipping sauce and to accompany grilled fish. Ginger's young tender stems are pickled for use as an edible garnish for grilled or roasted foods.

Fine slices of the pink flower buds of *myōga* (*Zingiber mioga*), a ginger relative, are used as an edible garnish, lending their flowery aroma and color to fish dishes and soups. *Myōga's* tender stems are also pickled as edible and aromatic garnishes for grilled and roasted dishes.

Besides the familiar round yellow or white onion and spring onions, the Japanese kitchen relies heavily on the local leek, *naga negi* (literally "long onion," *Allium fistulosum*). It is more frequently used in Japanese dishes than onions (known as *tama negi*, "round onion"). Garlic chives (*nira*, *Allium tuberosum*) are used to flavor *gyōza* (pan-fried dumplings or pot stickers). Garlic, rarely used in traditional Japanese dishes, is used in Korean-style grilled meats and pickles, Chinese-style dishes, and Western-style dishes. Contemporary cooks are using more garlic.

The stalks and leaves of the water dropwort, *seri* (*Oenanthe javanica*), are valued in one-pot dishes for their sharp herby scent. *Seri* is also one of the seven pot herbs of spring. The Japanese trefoil, *mitsuba* (*Cryptotaenia japonica*), is often called Japanese parsley because it is frequently used to adorn dishes. However, its scent is more delicate than that of parsley. The name *mitsuba* is literally "three leaf," as each leaf has three leaflets joined at the base.

*Shisō*, both green and red types, are the leaves of *Perilla frutescens*. Green *shisō* usually adorns a dish of sashimi and is often combined with the paste of the pickled Japanese plum (*umeboshi*) in hand-rolled sushi. Red *shisō* leaves are used to flavor and color plum pickles called *umeboshi*. The flower stalks, called *hōjiso*, often served with sashimi, are not only decor: the buds are meant to be stripped from the stalk and dropped into the dipping bowl, contributing their herbal scent to the soy sauce.

*Tade*, water pepper's (*Polygonum hydropiper*) baby leaves, come in both green and red. The red type often accompanies sashimi, and the green type is mixed with vinegar for a dip to go with grilled sweetfish (*ayu*). True to its name, it tastes peppery.

*Yuzu* (*Citrus junos*), though technically not a spice or herb, is a citrus fruit treasured for the distinctive aroma of its rind, thin slivers of which are often used sparingly as decor for *chawan mushi* and clear broths. The juice is often mixed with soy sauce for dipping. *Yuzu* was brought over from China as a medicinal plant during the Asuka or Nara period. It is traditionally floated whole or in slivers for a midwinter bath. Another citrus fruit used as flavoring is *daidai*, bitter or Seville orange (*Citrus aurantium*), with its juice added to soy sauce dips. Similarly, the juice of *kabosu*, a green-skinned citrus fruit (*Citrus sphaerocarpa*), is added to soy sauce dips for hot-pot dishes (*nabemono*).

*Shichimi tōgarashi*, literally seven-flavor chili pepper, is a mixture of fine and coarsely ground dry spices whose seven ingredients vary according to the preferences of the shop or brand or the particular region of the country. When bought from a specialist shop, the customer can choose which spices and how much heat (in the amount of chili pepper) to include in the mixture. The most common spices found in *shichimi* (for short) are chili pepper (the main spice), *sanshō* (Japanese mountain pepper), hemp seed, green nori flakes, black or white sesame seed, ginger, poppy seed, green *shisō*, and roasted orange peel. In the Kanto region, *shichimi* is more fiery, in keeping with the general preference of Tokyoites for robust flavoring. The Kansai region prefers its *shichimi* to be aromatic rather than peppery.

## Vegetables

### Leafy Vegetables

The Japanese kitchen uses many leafy vegetables, of which the most common are Chinese cabbage (*hakusai*) and spinach (*horensō*). Chinese cabbage tastes best between late fall and winter, as exposure to frost makes it sweeter. Japanese spinach has smooth leaves and tender stalks, and is not astringent like the Western variety. The season for spinach, as with Chinese cabbage, is late fall to winter. Leafy greens are often prepared as *ohitashi*—blanched and flavored with *dashi* and soy sauce, sometimes sprinkled with bonito flakes (*katsuobushi*).

The cabbage family (*Brassicaceae*) contributes the most greens to the Japanese kitchen: *komatsuna* with leaves like turnip greens; *kyōna* (or *mizuna* in the Kansai region) and its close relative *mibuna* with serrated, mild-tasting leaves; and flowering rape shoots (*nanohana, Brassica napus*). Recently these greens have also become popular outside Japan. The season for leafy greens is late fall to winter. The aromatic leaves of edible chrysanthemum (*shungiku, Chrysanthemum coronarium*), often combined with their tiny yellow flower petals, are rapidly blanched and flavored with stock and dried bonito flakes (*katsuobushi*) for *ohitashi*. Chrysanthemum greens are also included in one-pot dishes (*nabemono*). Mitsuba (*Cryptotaenia japonica*), or trefoil, is a green herb much appreciated for its aroma. Often called Japanese parsley, it is unrelated to Western parsley, and its delicate flavor is not at all similar. It is used as a vegetable in its own right, as well as a garnish.

### Root Vegetables

The giant radish, *daikon*, is the most versatile of Japanese vegetables, often found in miso soups as dice or short strips. Thick cylinders are slowly braised for *furofuki daikon*, a warming winter dish. Lacy *daikon* "fishing nets" often garnish sashimi. Finely grated as *daikon oroshi*, it is mixed with grated fresh ginger for dipping tempura. Finely grated *daikon* often appears alongside grilled fish, drizzled with a bit of soy sauce, as a condiment, and is also stirred into soup called *mizore jiru* ("sleet soup").

Daikon is most often made into *takuan* pickles. Its flesh is dried as *hoshi daikon*, to be rehydrated before cooking. No part of the daikon is wasted: the leaves are blanched and dressed for *aemono*, and can also be dried and rehydrated. Even the peelings are useful: they are used to prime the pickling bed for rice bran pickles (*nukazuke*).

Burdock (*gobō*) has an earthy aroma and crisp texture, quite similar to a nonsweet parsnip. It is often paired with carrot in *kinpira gobō*. Burdock was originally brought to Japan from China as a medicinal plant, but Japanese horticulturists developed it into a much-appreciated ingredient for stews (*nimono*), salads (*aemono*), and New Year dishes.

Bamboo shoots (*takenoko*) are the undeveloped culms of several varieties of bamboo, dug up as soon as half an inch becomes visible above ground. Once the shoot has completely broken through the soil, it becomes too woody to be edible. Thus, harvesting bamboo shoots is a race against time. The tenderest bamboo shoot is from the *mōsō* bamboo (*Phyllostachys edulis*). The ones specially grown in Kyoto are famous. The season for bamboo shoots is late fall to early winter in southern Japan (Kagoshima) and spring in central Japan.

Taro is known as *sato imo* ("field tuber"). A vegetable soup with tiny taro tubers, called *imonoko jiru*, is an autumn specialty of Akita Prefecture. To prepare taro, all remaining soil is washed off, then they are peeled and rubbed with salt to remove their slipperiness. They are then soaked in cold water to remove any irritants (*aku*). *Ebi imo* ("shrimp tuber"), so named because it curves like a cooked shrimp, is a type of taro specially grown in Kyoto.

True yams (not sweet potatoes) include *yamaimo* (also *yama no imo*, literally "mountain yam" *Dioscorea japonica*) and *nagaimo* (long yam, *Dioscorea polystachya*). These are often eaten raw. *Yamaimo* is finely grated to a snowy fluff, called *tororo*, mixed with hot rice for breakfast, or with cold buckwheat noodles (*zaru soba*). *Nagaimo* is not as sticky as *yamaimo*, and is usually sliced raw into strips for salads (*aemono*). These yams are relished for their viscosity as well as their nutritional minerals and vitamins.

## Soy and Other Beans

The soybean is ubiquitous in Japanese food culture. The fresh pods with unripe beans, called *edamame*, are blanched and salted, and the green beans inside are perfect for summer snacking with drinks. Puréed *edamame* paste called *zunda* is used in sweet pastries. The dried beans are pressed for soy milk, a product in its own right, as well as the basis for

## Influential Ingredients

other products. Soy sheets called *yuba* are dried, to be reconstituted before use, or used fresh to wrap vegetables or other ingredients into rolls for steaming or braising. Bean curd (*tōfu*) comes in two types: *momen dōfu*, sieved through a cotton (*momen*) filter, and *kinugoshi dōfu*, filtered through silk (*kinu*). *Yakidōfu* is grilled tofu with charred bars on its surface. Bean curd can be fried as well; the thin-walled kind, called *aburaage*, puffs up to create a pocket for stuffing. Thick-walled fried bean curd is called *atsuage* ("thick fried"). Freeze-dried bean curd, called *kōya dōfu*, must be rehydrated before cooking. The lees (*okara*) that remain after processing diverse soybean products are not discarded; instead, they are added to dressed salads (*aemono*). Soybean flour (*kinako*) is used to dust rice cakes for easier handling and eating. *Kinako* comes in both pale brown and green; green *kinako* is made from green soybeans.

> The soybean is an important food. While the pods are green and the beans inside not fully ripe, they are harvested as *edamame* (literally, "branch bean"). Quickly parboiled and seasoned with salt, *edamame* are the usual summer accompaniment to cold beer. Pureed and mixed with sugar, *edamame* becomes *zunda*, a filling and coating for rice cakes (*mochi*) in northeastern Japan. The mature beans are boiled and pressed to produce soymilk, which can be further processed into soybean sheets (*yuba*) and soybean curd (*tōfu*). *Tōfu*, when fried, becomes *aburaage* and *atsuage*. The mature beans, when fermented, become the important Japanese seasonings soy sauce, miso, and tamari.

Steamed soybeans are fermented with special bacteria into a fermented viscous delicacy called *nattō*, commonly served for breakfast in the Kanto region, but not so popular elsewhere because of its strong smell. Regular *nattō* consumption is considered to contribute to intestinal and overall health. Since the coronavirus pandemic in 2020, sales and consumption of *nattō* have increased. *Hama nattō* is a dark, dry type of fermented soybeans, originally processed in China and brought to Japan by Buddhist monks. Aside from being used in Buddhist temple cuisine, it is also used by professional chefs as a hidden flavor (*kakushi aji*) to enhance the taste of special dishes.

Small red beans called *azuki* (also spelled adzuki in English) are made into sweet fillings for rice cakes. Red bean paste is the basis for a sweet soup with tiny rice balls. *Azuki* beans are cooked with rice for a celebratory dish called *sekihan* ("red rice").

*Saya endō*, sugar pea pods, are used for stir-fries, salads, and as garnish.

The sword bean (*nata ingen, Canavalia gladiata*), so called because of its length (about 12 inches), is widely cultivated and eaten in southern Japan (Kagoshima, Kyushu, Shikoku, and Okinawa).

## Other Vegetables and Fungi

Small, mild-tasting green peppers called *shishitōgarashi*, or *shishitō* for short, are often used for *yakitori* and tempura. Several types of eggplant (*nasu*) are used in the Japanese kitchen: tiny ones no larger than 2 inches long to large, wide, oval ones about 6 inches long (*bei nasu*), often sliced lengthwise, topped with miso, and grilled. Eggplants are frequently braised, as they are noted for their capacity to absorb flavoring.

Japanese squashes (*kabocha*) are firm, sweet, and nutty and lend themselves to slow cooking.

Cucumbers (*kyūri*) in Japan are harvested earlier than their Western counterparts (before seeds form), and are slimmer and mild tasting without bitterness. They are also rather spiny. They are used raw in salads (*aemono*) and occasionally cooked in stir-fries.

Bitter melon (*niga uri* or *gōya, Momordica charantia*) is a distinctive ingredient of Okinawan cooking. It resembles a cucumber with dark green wavy ridges. Its bitterness is regarded as a health promoter, and many Okinawans attribute their longevity to it. (The bitter melon is known to lower blood sugar in diabetics.)

*Hayato uri* (*Sechium edule*) is christophene or chayote, originally from Mexico, but introduced in 1917 to Kagoshima. It has a mild taste and crisp texture, and is most commonly eaten in Okinawa and Kagoshima.

The spring shoots of mountain greens called *sansai* ("mountain vegetables") include the fiddleheads (curled young shoots) of ferns, such as *warabi* (common bracken, *Pteridium aquilinum*), *kogomi* (ostrich fern, *Matteuccia struthiopteris*) and *zenmai* (Asian royal fern, *Osmunda japonica*). *Warabi* is soaked in lye water overnight to neutralize irritants (*aku*). The fern fiddleheads are prepared as tempura, blanched for *ohitashi*, and dressed for salads (*aemono*). The buds of the Japanese butterbur (*fuki no tō, Petasites japonica*) are prepared as tempura, as are the tender shoots of horsetail (*tsukushi, Equisetum arvense*).

The sheer variety of mushrooms used in the Japanese kitchen is astounding. They include the thick, flavorful caps of *shiitake* (fresh and dried), needle-like clumps of *enokidake*, gray- and beige-capped *shimeji*, coral-like *maidake*, and aromatic, prized *matsutake* (pine mushroom), an autumn delicacy.

*Influential Ingredients* 39

The lotus is highly regarded for its flowers and edible root. The root with its interior chambers is regarded as auspicious and thus is often prepared for New Year feasts and special occasions. It is peeled and soaked in cold water before using, to prevent it from turning brown.

Water chestnuts (*kuwai*) are the tubers of the arrowhead plant (*Sagittaria trifolia*). They are appreciated for their crisp texture and, like the lotus root, are often used in New Year dishes.

### Lotus Root with Walnut Miso Dressing, *Renkon no Kurumi Miso Ae*

In Akita Prefecture in Northern Honshu, walnuts are a common crop, often used to add body and flavor to *aemono*. This autumn dish uses freshly harvested walnuts combined with miso as dressing. The flavorful dressing is versatile, and can be used with other vegetables such as lettuce, arugula, or baby spinach. It is equally good on blanched kale, asparagus, broccoli, cauliflower, leek, beets, carrots, cabbage, baby onions—the choice is yours. This dish is also good to complement beer or *sake*.

*Yield:* 4 servings

**Ingredients**
1 cup walnut meats
3 tablespoons *sake*
3 tablespoons mirin
3 tablespoons miso, red or white
1 teaspoon sugar, or to taste
1 pound fresh lotus root, washed
5 tablespoons vinegar
2 cups water
¼ teaspoon salt
4 stalks green onions (green part only), or chives

**Procedure**
1. Prepare the walnut miso paste. Dry-toast the walnut meats in a heavy-bottomed frying pan at low heat until aromatic. Let cool to room temperature.
2. Reserve 4 tablespoons of walnuts and roughly chop. Place the rest of the walnuts into a food processor, and add the *sake*, mirin, and miso. Process to a paste. Add a bit more *sake* or mirin if too thick. Taste and add sugar only if necessary to balance the saltiness of the miso. The sweetness imparted by the mirin may be enough.

3. Prepare the lotus root. Peel the lotus root and slice into ¼-inch-thick rings. Slice the rings in half. Place the slices at once into a bowl of water with 2 tablespoons of vinegar to prevent discoloring.
4. Bring to a boil the remaining 3 tablespoons of vinegar, water, and salt over high heat. Add the lotus root slices and parboil briefly, until they are translucent but still crisp. Drain thoroughly and pat dry with paper towels.
5. Place the lotus root slices into a mixing bowl. Gently stir in 6 heaping spoonfuls of the walnut miso paste until the lotus root slices are all coated. Arrange into mounds in 4 small bowls. Sprinkle with finely sliced green onions or chives.
6. Alternatively, arrange the lotus root slices in mounds in 4 small bowls. Place about 1 ½ heaping spoonfuls of the walnut miso paste in the center of the mound, taking care not to totally obscure the lotus root slices. There should be a clear division between the white lotus root and the brown-beige walnut miso paste. Top with a sprinkling of finely sliced green onions or chives.

*Serve at once, as the walnut miso dressing tends to separate if left standing.*

*Any remaining walnut miso paste will keep in the refrigerator for about a week. Mix well before using.*

## Blanched Trefoil, *Mitsuba no Ohitashi*

Substitute young spinach, Chinese cabbage, arugula, spring chrysanthemum (*shungiku*), or green pea shoots if *mitsuba* is unavailable.

Yield: 4 servings

**Ingredients**
1 pound *mitsuba*, washed well, with roots intact
1 cup freshly made *dashi*
1 tablespoon mirin
3 tablespoons soy sauce
4 tablespoons *katsuobushi*

**Procedure**
1. Prepare a large bowl of ice-cold water and set aside.
2. Blanch the *mitsuba*. In a large saucepan, bring to a boil 1 quart of water with a pinch of salt. As soon as the water boils, add *mitsuba*. When water returns to a boil, in about a minute or less, remove *mitsuba* and

plunge into ice-cold water to stop cooking and prevent discoloring. Drain *mitsuba*, and lightly press to remove excess water.
3. Prepare *hitashi* dressing. In a saucepan over medium heat or in a microwave, heat *dashi*, mirin, and soy sauce just below boiling point. Mix and adjust seasoning. Turn off heat and let cool.

*To serve:* Cut mitsuba *into 3-inch lengths. Place heaped mounds into 4 small deep bowls. Spoon flavoring sauce gently over* mitsuba. *Sprinkle* katsuobushi *on top.*

*If not eaten at once, cover bowls with plastic wrap and refrigerate. Top with* katsuobushi *just before serving.*

## Bamboo Shoot Taro in Shirazu Dressing,
### *Takenoko Imo no Shirazu Ae*

Bamboo shoot taro is a specialty of Miyazaki Prefecture, but is commonly used in Kyoto cookery. This taro is the longest variety of taro (up to 2 feet long), and is so named for its physical resemblance to bamboo shoot. Substitute regular taro, called *sato imo*, if bamboo shoot taro is unavailable. Taro has a natural slippery or viscous texture that is appreciated by Japanese diners. The tubers' slipperiness is reduced by rubbing them with salt, rinsing, then blanching before further cooking. To serve, choose 4 small deep ceramic bowls with a dark glaze to contrast with the pale taro and dressing.

*Yield:* 4 servings

**Ingredients**
½ pound bamboo shoot taro or regular taro, washed thoroughly
½ teaspoon salt
1 ½ cups dashi
4 small slices *yuzu* zest (or lemon zest) for garnish

*Dressing*
1 block silk (*kinugoshi*) tofu, well drained
1 ½ tablespoons white miso
1 tablespoon rice vinegar
2 tablespoons mirin
2 tablespoons *sake*

**Procedure**
1. Prepare the taro: Peel, using a pair of disposable gloves, as taro contains crystals that sometimes irritate skin. Rub with salt and rinse. If using bamboo shoot taro, slice in 2-inch lengths. Leave regular taro whole if no larger than 2 inches. Soak in a large bowl with water to cover for about 30 minutes. In a large saucepan, place taro and enough hot water to cover; add ½ teaspoon salt. Bring to a boil over medium heat for 2–3 minutes. Take off heat and drain the taro. Rinse them and if still slippery, rub again with salt, rinse, and drain.
2. In a large saucepan, place the taro in a single layer, and cover with *dashi*. Let simmer over low heat for 20–25 minutes, or until a bamboo skewer easily pierces the taro.
3. Meanwhile prepare the dressing. Into a food processor bowl, place tofu, miso, vinegar, mirin, and *sake*. Process until thoroughly blended. Taste, and adjust seasoning. The vinegar's tanginess should be balanced by the sweetness of mirin and saltiness of miso. Chill dressing until ready to serve.

*To serve:* Mound taro with dressing into 4 small, deep bowls. Garnish with zest.

## Braised Squash, *Kabochani*

Autumn and winter are the seasons for enjoying squash. The best variety to use for this dish is the *kuri* (chestnut) *kabocha* type, with firm, nutty, sweet flesh. If this type of squash is unavailable, use butternut squash. *Shirasu* or *chirimenjako* both refer to dried sardine fry (immature or baby fish). The Kanto region calls them *shirasu*; the Kansai region calls them *chirimenjako*. They are usually sold in Asian food shops.

*Yield:* 4 servings

**Ingredients**
4 dried *shiitake* mushrooms
½ cup dried sardine fry (*shirasu* or *chirimenjako*) or dried whitebait
1 cup *dashi*
2 tablespoons mirin
2 tablespoons *sake*
2 tablespoons soy sauce, or to taste
1 pound kabocha squash (about ½ of a whole squash)
4 red maple leaves for garnish

*Influential Ingredients* 43

**Procedure**
1. Prepare braising stock. Rehydrate *shiitake* mushrooms in enough warm water to cover for 20 minutes. Cut the tip off stems and discard, but keep stems for making stock. Slice *shiitake* caps into quarters or eighths, if large. Place sliced *shiitake* and stems into a saucepan; add the dried sardine fry, *dashi*, mirin, *sake*, and soy sauce. Bring the stock ingredients to a boil and lower the heat to allow contents to simmer for 20 minutes. Remove *shiitake* stems, press to extract stock, and discard the pressed stems.
2. Meanwhile, prepare squash. After washing, remove and discard seeds and central membranes. Kabocha skin is edible, so there is no need to peel. However, for aesthetics, peel off skin randomly. If using butternut squash, peel off all the skin. Slice squash into 2-inch pieces.
3. Place squash in a wide saucepan in one layer. Pour braising stock over the squash, cover pan, and bring to a boil. Lower heat and simmer for 15 minutes, or until toothpick pierces through squash and very little liquid remains. Turn off heat, but leave squash in pan.

*To serve: Choose pale-colored bowls and mound the squash. Garnish each bowl with a maple leaf. Serve warm or cold.*

## Stir-Fried Bitter Melon, *Gōya Itame*

*Gōya* (bitter melon) is a vegetable typically used in Okinawa and southern Japan, though its popularity is spreading throughout the country. Bitter melon's bitterness can be reduced by salting and rinsing before cooking.

*Yield:* 4 servings

**Ingredients**
1 pound bitter melon
1 tablespoon salt
2 tablespoons cooking oil
½ pound belly pork, sliced into bite-sized pieces
2 tablespoons fresh ginger, grated
1 clove garlic, finely grated
1–2 tablespoons miso
2 tablespoons mirin
Tomato slices for garnish

**Procedure**
1. Slice bitter melon in half lengthwise. With a spoon, scoop out the seeds and central spongy membrane and discard. Slice the bitter melon halves into very fine half-rings. Place slices in a bowl and sprinkle with salt. Toss to let the salt touch all the slices. Let stand for 15 minutes, rinse well, and drain. This step reduces bitterness.
2. In a large frying pan over medium heat, put the oil and stir-fry the pork pieces until golden.
3. Stir in ginger, garlic, miso, and mirin, followed by the drained bitter melon.
4. Stir-fry until the bitter melon is tender but still crisp.
5. Adjust seasoning, and turn off heat.

*To serve: Mound into small bowls and garnish with tomato slices. Serve as a side dish with rice.*

## Fish and Seafood

The Japanese consume more than 860 species of marine and freshwater fish. Around 600 marine species—half of them fish—are traded at Toyosu (which replaced the world-famous Tsukiji market) in Tokyo, the largest fish market in the world. The majority (86%) of fresh, live, and frozen fish are caught by the Japanese fishing fleet; 14% are imports. Crustaceans (such as shrimps, prawns, crabs, and lobsters) and cephalopods (squid, cuttlefish, octopus) account for the remainder. Japan caught almost a quarter of the world's total marine capture volume of 94 million tons in 2015. Nevertheless, Japan still imports much of its marine food—it is the world's second largest importer of fish and top importer of seafood from the United States, China, Chile, Thailand, Russia, Taiwan, Canada, and more than 100 other countries.

Fish, seafood, and other marine products, such as seaweeds, appear on the Japanese dining table at least once daily, even if only as *dashi*. In 2006, nationwide consumption of fish totaled 8 million tons. In 1997, Japan topped worldwide fish consumption at 66.7 kilograms (147 lbs.) per capita. By 2014, consumption had dropped to less than a third, at 27.3 kg (60.2 lbs.), because meat consumption has gone up. (In comparison, the average annual consumption of fish in the United States in 2016 was 14.7 lbs of fish per capita, a tenth of Japanese consumption in 1997.) The most commonly eaten fish varieties are described here.

### *Aji*, Japanese Horse Mackerel

*Aji* is a popular marine fish for home cooking whose name derives from the word "taste" (*aji*), owing to its good flavor. When fresh, it is best as sashimi, *tataki*, sushi, or marinated in vinegar (*aji suzuke*). Fresh aji is found in the famed *obentō* (boxed meal) called *aji no oshizushi* (pressed *aji* sushi). It is frequently salt-grilled (*shioyaki*), fried, and then marinated Southern Barbarian style (*aji nambanzuke*), or dried overnight and grilled for breakfast (*hitoyazuke*). Thicker-fleshed varieties are made into a salted and dried condiment called *kusaya*, a strong-smelling delicacy often served with *sake*. *Aji* are available all year round, but the small ones caught from May to July taste best. Larger, thicker-fleshed *aji* caught from fall to winter are considered inferior.

### *Akōdai*, Red Rockfish

*Akōdai* is a deep-sea fish with firm, white flesh noted for good flavor. It belongs to the scorpionfish family, which provides the most species for the Japanese table. Its season is winter. It is suitable for sashimi, and its firm texture lends itself to slow braising.

### *Ayu*, Sweetfish

*Ayu* is a freshwater fish, 4 to 6 inches long, prized for its delicate sweetness and white flesh. It is in season during summer, and is served quickly grilled at high heat—no more than 10 minutes—just until the flesh nearest the bone is cooked. Its diet of river algae gives its innards a bitter flavor that gourmets appreciate. Like the salmon, to which it is related, it spends the winter in the sea and returns inland to spawn in spring. It only lives for a year.

### *Buri*, Yellowtail, Japanese Amberjack

*Buri* is related to *aji*. Its name changes as it matures—at 6 inches long, in the Tokyo area it is called *wakashi*. Between 14 and 15 inches, its name becomes *inada*, whereas in the Osaka area it is known as *hamachi*. Farm-raised *buri* are also called *hamachi*. At 2.5 feet and longer, it is called *buri*, both in Tokyo and Osaka. Over winter, *buri* builds up fat reserves and is regarded as the best-tasting fish. Its fine flavor and firm texture make it suitable for sashimi, sushi, frying, salt-grilling, teriyaki, and braising. It is a celebratory dish for New Year.

### *Katsuo*, Skipjack Tuna, Bonito

*Katsuo* is in season from early summer to autumn. It is often served as a summer delicacy called *katsuo tataki*—as a fillet quickly seared and plunged into ice water to keep the center raw. It is then served with freshly grated garlic and/or ginger and chopped green onions. It is also made into teriyaki, although most *katsuo* are dried for *katsuobushi*, the dried flakes for fish stock. *Katsuobushi* flakes also serve as garnish.

### *Maguro*, Atlantic Blue-Fin Tuna

*Maguro* is a large fish, 3–9 feet, popular for sashimi and sushi. Its fatty ventral section, called *toro*, is highly appreciated. The globalization of sushi has pushed demand sky-high, endangering world stocks of *maguro*. It tastes best when caught in early summer, but is available year-round.

### *Saba*, Pacific Mackerel

*Saba* is one of the most common food fishes in Japan, appreciated for its flavor and reasonable price. It is in season from October to November, when its fat content rises from 16.5% to more than 20%, which makes it even tastier. It is best prepared salt-grilled or braised in miso, and served with shredded fresh ginger. *Saba* is rarely eaten raw, because it spoils rapidly. However, it is often salted overnight and marinated in vinegar for *shimesaba*, a popular sushi topping. Thus pickled, it appears in the Osaka dish called *battera*. Out of season, its fat content is lower, and it is often fried and eaten as is, or subsequently marinated Southern Barbarian-style (*nambanzuke*).

### *Sake*, Chum Salmon

Written "*sake*" but pronounced "sha-ke" by Tokyoites, salmon spends most of its life in the sea, returning to rivers to spawn. It is in season in spring and fall. Wild-caught salmon is rarely prepared fresh as sashimi or sushi because of parasites. However, deep-freezing kills the parasites, and the thawed salmon is considered safe for preparing as sushi and sashimi. Farm-cultured salmon is safe to use fresh for sushi and sashimi. Salmon is also preserved in salt or miso and grilled for breakfast. Teriyaki, frying, one-pot cooking (*nabe*), and smoking are other methods of preparing salmon. Salmon eggs are also salted, and called *sujiko* or *ikura*. *Ikura* is a prized, and high-priced, sushi ingredient.

### *Suzuki*, Japanese Sea Bass

*Suzuki* is another fish whose name changes with age. At one year old and less than one foot long, it is called *seigo*. At two to three years, it becomes *fukko*. At four years and longer than two feet, it finally attains its adult name of *suzuki*. Its season is June to September, and it is best for summer sushi and sashimi. Its white flesh, tinged pink from its diet of young crab, is fine flavored and suitable for all kinds of dishes—steamed, fried, salt-grilled—and as an addition to Japanese clear soups.

### *Tai*, Sea Bream

*Tai* is the celebratory fish in Japan, owing to its homonym in the word for congratulations—*medetai*. Highly appreciated for its shape, pink color, firm texture, and fine flavor, it is considered the king of marine fish, and no special occasion is without it. Although it reaches more than three feet in length, the most convenient size for cooking is between two and two and a half feet. In season from March to April and again from late fall to winter, *tai* is best as sashimi. It is also salt-grilled, braised, steamed, and included in one-pot cooking (*nabe*). For special occasions, it is cooked and presented as a whole fish. The head and cheeks are added to clear soups. There are several species of sea bream: *madai* (the largest, growing to three feet), *chidai* (similar to *madai* in appearance, but smaller), *kidai* (whose flesh is tinged yellow), and *kurodai* ("black tai").

The name *tai* is also used for fish with similar firm flesh and shape, though not from the sea bream family—*amadai*, *akōdai*, *ishidai*, *ibōdai*, *kinmedai*. They are more affordable for everyday dishes.

## Seafood

### *Ebi*, Shrimp, Prawn

Shrimps and prawns are highly appreciated for their shape, color, texture, and flavor. Their name in Japanese is written with the characters for "sea" and "old," because of their long "whiskers" and crooked posture when cooked. Hence, shrimps, prawns, and crayfish (*Ise ebi*) are symbols for longevity, and served during celebratory occasions, especially New Year. *Amaebi* are red-fleshed shrimps with sweet flesh, prized for sashimi and sushi; they are in season in winter. Wild (not farm-raised) *kuruma ebi* (literally "wheel shrimp") are in season from April to October. Mantis shrimp (*shako*) are an early summer sushi topping.

## *Ika*, Squid, Cuttlefish

There are 13 species of squid and cuttlefish that are commonly eaten. Squid is served as sashimi and sushi and in dressed salads (*aemono*). Its sweet, mild flavor makes it versatile, and it is fried, braised, stuffed and steamed, or grilled. Dried squid or cuttlefish (*surume ika*) is shredded as an accompaniment to beer or *sake*. Fresh squid innards with tentacles and flesh are chopped and preserved in salt (*ika no shiokara*) to accompany *sake* or beer.

## *Tako*, Octopus

*Tako* (octopus) is used for sushi, marinated dishes (*sunomono*), and salads. It is always cooked, never served raw. Though available all year round, it is best in winter.

## Clams

Freshwater clams such as *shijimi*, sea clams such as *asari* (short-neck clam), and *hamaguri* (hard clam, Venus clam) are often added to miso soup in their shells, or shucked for dressed salads (*aemono*). *Shijimi* clams are in season summer and winter, *asari* in early spring. They are also made into *kakiage* (fritters) and *tsukudani* (braised in soy sauce). Winter *hamaguri* are used for sushi, and can also be steamed and grilled. The horned turban shell (*sazae*), pen shell (*taira gai*), surf clam (*aoyagi*), *torigai* (Japanese cockle), and blood shellfish (*akagai*) are prepared for sushi.

## Crab

Of the some 5,000 crab species worldwide, roughly one-fifth are found in Japan. Winter is their season. The brown king crab, horsehair crab, helmet crab, king crab, and Pacific snow crab are specialties of Hokkaido.

## Meat

The traditional Japanese diet relied greatly on marine ingredients, but since the 1960s, meat consumption has increased. In 2017, Japan became the world's largest importer of meat. The United States, Australia, Canada, and New Zealand are the largest suppliers of meat to Japan. Around 50 years ago, the amount of meat eaten in Japan was about 8 pounds of chicken, pork, and beef combined per capita per year. By 2018, Japanese consumers were eating 900% of that, at 73 pounds per capita, of which just over 40% was chicken, 39% was pork, and about 20% was beef. Several reasons explain why this shift occurred. First, the liberalization of beef imports allowed cheaper meat to enter the Japanese market. Second, the price of fish had gone up, mainly as a result of depleted wild stocks and greater demand from other countries. Third, young Japanese families tend to eat Western-style, and the younger generation's food preferences center predominantly on meat. Fourth, preparing fish dishes is regarded as complicated. Lastly, younger diners regard eating whole fish as cumbersome due to its bones.

Meat is usually bought at supermarkets, or in the basement section of department stores (*depa chika*), located at major transportation hubs so that workers on their way home can conveniently shop. There are also specialist butchers that stock *wagyu* (premium Japanese beef), branded pork, lamb, and game. Upscale department stores' food sections also stock luxury meats. In addition, supermarkets that cater to foreign residents stock meat such as lamb, veal, turkey, goose, and other meat not found in regular supermarkets. Meat in Japan, in comparison to other developed countries, is pricey. The lower-priced meats are from Australia, New Zealand, the United States, and Canada. American beef retails at around 300 yen (about US$3) for less than ¼ pound, while *wagyu* is priced 2.5 times that.

In supermarkets, meat is neatly wrapped in small portions, usually less than 250 grams (about a pound) in weight, in ready-to-cook slices, boneless, or in bite-sized pieces easier to eat with chopsticks. The meat is trimmed so well that there is hardly any need to remove sinews or other undesirable bits at home. Meat, such as beef or pork, is rarely seen in huge chunks intended for roasting, such as those sold in the United States, and chicken is rarely displayed whole. The package label often indicates what kind of dish the meat is appropriate for: an example is *tebaniku itame yō* ("chicken wing meat for sautéeing"). Certain cuts are unique to Japan, such as chicken *sasami* ("bamboo grass flesh"), shaped like a bamboo leaf. It is the inner fillet under the chicken breast, commonly used for chicken sashimi and briefly cooked dishes—savory steamed custard (*chawan mushi*) and dressed salads (*aemono*).

Beef is the most expensive meat, especially *wagyu* from renowned specialist breeders in Matsusaka, Kobe, Omi, and Yonehara. Marbled beef—beef with fat evenly distributed throughout, thus resulting in tender and flavorful meat—is the national preference, and special care ensures that the resulting meat meets stringent quality standards. Interestingly, European and Korean breeds (Brown Swiss, Devon, Holstein, Shorthorn,

Korean Hanwoo) were imported for 10 years beginning in 1868 to develop superior meat and dairy cattle breeds suited to the Japanese environment. Four major breeds are recognized as *wagyu*: Japanese black, Japanese brown, Japanese shorthorn, and Japanese polled.

Although chicken is the most commonly consumed meat, Japanese families spend most of their meat budget on pork, the price of which is higher than chicken but lower than beef. A crossbreeding program for pigs similar to that for cows resulted in branded pork with distinctive characteristics. *Kurobuta* ("black pig") was bred in Kagoshima from the English Berkshire pig. As with *wagyu*, marbled fat is the sought-after characteristic of *kurobuta*, which makes for juiciness, tenderness, and sweetness. There are 400 pig breeds that produce branded meat, including *Agubuta* in Okinawa and *Mizunami Bono* in Gifu Prefecture. Most are noted for fine texture, marbling, and moistness. These are rarely found in regular supermarkets; most are sold directly to restaurants and specialty shops.

The Japanese preference is clearly for meat that is tender, juicy, and fine-textured. For beef and pork, marbled fat is desirable. Health-conscious consumers prefer chicken, white breast meat in particular.

## Dairy Products

Contrary to what was once thought—that the Japanese did not historically consume dairy products—the first recorded use of milk in Japan is from the mid-6th century AD, when medical books brought by a Korean Buddhist monk described the benefits of milk as a medicine, and dairy farming and milk production were initiated for medicinal use. The monk and his family were appointed as stewards of the imperial dairy and medical advisers to the Heian imperial court. Milk boiled down as curds, called *so*, became a tax collected by the imperial court for exclusive consumption by the aristocracy. Milk production and *so* tax collection ceased with the rise of the warrior class, and it was only during the Edo period that dairy farming was revived.

With the opening of Japan to Western trade during the Meiji period, milk, butter, cream, and cheese began to be produced, initially solely for the foreign community. The smell of butter was then considered revolting, and *bata kusai* ("butter stinky") was a derogatory term for anything foreign. Promotional campaigns for milk—as a substitute for mother's milk, a health food, an energy-provider, a builder of stronger bodies—were regularly undertaken, and eventually, with the publication in 1921 of a book on the use of milk and butter for cooking (*Katei Muke Gyūnyū Ryōri*, Milk for Home Cooking), butter and milk became generally accepted. Just prior to and during World War II and the immediate postwar years, dairy products were unavailable to the public because they were destined for military use. After the war, skim milk and other dairy products (among other necessary food items until national food production could be re-established) from UNICEF, the United States, Canada, and Australia were disseminated in school meals under a national nutrition improvement program.

From the 1960s onward, milk, cream, cheese, and butter from Hokkaido and Nagano Prefectures found their way into soups, stews, croquettes, and sweets. Sweet dairy products, in particular ice cream, became hugely popular, together with cream-filled pastries, cheesecakes, and butter-cream icing (for more details, see Chapter Five, Desserts). Fermented milk products, such as Calpis and Yakult, became popular due to the perception of lactobacillus and bifidobacteria as contributors to longevity, maintaining the ancient belief that dairy products promote health. Chapter Six has more details on dairy-based drinks.

## Fruits and Nuts

As mentioned before, Japan's geography spans subarctic, temperate, Mediterranean-like subtropical, and tropical conditions. Accordingly, fruits for the Japanese table reflect these diverse fruit-growing environments—from temperate fruits such as apples, cherries, pears, and plums; to Mediterranean/subtropical figs, quinces, loquats, and persimmons; and even tropical fruits. The three most widely grown fruits in terms of production volume are mandarin orange, apple, and watermelon. These are followed by Japanese pear (*nashi*), persimmon (*kaki*), melon, grape, strawberry, peach, and plum, in that order. Cherries, Japanese apricots (also called Japanese plums, *ume*), loquat (*biwa*), Japanese quinces (*karin*), Western quinces (*marumelo*), and kiwi fruits are also grown. Okinawa grows pineapples, papayas, and the endemic citrus fruits *tankan* and *shikwasa*. Besides locally grown fruits, Japan imports bananas from the Philippines and other tropical countries; citrus fruits such as grapefruits, lemons, oranges, and pineapples from the United States; and apples and kiwi fruits from New Zealand.

The Japanese fruit sector produces close to 4 million tons annually, and continuously develops new fruit varieties. The Fuji apple, for example, was developed in Northeastern Honshu in Aomori Prefecture (Japan's top apple producer) from two American apple varieties. It is currently one of the most popular and widely grown apples worldwide, and in 2016 was recognized as the third most popular apple in the United States.

Besides everyday fruits for the table, fruit growing in Japan also focuses on luxury fruits. Fruits of extraordinary size and shape, as well as outstanding flavor, are popular for gift-giving. Besides the main gift-giving periods during summer (*ochūgen*) and New Year (*oshōgatsu*), major life events, such as job promotions, school graduations, and recovery from serious illness, are occasions for fruit gifts. Even apologies are sometimes expressed with a basket of exotic fruit (as the author knows, having received one). The most well-publicized fruits in the foreign media are exorbitantly priced melons and square watermelons. Not so well-known are apples, grapes, Japanese pears, and strawberries specially grown for size and flavor.

The development of luxury fruits takes around 30 years until they can be brought to market. The Kyohō grape—each berry as big as a Western plum and seedless—is the best-known result of Japan's fruit breeding programs. Since its release in 1971, it has become the most widely bought grape in Japan. The intensive labor required to produce a perfect bunch of seedless black Kyohō grapes is reflected in its price, with one bunch costing about US$30. Each bunch on the vine is treated with gibberellic acid (a naturally occurring plant substance) twice to make it seedless and enhance berry size. Japanese table grapes have been developed from American native grape varieties Delaware, Campbell, Niagara, and Concord. Grapes are also grown for wine for the Japanese wine industry. Another fruit that has attracted the attention of special breeders is the strawberry, newly developed varieties of which are ultra-sweet with plum-sized (and often even larger) berries.

Most fruits are eaten fresh as snacks or after meals as dessert. Apples, persimmons, Japanese pears, and similar juicy fruits are usually peeled and sliced into quarters or eighths (if very large), with two slices placed on a small plate for serving. Mandarin oranges are a ubiquitous snack enjoyed throughout winter. They are frozen and then thawed as cold summer treats. They used to be sold together with well-chilled small bunches of grapes at train stations for summer travelers.

Of Japan's native citrus fruits, the *yuzu* is the one that has recently captured the attention of international chefs. Its zest has a unique aroma, much appreciated as a scented garnish. It is also used to flavor sorbets, juices, liqueurs, and Japanese and Western pastries. Other citrus fruits mainly grown in southern Japan include *daidai, kabosu, ponkan, tankan, natsu mikan* (summer mandarin), and Okinawa's unique mini-citrus, *shikwasa*, a popular addition to cocktails.

A fruit native to Hokkaido and Siberia and related to the honeysuckle is haskap (*Lonicera caerulea*). It resembles an elongated blueberry and is tart-sweet. It is currently cultivated in the United States and other countries as honey berry or May berry. The Ainu community calls it the fruit of longevity, attributing their good health and long life to its consumption. The haskap possesses high levels of antioxidants (anthocyanin) and vitamins. In Japan, it only grows in marshy areas of Hokkaido and ripens from June to August. It is made into juices and preserves, and mixed into yogurt and ice cream. Kiwiberries or baby kiwi, from the same plant family as the familiar kiwi fruit developed in New Zealand, are actually native to the forests of Japan. However, they are not raised commercially in Japan, and Japan imports kiwiberries from Chile and China.

Some local fruits cannot be eaten fresh. These are the astringent variety of persimmon (*shibugaki*), Japanese apricot or plum (*ume*), Japanese quince (*karin*), and Western quince (*marumero*). Astringent persimmons, when air-dried, are transformed into sweet delicacies eaten in autumn and winter. Raw *ume* contains high levels of toxic hydrocyanic acid, but the toxicity is neutralized when *ume* fruits are salted into the pickles called *umeboshi* or into a sweet alcoholic drink called *umeshū*. *Karin*, the Japanese quince, much like its Western counterpart, the *marumero*, is astringent when raw. Cooking enhances both quinces' aroma and flavor. The Western quince was brought to Japan by Portuguese traders and is made into fruit liqueur and fruit syrup, a folk treatment for sore throats.

Only a few nuts are native to Japan. Japanese chestnuts, depending on variety, grow throughout the country, from Hokkaido to Okinawa, but the most well-known is the Tanba chestnut, grown near Kyoto. Chestnuts ripen in autumn, and are most popularly cooked with rice (*kuri gohan*) to welcome the season. Japanese walnuts, slightly smaller than California walnuts, are grown mainly in northern Honshu. They are often chopped or finely ground, then mixed with miso as salad dressing. Ginkgo nuts ripen in autumn, and because ginkgos are often used in public planting, the nuts (actually the seeds, which are rather malodorous from the ripening fruits) can often be found together with the fallen yellow leaves under the trees. These pale green nuts are most often cooked in steamed savory custards or skewered and roasted over coals.

Other nuts widely eaten as snacks on their own or added to confectionery, such as macadamia, cashew, pine, almond, walnut, pecan, and hazelnuts, are imported. Nuts are also popular accompaniments to soft and alcoholic drinks. Almonds, walnuts, pecans, and pistachios are sourced from the United States, with almonds and walnuts comprising half of Japan's total nut imports in 2018. Australia supplies macadamia nuts, and Turkey, hazelnuts.

Japan has its own hazelnuts, the beaked hazelnut (*tsuno hashibami*, *Corylus heterophylla*, var. *thunbergii*, also known as *Corylus sieboldiana*). It grows in forests in Hokkaido, Honshu, and Kyushu, but has not been developed into a commercial product. In recent years, nut tree cultivation—pecans in Saitama Prefecture and Italian hazelnuts in Nagano Prefecture—is being promoted as a less labor-intensive agricultural niche, in light of the current shortage of agricultural workers.

## Food Preparation and Slicing

For certain plant ingredients, particularly those gathered from the wild, such as young fern fronds, leaching (*aku nuki*) is necessary to remove bitterness or irritating substances. In most cases, this involves a simple soaking in cold water overnight and rinsing before use. Carrots, giant Japanese radishes, and turnips are peeled (with a knife rather than a peeler), then sliced into familiar shapes: thin matchstick (julienne) strips; slightly thicker ones the size of French fries; circles; half-moons (half circles); ginkgo-leaf shape (quarter circles); dice; or flat strips.

Slicing methods unfamiliar to non-Japanese include *rangiri* (random cut)—slicing carrots or eggplants on the diagonal and making a half-turn for the next slice to expose more surfaces to heat; *kakushi bōchō* (hidden knife)—partial cuts through thick cylinders of hard-fleshed vegetables, such as turnip or giant radish, made to enable faster cooking; and chamfering (*mentori*) the edges of vegetables (e.g., giant radish) cylinders to preserve their shape during braising.

Some decorative slices (*kazari kiri*) are standard: for instance, carrots trimmed into five-petalled plum flowers, or shiitake caps etched with a starburst. For New Year dishes, lotus root and water chestnuts are fashioned into auspicious symbols, such as arrows and chimes. Other fortuitous symbols carved from vegetables, besides the plum flower, are bamboo leaves and pine cones or pine needles. Professional kitchens have an extensive repertoire of decorative slicing, and apprentices are tested on their ability to reduce a giant radish into a continuous gossamer sheet.

## Cooking Methods

Most methods used in the Japanese kitchen are similar to those used elsewhere: boiling (*yuderu*); blanching (*hitasu*); steaming (*musu*); stewing or braising (*niru*); deep frying (*ageru*); stir-frying (*itameru*); roasting or grilling, usually directly over coals or over a flame (*yaku*); and combining or dressing (as for a salad, *aeru*). Baking at home is recent, as ovens were not common in traditional home kitchens.

## Kitchen Equipment

Most kitchens have an electric rice cooker that simplifies the cooking process. It comes with a cup for measuring rice, and the inner pan is marked with the corresponding water level. The latest electronic models have timers to set cooking for a specific time and to keep the rice warm until needed. Microwave ovens are common, and some come with a baking function. Most cooking stoves have a small grilling compartment below the two gas burners.

Sharp knives are a must, and most kitchens have at least two: a versatile knife with a rectangular blade (*hōchō*) and another with a leaf-shaped blade (*deba bōchō*). A fish filleting knife would be a third.

Other pieces of equipment common in the Japanese kitchen are bamboo cooking chopsticks, longer than ones for eating; soup ladles; fish turner; skimmer; small rectangular trays called *batto* for ingredients; steamer or double boiler; grater; rice scoop; rice canister for serving; frying pan; metal mesh for grilling; stewing pans; rectangular omelet pan; metal/cast iron pan or stoneware pan for tabletop cooking; and tabletop burner for hot-pot cooking.

## Tableware

Basic tableware consists of rice bowls (ceramic or stoneware), soup bowls with lids (usually lacquerware), small deep bowls for salads or stews (ceramic or lacquerware), rectangular or round plates for main dishes (ceramic or stoneware), tea cups with or without lids (ceramic or stoneware), chopsticks (plain wood or lacquered), and chopstick rests. These are intentionally chosen to have dissimilar patterns. The choice of color or glaze of ceramic ware or stoneware is dictated by the (envisioned) foods that will be laid or placed on it. In principle, *shibui* (unobtrusive, subtle) colors or glazes and simple patterns are preferred.

CHAPTER THREE

# Appetizers and Side Dishes

## Structure of a Traditional Meal

A traditional Japanese meal comprises a staple (*shushoku*, main meal) and side dishes (*okazu* or *osōzai*). The staple was traditionally one of several cereals: three kinds of millet, barley, and rice. Until the 1960s, rice had not always appeared on everyone's table in its present form. The average Japanese would have had some other grain mixed with rice. To have unmixed rice—"white" rice, not speckled with barley or millet grains—was considered the ultimate luxury that historically was only available to the very wealthy and the elite. That ideal was reached for the majority just a few decades ago. Rice partnered with a soup (clear broth or *miso shiru*) and pickled vegetables constituted the foundation of a traditional meal, and in less prosperous times this was the daily meal for most common people. Even now, a farmer in Kyoto recently breakfasted on rice mixed with barley, miso soup, and pickles. This is nutritionally sound: rice and barley provide carbohydrates for energy, and the vegetable pickles, usually fermented through lactic acid fermentation, provide supplementary nutrients. Miso soup supplies proteins from the soybean-based miso paste; additional protein, minerals, and vitamins from the *katsuobushi* stock and tofu (if included); and more nutrients from fresh vegetables, such as giant radish (*daikon*), carrots, and green vegetables. This basic meal was eaten at breakfast, lunch, and supper.

Besides rice, miso soup, and pickles, all other dishes are called *okazu* or *osōzai* (the prefix "o" in both cases signify politeness). *Okazu* and *osōzai* both mean "side dish," and are further classified into main side dish (*shuzai*) and subsidiary side dish (*fukuzai*). Common ingredients for main side dishes are fish, seafood, meat (pork, beef, chicken, duck), or, for vegetarians and vegans, different variants of *tōfu* (fresh, fried *aburaage* or *atsuage*, or freeze-dried *kōya dōfu*). Occasionally lamb, wild boar, and whale meat may be featured, depending on the region. *Fukuzai* are usually based on vegetables, and include cultivated vegetables and mushrooms as well as wild gathered greens

> Traditional side dishes usually consist of seasonal vegetables prepared in several ways. The most common way and easiest to prepare is *ohitashi*, made from greens such as spinach, Chinese cabbage, or other leafy vegetables such as *mizuna*. These are briefly parboiled, rapidly cooled in an ice bath to stop further cooking and help retain their green color, then flavored with fish stock (*dashi*) and served garnished with *katsuo* flakes (*katsuobushi*), and sometimes roasted sesame seeds. Another common way of preparing vegetable side dishes is by braising in *dashi* after an initial frying; this method is often used for eggplants.

and fungi. Green vegetables, collectively called *nappa*, and root vegetables such as burdock (*gobō*), taro (*sato imo*), and giant radish (*daikon*) frequently appear as subsidiary side dishes. Seaweeds are also frequently used.

## Appetizers and Side Dishes

For a home-cooked traditional Japanese meal, the concept of appetizers as an initial course does not apply, as all dishes—rice, soup, main dish, side dishes—appear on the table at the same time. However, formal meals for the tea ceremony (*cha kaiseki*) and specialist restaurants (*kaiseki*), as well as drinking parties (*shuseki*) and formal banquets (*enkai*), where individual courses are served in sequential order, will have appetizers called *zensai*. A drinking party's appetizers may also be called *sakizuke*. Appetizers for formal meals are akin to *amuse bouche* or hors d'oeuvres. For home meals, the dishes in this chapter can serve as appetizers or side dishes.

## Dressed Salads, *Aemono*

*Aemono* stems from the two words *aeru*, which means "to bring together," "to make (things) meet or harmonize," and *mono*, meaning "things, foods."

> A common side dish is *aemono*, which is essentially a salad of two or three types of seasonal vegetables, finely chopped, with or without seafood or meat, and bound with a thick dressing. The vegetables and seafood may be raw or parboiled. The thickness of the dressing comes from the use of ingredients that have body, such as tofu or the lees (the solids that remain after filtering liquids) from *sake* or tofu manufacture. Other dressing bases are inherently oily, such as sesame seed paste, or have a viscous or slippery quality, such as finely grated or puréed mountain yam (*yama imo*) or *nameko* mushrooms.

*Appetizers and Side Dishes*

*Aemono* are composed from any ingredient in season—vegetables, cooked or raw shellfish or seafood, cooked meat of any kind, or a mixture of these—and they are meant to complement the main dish. The dressing, which also serves as a binder for the salad ingredients, may contain miso, mashed tofu, sesame paste, or *sake* lees (*okara*).

### Squid and Vegetables in Mayonnaise and Sesame Miso Dressing, *Ika to Yasai no Mayonēzu Goma Miso Ae*

Ready-to-use squid tubes are often sold frozen in Asian food shops; thaw before using. Use young cucumber for this dish, ideally before seeds have formed. If not available, remove the seed-bearing core. Mayonnaise is widely used in contemporary Japanese cuisine, although combined with classic Japanese flavorings. Black sesame seeds make a striking contrast against the light-colored dressing and white squid. Serve this as an appetizer or as accompaniment to drinks.

*Yield:* 4 servings

**Ingredients**
1 whole fresh squid, about ½ pound dressed weight, cleaned (i.e., without head and tentacles, dark outer skin removed, leaving a white tube), or 1 whole frozen ready-to-use squid tube, about ½ pound
1 small cucumber, about 6 inches long, peeled
1 small carrot, peeled
½ teaspoon salt
4 tablespoons sesame seeds
¼ cup mayonnaise
1 teaspoon wasabi paste, or more to taste
1 tablespoon light-colored miso, or more to taste

**Procedure**
1. Slice the squid into very fine strips, about 1 inch long.
2. In a saucepan, bring to a boil 2 cups of water; turn off the heat and immediately add the squid slices. As soon as they turn opaque, remove them. Do not overcook, as they will become tough. Drain thoroughly, pat dry with paper towels, and refrigerate until needed.
3. Slice the cucumber and carrot into fine strips, 1 inch long, place them in a bowl, and sprinkle salt over them. Once the vegetables have softened, rinse them and place on a sieve to drain. Pat vegetables dry with paper towels, and refrigerate until needed.

4. Prepare the dressing. Dry-roast the sesame seeds in a frying pan until aromatic. They scorch easily, so keep a watchful eye. Transfer the sesame seeds to a bowl and set aside.
5. In a large bowl, mix the mayonnaise, wasabi paste, and miso. Taste, and add more wasabi and miso, if needed.
6. Reserve 3 carrot strips per serving and 1 teaspoon of the sesame seeds for garnish.
7. Add the chilled squid, vegetables, and sesame seeds to the mayonnaise mixture, ensuring that each ingredient is coated with dressing.

*To serve: Spoon the salad into 4 small bowls, preferably of a dark color to contrast with the white ingredients, keeping the center of the salad mounded. Place three reserved carrot strips, criss-crossed, on top of each mound. Sprinkle with reserved sesame seeds. Serve at once.*

## Fried Eggplants in Tempura Sauce, *Agenasu ni Tentsuyu*

Small Japanese or Chinese eggplants are in season during summer (available in Asian food shops). Choose ones that are no more than 3–4 inches long. The eggplants are first fried and then marinated in tempura sauce. To serve, the eggplants are topped with finely sliced green onions and a layer of snowy grated radish. Accompany each bite of the eggplant with a mixture of the grated radish and green onions. This appetizer can also accompany drinks.

*Yield:* 4 servings

### Ingredients
8 small eggplants, 3–4 inches long
½ pound giant radish (daikon), peeled
1 inch ginger, peeled and finely grated
1 small bunch green onions
Oil for deep frying

Tempura *sauce*
2 cups *dashi*
½ cup mirin
½ cup soy sauce

### Procedure
1. Cut off and discard the stem and calyx at the top end, and about ⅛ inch off the tail end of the eggplants. Make several shallow, lengthwise slits into the eggplant about ½ inch apart. Take care not to slice all the way

*Appetizers and Side Dishes*

through—keep the eggplants whole. The slits enable the heat to pass through the center of the eggplant, thus cooking it more rapidly and evenly. Thoroughly pat-dry the eggplants and set aside.

2. Grate the radish as finely as possible, enough to fill 1 cup. Divide the grated radish into four equal portions, squeeze lightly to extract the excess liquid, and form into small balls. Top each ball with a portion of the grated ginger. Set the radish and ginger balls aside until needed.
3. Slice finely the green onions, both the white and green parts, enough to fill 1 cup. Place sliced green onions in a piece of cheesecloth (or clean kitchen towel) and soak in cold water for 5 minutes. Squeeze the cheesecloth to remove excess water from the onion. Set the green onions aside until needed.
4. In a frying pan, heat about an inch of oil over medium heat. Test the heat of the oil before using: dip the end of a chopstick into the oil and if small bubbles form around it, begin frying. Otherwise, use a cooking thermometer to check; the temperature should be between 320° and 330°F.
5. Fry the eggplants, turning them frequently to expose all sides to the hot oil. Fry them until completely soft and tender all the way to the center. Check by using a pair of heat-proof tongs or chopsticks and squeezing the eggplants at the middle. Drain the eggplants and place them in four small bowls, two for each person. Each serving should have the eggplants facing the same way.
6. Prepare the tempura sauce. In a saucepan, mix together the *dashi*, mirin, and soy sauce. Place over medium heat just until the mixture begins to boil. Turn off the heat.
7. Pour the hot tempura sauce over the eggplants. Arrange a layer of green onions at the center of the eggplants. Try to keep the green onions from dropping into the sauce. Top the green onion layer with the grated radish and ginger ball.

*Serve at once.*

## Spinach Nori Rolls, *Horensō no Norimaki*

Japanese spinach is different from that grown in the United States. Its leaves are smooth and triangular in shape, and the stalks close to the roots are tinged pink. Its taste is less astringent than American spinach, and the stalks have a sweetish aftertaste. However, fresh young American spinach or watercress can be used in this dish. Another alternative is tender green asparagus. A modern and colorful spin on this traditional roll would be to include thin slices of carrot (sprinkled with a bit of salt to wilt them and make them pliable enough to roll) and perhaps a julienned white or pale green vegetable alongside the spinach. This is suitable as an appetizer and drinks accompaniment. If *nori* is unavailable, use a thin omelet sheet instead.

*Yield:* 4 servings

**Ingredients**
1 pound fresh spinach (preferably Japanese, but American young spinach is fine)
½ teaspoon salt
Water for blanching
Ice-cold water, as needed
4 sheets *nori*
4 tablespoons sesame seeds
4 tablespoons *katsuobushi* (optional)

*Dipping sauce*
½ cup *dashi*
2 tablespoons *sake*
1 tablespoon mirin
2 tablespoons soy sauce
½ teaspoon sesame oil (optional)

**Procedure**
1. Wash spinach well, taking care that no sand or soil remains on the leaves or stalks. If using Japanese spinach, keep the roots intact but clean them well of any remaining sand.
2. In a large saucepan, bring to a boil 4 cups of water and salt. Add the spinach and leave to blanch for 1 minute until the leaves turn a darker green. Immediately remove and plunge into ice-cold water in a large bowl to stop further cooking. Set aside until needed.
3. Make the dipping sauce: in a small saucepan, put the dashi, *sake*, mirin, and soy sauce. Heat over medium heat just until bubbles appear at the edges of the pan. Turn off heat and add sesame oil, if using. Let the sauce cool to room temperature.
4. Take the spinach from its ice-cold bath and drain well, squeezing to extract all the remaining water. Cut off the roots, if using Japanese spinach.
5. On a sushi rolling mat, lay a sheet of *nori* shiny side down. Place a quarter of the well-drained spinach along the length of the *nori* sheet, 2 inches from the edge. Roll the mat in one swift movement over the spinach, then tighten the mat around the spinach, moving your fingers all

*Appetizers and Side Dishes*

along its length. Raise the edge of the mat that was closest to the spinach, and continue rolling until all the *nori* has surrounded the spinach. Take the roll off the mat and let it rest on a tray, with the edge of the *nori* roll facing down. Continue rolling the rest of the spinach with the remaining *nori* sheets.
6. Slice the *nori* rolls with a sharp knife crosswise into 1 ½- or 2-inch slices. Arrange on four bowls or small flat dishes, cut side up. Sprinkle with the sesame seeds and *katsuobushi* flakes (if using). Divide the dipping sauce into 4 small bowls and set alongside the spinach rolls.

## Blanched Chinese Cabbage, *Hakusai no Hitashi*

The simplest and best way of serving green vegetables is to quickly parboil them and flavor them with *dashi* and soy sauce. The resulting dish is called *hitashi* (or politely, *ohitashi*), from the word *hitasu*, meaning to steep or to blanch. The current way of preparing *hitashi* has been streamlined so that after parboiling the vegetables, they no longer need to be steeped in flavored *dashi* stock. Instead, *dashi* is poured over them and soy sauce is added at the table before eating. Instant *dashi* powder, also called *hondashi*, makes the preparation of this dish convenient.

*Yield:* 4 servings

### Ingredients
½ head Chinese cabbage
¼ teaspoon salt
2 cups water
1 teaspoon *hondashi*
2 tablespoons soy sauce, or to taste
2 tablespoons mirin or *sake*
2–3 tablespoons grated fresh ginger

### Procedure
1. Remove the central core of the Chinese cabbage, and separate the leaves. Wash well to remove any remaining soil.
2. Prepare a large bowl of water with ice cubes, and place near the kitchen sink.
3. In a large saucepan over high heat, bring 6 cups of water to a rolling boil. Parboil the cabbage briefly, until tender but still crisp and the color of the leaves is still bright.

4. Turn off the heat, and at once take out the cabbage leaves and plunge them into the ice-cold water to stop them cooking further. Take the cabbage leaves out after 2–3 minutes, and drain them, pressing lightly.
5. Align the stems and slice the cabbage leaves crosswise into 2-inch lengths.
6. Meanwhile, prepare the flavoring sauce. In a small saucepan over medium heat, bring the 2 cups of water to a boil. Turn off the heat. Stir in the *hondashi*, soy sauce, and mirin or *sake*. Taste and adjust the seasoning, adding more soy sauce or mirin as needed. Let the sauce cool to room temperature.

*To serve: Distribute the cabbage, mounding it into 4 small, deep bowls. Pour the flavoring sauce around the cabbage. Spoon the grated ginger on the top of the mound of cabbage.*

*Serve as a side dish for a traditional Japanese meal at any time.*

## Braised *Wakame*, Bamboo Shoots, and Sugar Pea Pods, *Take no Ko to Wakame to Saya Ingen no Takiawase*

Fresh bamboo shoots are available in late winter or early spring. In neighborhood greengrocers in Japan, they are usually kept soaking in large tubs of water. The flavor of fresh bamboo shoots is the flavor of spring. If you can get them already parboiled and peeled, ready to be used, that would be preferable, as peeling them yourself is not advisable. Some specialty stores carry frozen or bottled bamboo shoots. Choose the narrower shoots, preferably unflavored. This recipe uses the canned variety. Dried *wakame* are available in small packages in Japanese or Korean food shops. Choose uncut *wakame*, and check that the *wakame* you buy is not packed with harmful chemicals. If vegetarian *dashi* powder and *dashi* are used, this qualifies as a vegetarian and vegan side dish.

Yield: 4 servings

**Ingredients**
1 ounce dried uncut *wakame*
2 19-ounce cans bamboo shoots (drained weight per can is 10 ounces)
½ pound fresh sugar pea pods or string beans
1 ½ cups *sake* or mirin
2 tablespoons soy sauce

*Appetizers and Side Dishes*

Salt to taste
2 teaspoons *dashi* powder
Sugar to taste
5 cups prepared *dashi*

**Procedure**
1. Check the dried *wakame* for sand or other debris. Shake it or quickly give it a rinse under running water. Place the *wakame* in a large bowl and reconstitute in warm water to cover. It will expand to about two and a half times its original volume when fully hydrated.
2. Once the *wakame* has softened, cut off the middle vein. Slice the *wakame* crosswise into 1-inch lengths.
3. Place the *wakame* in a pan with 3 cups of water, ½ cup *sake* or mirin, 1 tablespoon soy sauce, sugar (if using), ¼ teaspoon salt, and 1 teaspoon *dashi* powder. Let it come to a boil over medium heat. Skim off all scum that arises, and lower the heat. Keep a close eye on the *wakame*; stir it from time to time, and top with water as needed, because *wakame* scorches very easily. Let the *wakame* simmer until tender. Once done, let it remain in the pan until needed.
4. Rinse the bamboo shoots and slice into 2-inch pieces. Set aside.
5. In another pan, place 5 cups of *dashi*, 1 cup *sake* or mirin, ¼ teaspoon salt, 1 tablespoon soy sauce, and 1 teaspoon sugar (if using). Place the pan over medium heat and add the bamboo shoots. Let it come to a boil, then turn down the heat and let the bamboo shoots simmer until tender, and they have taken on the flavoring of the braising liquid.
6. Add the sugar pea pods and cook only briefly to retain their bright green color and crispness.

*To serve: Distribute bamboo shoot slices evenly and place at the bottom of small bowls. Place* wakame *to one side, and sugar pea pods on the other. Spoon the braising liquid over all to reach ⅓ of the way up the sides of the bowl.*

## Steamed Dishes, *Mushimono*

*Musu* means "to steam"; hence, *mushimono* are steamed dishes. Steaming is a common method of preparing dishes that feature delicate ingredients, such as eggs, tofu, and seafood. The most popular steamed dish is *chawan mushi* (literally, teabowl steam).

Diners who are eating *chawan mushi* for the first time are invariably surprised by it. It is usually presented in a lidded cup or bowl, warm or hot. When the lid is lifted, the aroma of soup wafts up from what looks like a custard within, with a decorative sprig of *mitsuba* or other garnish. The diner proceeds to dip into the custard with the spoon provided, and unexpectedly encounters a savory and pleasant flavor. Deep inside are morsels of mushrooms, ginkgo nuts, sometimes shrimp, chicken, or small pieces of firm-fleshed fish. The custard ends about midway down the cup or bowl, and what remains beneath is a flavorful clear broth. One can either continue to use the spoon provided to sip the broth, or bring the cup or bowl to the lips with both hands and drink the remaining soup thus. Chopsticks are alternately used with the spoon to fish out the morsels hidden in the custard.

---

### Savory Custard Soup with Sea Bream, *Madai no Chawan Mushi*

This recipe is a departure from the usual Tokyo- or Kanto-style *chawan mushi* that contains chicken and shrimp, and instead uses sea bream flavored with ginger. Fish is a common ingredient in *chawan mushi* in the Kansai area, especially around Lake Biwa where it is made with freshly caught local fish. Clear chicken stock can be used instead of *dashi*, if *dashi* is unavailable.

*Yield:* 4 servings

**Ingredients**
¼ pound sea bream boneless fillets, or any mild fish such as salmon or trout, washed and patted dry
1 inch knob of ginger, washed and peeled
2 tablespoons *sake*
¼ teaspoon salt
16 ginkgo nuts, fresh or canned, or 4 large raw chestnuts
4 large fresh or dried *shiitake* mushrooms
12 stalks fresh *mitsuba*, or 1 cup arugula or watercress, washed and drained, for garnish
*Wasabi* paste, optional

*Custard*
3 large eggs
¼ teaspoon salt, plus additional to taste
2 tablespoons mirin
1 tablespoon light soy sauce
3 cups *dashi*, at room temperature

*Appetizers and Side Dishes*

**Procedure**
1. Prepare the solid ingredients. Slice the sea bream into bite-size pieces, and place in a bowl. Finely grate the ginger, and firmly press the juice through a fine sieve into a small bowl. Discard ginger solids. Add *sake* and salt to the bowl, mix well, and pour over the fish pieces. Turn the fish to make sure all have been coated with the marinade. Set aside for 5 minutes.
2. If using fresh ginkgo nuts, shell them, wash, and pat dry. If using canned, rinse thoroughly and drain, then pat dry. If using fresh chestnuts, be careful while peeling the tough outer shell; it is best to use a pair of thick cotton gloves to protect your hands. Using a knife or vegetable peeler, peel off the inner brown-grey coat, then slice into bite-sized pieces. Leave the slices to soak in cold water so as not to discolor, until needed.
3. For fresh shiitake mushrooms, cut off the stalk, and slice the cap into quarters. If using dried ones, soak in ½ cup warm water for 15 minutes or until rehydrated; then slice the cap into quarters, and cut off and discard the stems. Add the sieved soaking liquid to the *dashi*.
4. To use *mitsuba*, take 3 stalks and gently bend them to form a loose knot. Cut off the stems 2 inches below the knot. Slice the remaining stems into 1-inch pieces. Set aside. If using arugula or watercress, slice them into bite-size lengths and set aside.
5. Prepare the custard. In a bowl, gently beat the eggs with salt and mirin. Take care not to incorporate air that would cause bubbles or froth. Taste the *dashi*, add salt if needed, and gently stir into the egg mixture.
6. Assemble the *chawan mushi*. Drain the fish slices and discard the liquid.
7. Into 4 custard cups or Japanese lidded cups or bowls, lay the sliced stems of the *mitsuba*. Next, distribute the drained fish slices. Add the ginkgo nuts and *shiitake* mushrooms. With a ladle or large spoon, gently pour the egg-*dashi* mixture over. If using Japanese cups, cover with the lids. Cover custard cups or bowls with foil.
8. Place covered cups to steam in a double boiler or steamer at medium heat, and cover. The boiling water must not touch the bottom of the cups. Let steam for 20 minutes (begin counting the time as soon as steam rises from underneath the lid of the steamer or double boiler). Turn off heat.
9. Uncover the bowls and place the *mitsuba* wreaths (or arugula or watercress) on top of the custard. Replace the covers. The greens will continue to cook in the remaining heat.

*Serve at once while hot, with a small spoon on the side. If using Japanese lidded cups, bring them to the table with the lids on. The plastic wrap or foil covers can stay on until just prior to serving. A small dab of wasabi paste may be added next to the mitsuba or substitute greens, if desired.*

## Savory Custard with Wakame Seaweed, *Wakame no Chawan Mushi*

*Wakame* (*Undaria pinnatifida*) is a commonly used ingredient in salads and miso soups. It is considered a healthy food for its high levels of omega-3 fatty acids, as well as other nutrients such as sodium, iodine, niacin, calcium, and thiamine. This simple *chawan mushi* is good as a side dish to accompany a fish or meat dish. If made with *konbu* or shiitake *dashi*, this dish is vegetarian. *Wakame* can be found in Japanese or Korean food shops in dried form in small packages. Some dried *wakame* also comes pre-cut.

*Yield:* 4 servings

### Ingredients
½ ounce dried, cut *wakame*
4 cups boiling water
1 square pre-fried tofu (*aburaage*)
3½ cups *dashi*
1 tablespoon soy sauce
Salt to taste
3 eggs
2 tablespoons grated fresh ginger

### Procedure
1. In a bowl, soak the *wakame* in cold water for about 5 minutes until rehydrated. Slice the *wakame* into 1-inch strips. Set aside to drain on a sieve.
2. Place the *aburaage* in a heat-proof bowl, and pour boiling water over it. Turn the *aburaage* so that all sides come into contact with the hot water. This step removes surface oil from the *aburaage*. Wipe the *aburaage* dry with paper towels, and dice. Set aside.
3. Prepare the savory custard: in a large bowl, put the *dashi* and stir in the soy sauce. Taste the mixture, and add salt if needed.
4. Break eggs into a separate bowl. Beat gently but thoroughly to mix the yolks and whites, taking care not to raise bubbles. Stir the beaten eggs into the *dashi*.
5. Into 4 custard cups or Japanese tea cups, distribute the slices of *wakame* and the diced *aburaage*. Ladle the egg-*dashi* mixture into the cups. Skim off any bubbles, as they will mar the desired smooth surface of the finished custard. Cover the cups tightly with foil.

*Appetizers and Side Dishes*

> 6. Place a double boiler or steamer over medium-high heat. When the water boils, place the cups in the container and lower the heat to medium. Leave the cups to steam for 15 minutes. Turn off heat.
> 7. Serve at once, or while still warm.
>
> *To serve: Remove foil just prior to serving. Shape the grated ginger into small cones, and place one cone atop each custard.*
>
> *To eat: Stir the ginger into the custard, and eat with a spoon.*

## Stewed or Braised Dishes, *Nimono*

*Nimono* are stewed or braised dishes. To braise or stew is *niru*, and is often used in its short form "*ni.*" *Tsukudani* is a method of stewing or braising in soy sauce, once used to preserve foodstuffs at room temperature before the days of refrigeration. It is a method that originated in Tsukuda, a place in Tokyo. Fish or seafood and seaweed (such as nori and kelp), as well as vegetables that can be cooked for a long time without disintegrating, are often made into *tsukudani*. The flavoring mixture consists of soy sauce, *sake*, mirin, water or *dashi*, and occasionally sugar. The ingredients are simmered uncovered until only a small amount of liquid remains. As a result of the long simmering and the sauce ingredients, *tsukudani* dishes have a natural, attractive gloss. It was, and still is, a good dish to have at hand for unexpected guests, or as an after-meal savory to finish off any rice remaining in one's bowl. Besides small fish such as anchovies and sardines, uniform cubes of larger fish, as well as beef, pork, and other meat, are also made into *tsukudani*.

The name *Tsukuda* refers to Tsukuda Island (Tsukudajima) in old Edo (now Chuo Ward, Tokyo). Four hundred years ago, during the reign of Tokugawa Ieyasu, a group of fisher-folk from Tsukuda village in Osaka were resettled in the island when Ieyasu made Edo his capital. This magnanimous gesture was in return for their saving his life when he was being pursued by assassins. The original products were the small fish and shellfish that were caught nearby, and stewed using a process widely practiced in their former village. The resettled folk named their new home after their old Osaka village. As a result of Ieyasu's patronage and their quality, the preserved products became highly sought after, not only in old Edo, but throughout the country. *Tsukudani* continues to be extensively manufactured as a commercial product in Tokyo, Hiroshima, Aichi, and Osaka.

## Green Beans Tsukudani, *Ingen no Tsukudani*

This dish uses the *tsukudani* process of braising in a mixture of soy sauce, *sake* or mirin, a traditional way of preserving food. *Tsukudani* no longer requires long cooking as was customary in the past, nor with such a great amount of soy sauce. Firm, fresh green beans are usually available all year round, but substitutes are asparagus, small green peppers (*shishitōgarashi*), fresh *shiitake* or white mushrooms, lotus root slices, or Okinawan bitter melon (*gōya*) slices.

*Yield:* 4 servings

**Ingredients**
1 pound fresh green beans, washed
1 small red chili pepper, washed (or ¼ teaspoon *shichimi tōgarashi*)
2 tablespoons cooking oil
½ cup *sake*, or ¼ cup *sake* and ¼ cup mirin
½ cup *dashi*
3–5 tablespoons soy sauce, or to taste
2 teaspoons white sesame seeds, for garnish

**Procedure**
1. Prepare the beans. Trim only the stalk end from the green beans, and cut into halves or thirds.
2. Dry the beans thoroughly with a paper towel.
3. Slice the chili pepper pod into fine rings. Remove and discard the seeds. If using *shichimi tōgarashi*, sprinkle over the beans only when finished cooking, or just before serving.
4. Place a heavy-bottomed shallow saucepan to warm over medium heat. When hot, add the oil.
5. Add the beans and stir-fry, making sure to coat each piece with oil.
6. Prepare the flavoring sauce. Mix the *sake*, *dashi*, and soy sauce in a small bowl, and pour over the beans.
7. Reduce the heat to the lowest setting, and let the beans simmer uncovered, stirring them from time to time, until just a very thin film of liquid is left at the bottom of the pan. Keep a close eye at the end, so that the beans do not burn. Turn off the heat and transfer the beans at once to a plate. Set aside and allow the beans to cool thoroughly before serving.
8. In a small frying pan over low-medium heat, dry roast the sesame seeds, stirring continuously for a minute or so until the seeds release their aroma. Watch carefully, as sesame seeds tend to scorch rapidly. Transfer at once from the pan to a plate, and cool to room temperature.

*Appetizers and Side Dishes* 71

*To serve:* Place mounds of the beans into small bowls (the center of the mound must be higher than the sides). Sprinkle with sesame seeds. If using shichimi tōgarashi, *sprinkle over sesame seeds.*

Serve as an appetizer to accompany drinks, or as a side dish to eat with rice and a main dish, at any time (breakfast, lunch, or supper).

## Braised Giant Radish, *Furofuki Daikon*

As soon as cold weather starts, there is perhaps no more comforting dish than braised giant radish topped with a miso-based sauce. If giant radish is unavailable, turnips (*kabu*) are a good substitute. It is customary to re-use the water used for washing rice for cooking the radishes, as it is believed to reduce the pungent smell of cooking radish. The rice grains in this recipe are a substitute for rice-washing water.

*Yield:* 4 servings

**Ingredients**
1 giant radish (*daikon*), roughly 1 ½ pounds
1 tablespoon raw rice grains
1 4-inch square *konbu*
4 cups *dashi*
2 teaspoons soy sauce

*Miso-meat sauce*
2 tablespoons oil
1 pound ground chicken meat or pork
1-inch piece fresh ginger, peeled and finely grated
1 cup finely chopped leek (white part only) or green onions
3 tablespoons *sake*
2 tablespoons mirin
2 tablespoons miso, or to taste
2 teaspoons soy sauce
½ tablespoon cornstarch
3 tablespoons water
2 teaspoons *sanshō* (Japanese mountain pepper) for garnish
Radish shoots (*kaiware sō*), watercress, or micro-greens for garnish

**Procedure**
1. Peel the radish and slice crosswise into 4 equal cylinders about 2 to 2 ½ inches tall. Do not discard the peelings; use them for another dish. (Optional: trim the cut edges to bevel them slightly. This cut, called *mentori*, prevents the cylinders' edges from splitting during cooking.)
2. Make an X-shaped cut through the middle of each cylinder, to about 1 inch deep halfway. This cut, called *kakushi-bōchō* ("hidden knife"), is done to thick root vegetables to enable heat to penetrate faster, shortening cooking times.
3. Place the *konbu* at the bottom of a pan wide enough to take the radishes in one layer, and lay the radish cylinders on it vertically. Add the rice grains and enough water to cover the radishes. Bring to a boil over high heat, turn down the heat, and allow to simmer for about 25–30 minutes, or until a bamboo skewer pierces through the radishes without resistance.
4. Drain the radish cylinders, taking care to handle them gently so that they keep their shape. Discard the *konbu* and rice and wash the pan. Place the radish cylinders to soak in a large bowl with enough fresh water to cover them for 10 minutes to reduce their pungent smell.
5. In the now-washed pan, put the *dashi* and soy sauce, return the radish slices, and let them simmer, uncovered, at medium heat for 20 minutes, lowering the heat so the liquid stays at a gentle simmer. Turn off the heat after 20 minutes, and let the radish cylinders stay in the braising liquid.
6. Meanwhile, prepare the miso-meat sauce. In a frying pan over medium heat, heat the oil, and stir-fry the ground chicken meat. Once it has started to turn slightly golden, stir in the grated ginger, chopped leek, *sake*, mirin, soy sauce, and miso. Add ½ cup of the braising liquid, and simmer for about 10 minutes.
7. Thicken the sauce: mix the cornstarch with 2 tablespoons water to make a slurry. Stir slurry into the simmering miso-meat sauce until thickened.

*To serve: Place one radish cylinder per serving in a small deep bowl. Spoon enough braising liquid over the radishes to reach a third of the way up the radish. Top radishes with miso-meat sauce. Garnish with radish shoots and* sanshō.

## Kinpira-Style Burdock Root, *Kinpira Gobō*

Burdock root, *gobō*, is often added to braised or stewed dishes, as it lends itself to long, gentle cooking. *Kinpira* (pronounced "**kim** pira") is a style of cooking firm and crunchy root vegetables such as burdock, carrot, and lotus root. The vegetables are first fried in oil, then soy sauce or mirin (or both) and *dashi* are added, and the result sprinkled with sesame seeds.

*Appetizers and Side Dishes*

Burdock is often paired with carrot, as the carrot's color contrasts with the burdock's beige-brown. The name *kinpira* was given to this dish during the Edo period, because it was believed that eating burdock, carrot, or lotus root made in this style bestowed stamina and energy. The dish is named after the famous strongman Sakata no Kinpira, the son of Sakata no Kintoki, also known as Kintarō, one of Minamoto Yorimitsu's bodyguards, who was himself famous for his superhuman strength. There are many myths surrounding the source of his strength: one holds that his mother was a mountain crone (*yama uba*) and his father a dragon.

*Yield:* 4 servings

### Ingredients
2 sticks *gobō* (burdock root), about 2 pounds (available fresh or frozen from Asian food shops)
2 carrots
2 tablespoons oil
1 tablespoon soy sauce
2 tablespoons mirin or *sake*
½ cup *dashi*
1 red hot chili pepper, sliced into rings (option: seeds discarded if you prefer a milder dish)
3 tablespoons sesame seeds
½ teaspoon sesame oil

### Procedure
1. Wash the *gobō* well. If it has traces of soil or mud, rub it lightly with a crumpled sheet of aluminum foil surrounding the root. Do not peel it, as much of the flavor of *gobō* lies in the peel.
2. The traditional way is to score it lengthwise into quarters, then shave it with a knife into even ⅛-inch-thick shreds, rotating the *gobō* as you progress. Otherwise, slice it into julienne strips, and immediately soak it in a large bowl of water with 1 tablespoon vinegar, to stop it oxidizing (turning black).
3. Peel the carrots and slice them in the same manner and the same size as the *gobō*.
4. Dry roast the sesame seeds, and set aside.
5. Place a frying pan over medium heat, add oil, and stir-fry the *gobō* and carrot until they are evenly coated with oil. Stir in soy sauce, mirin, or *sake*, mixing the seasonings well with the vegetables. Then add the *dashi*, and cover the pan to allow the vegetables to absorb the seasonings and become just a bit tender. The character of this dish lies in the crispness of the vegetables, so only cook them briefly.

6. Add the sliced chili pepper just before turning off the heat. Sprinkle with sesame oil, and mix well.

*To serve:* Mound the gobō *and carrots into individual bowls. Sprinkle with sesame seeds.*

CHAPTER FOUR

# Main Dishes

### Contemporary Home-Cooked Meals

The format of home meals is evolving with changes in contemporary lifestyles. With greater opportunities for international travel and direct experience of enjoying other cuisines, as well as instantaneous exposure to foreign food trends through digital communication and social media, the concept of a traditional Japanese meal—with its historical format of rice-miso soup-pickles, with a main side dish of fish or seafood, and two vegetable dishes—is being eroded. Increasingly, Japanese meals and ways of eating and cooking are taking on what is popularly called *mukokuseki* style: in other words, meals with no (recognizable) national origin. This trend became prevalent from the mid- to late 1960s. Those born after this period—during Japan's rise as an economic power—prefer preparing and eating meals that mix and match dishes from all over the world, a trend evidenced by cookery books and women's journals published during this period that feature mostly non-Japanese dishes. Those born before, in contrast, prefer the more traditional Japanese meal format.

However, this mixing and matching of foods is not a recent trend. The uptake of foreign foods and foreign methods of cooking has been ongoing for more than three thousand years, dating back to the waves of migration from mainland Asia via Korea: essentially, a continuous process of globalization of the Japanese table and kitchen. The one difference is that the historical adoption of foreign foods and culinary traditions was limited to a select few (the elite and imperial court), and it took quite a long time for these imports to trickle down the social scale. Today, with television, the internet, and various social media, everyone can acquire knowledge of global food ways and trends. Anyone in Japan interested in cooking and eating adventurously can mix and match food ingredients and cooking processes. This situation is particularly conspicuous in major Japanese cities, especially Tokyo and Osaka, where fusion Italian, French, and Japanese cuisines co-exist happily with their purist versions.

Precisely how is the Japanese home-cooked meal changing? The historical notion of a main side dish with several subsidiary side dishes is being supplanted by the concept of one main dish, or, in Japanese, "one-plate" (*wan purēto*) style. This simplifies home meals: rice can be a main dish in itself with the incorporation of meat or fish and vegetables while it is being cooked—not so different from the traditional Japanese dish *takikomi gohan*, though influenced by international rice dishes, such as Spain's paella, Italy's risotto, or Louisiana's jambalaya. Salads are transformed into main dishes with sausages, ham, roast chicken or pork, or tofu. The same goes for soup, as young families forgo miso soup for nutrient-dense potages with cream or milk and meat for their growing children. A streamlined meal of a main dish with vegetables makes for fewer plates to be washed and put away, a boon for today's cooks.

> The main dish for a traditional home-cooked meal features fish or seafood. For breakfast, the fish would usually be preserved overnight in salt or miso (*hitoyabōshi*, "overnight dried"), and quickly grilled over a flame. For lunch or dinner, fresh fish would be served as sashimi, or grilled, fried, or braised. These days, young families prefer meat in the form of chicken, pork, and less often beef (pricier than the first two). Ground meat formed into burgers and served with rice, curried pork or chicken, and pork sautéed in ginger sauce (*butaniku no shōga yaki*) are among the most popular main dishes.

Seasonings, condiments, and preparation methods from other cuisines are being borrowed and applied to Japanese ingredients and dishes. Modern health and power foods, such as chia seeds, goji berries, yogurt, coconut oil, quinoa, brown and other colored rice, are being included in contemporary home-cooked dishes. Vietnamese and Thai cuisine's use of cilantro (*pakuchi*) and fish sauce (*nampla*) is common, as are spice mixtures from Turkey, Malaysia, Central Asia, and Bhutan. Guam's finadene sauce, Philippine-style spring rolls, African peanut-based dishes, cous cous instead of rice, Korean spicy miso seasoning (*gochujang*), Lithuanian potato gratin, and Turkish *imam bayildi* were recent suggestions for evening meals in the website *Kurashi Jōzu* (Skillful Living). With most young working couples eating out for lunch (and often dinner, too) or buying ready-prepared foods, this website's daily suggestions for unusual, easy, and quickly prepared (most in 30 minutes or less) dishes for the evening

# Main Dishes

meal help make cooking from scratch and eating at home an attractive and healthy option.

## Breakfast

Breakfast for most urban Japanese of working age is usually bread-based. Bread comes in various forms—rolls, baguette, slices from a loaf. A typical breakfast would be toast with butter and jam, a soft- or hard-boiled egg, ham or sausages, and to drink, orange or other fruit juice, coffee for adults, and milk for children. A set breakfast at restaurants and cafés is called morning service (*mōning sābisu*), reasonably priced for working people. This comes with coffee or black tea and orange juice, thick toast with butter, and fried egg(s) with ham or bacon or sausages. A small bowl of fresh vegetable salad and fresh fruit, such as half a grapefruit or fresh fruit salad, may also be included.

The older generation tends to have a traditional breakfast of hot rice, miso soup, grilled salted fish, a fresh vegetable salad, and/or traditional Japanese pickles, with green tea. Another traditional option is rice gruel, with side dishes of *tsukudani* (soy sauce preserves), crisp-fried baby anchovies (*chirimenjako*), and assorted pickles. Some even have curry rice for breakfast.

---

### Grilled Overnight-Dried Salmon, *Sake Hitoyaboshi Shioyaki*

Grilled fish is a main dish for any traditional Japanese meal, whether breakfast, lunch, or supper. Drying fish was a method of preservation before refrigerators became commonplace. *Hitoyaboshi* means overnight drying, and the fish is lightly salted because it is intended for eating the following day. Substitute gilt-head bream, *aji*, or other firm-fleshed fish.

*Yield:* 4 servings

**Ingredients**
4 salmon fillets
1 ½ tablespoons coarse salt
¼ cup *sake*
2 tablespoons mirin
2 tablespoons oil
½ cup finely grated giant radish (*daikon*)

**Procedure**
1. Rinse the fillets and wipe dry with paper towels.
2. Lay the fish flat on a grid placed on a tray that will fit your refrigerator shelf.
3. Dissolve 1 tablespoon salt in ¼ cup of *sake*. Brush the fish on both sides with the *sake*-salt mixture. After 30 minutes, wipe the fish dry.
4. Sprinkle the fish with the rest of the salt and leave to dry, uncovered, overnight in the refrigerator.
5. Preheat the oven grill to medium or 350°F.
6. Brush the surface of the fish with mirin and oil.
7. Grill the fish for about 8 minutes on each side, or until just done (timing will depend on the thickness of the fillet). Increase the heat to high, and grill each side for about 1 minute more. Take care not to overcook the fish.

*To serve: Place each fish on a plate, and garnish with a cone of grated* daikon. *The grated radish serves as a condiment to eat with the fish.*

## Crisp-Fried Baby Anchovies, *Karikari Shirasu*

*Shirasu* or *chirimenjako* (in Osaka dialect) are semi-dried sardine fry, often sold in small packets in Asian food shops. Substitutes are dried anchovies or dried whitebait. *Karikari* is onomatopoeic for "crisp" or "crunchy."

*Yield:* 3–4 servings

**Ingredients**
Oil for deep frying
2 cups *shirasu* or *chirimenjako*

**Procedure**
1. In a deep frying pan, slowly heat the oil.
2. Add the *shirasu*, and fry them until they are crisp.
3. Drain the fried *shirasu* on paper towels to absorb excess oil.
4. Taste and sprinkle with salt if needed.

*Serve with rice gruel for a traditional Japanese breakfast.*

# Poached Egg and Ham Salad, *Pōchito Eggu to Hamu no Sarada*

Turning a salad into a main dish by adding meat, fish, seafood, or other form of protein, such as tofu, is becoming popular. Alternatives to ham are sausages or leftover roast chicken or perhaps slices of a pork cutlet from a previous meal.

*Yield:* 4 servings

**Ingredients**

*Salad*
1 head Lollo Rosso or other lettuce
1 bunch enoki mushrooms (*enokidake*)
1 red bell pepper
4 small red radishes
Juice of 1 lemon
Salt
Freshly ground black pepper
¼ cup olive oil
1 teaspoon mustard

*Poached eggs and ham*
8 slices smoked ham
1–2 tablespoons oil, or as needed
3 cups water
¼ cup rice vinegar
4 large eggs

**Procedure**
1. Prepare the salad. Wash the vegetables and pat dry.
2. Tear lettuce into bite-size pieces.
3. Trim and discard the roots from the enoki mushrooms, and separate into filaments.
4. Remove the seeds and white membrane from the bell pepper and slice finely lengthwise.
5. Trim the roots and stems of the radishes and slice the radishes into fine disks.
6. Arrange the salad vegetables nicely into 4 dishes.

7. Combine the lemon juice, salt, black pepper, olive oil, and mustard in a bowl and mix well. Place into a small bowl for passing around at the table.
8. Heat a heavy-bottomed frying pan over medium heat. Add 1–2 tablespoons of oil, then the ham, just to heat through. Turn off the heat, and leave ham in the pan until needed.
9. Prepare the poached eggs. In a saucepan over low-medium heat, bring 3 cups of water and ¼ cup of rice vinegar to a gentle simmer.
10. Break one egg into a small bowl. Gently slide the egg into the simmering water. Poach the egg for 3–4 minutes for a runny yolk. Use a slotted kitchen spoon to pick up the egg. Place the egg on a paper towel to absorb moisture before putting it in the middle of the salad.
11. Repeat with the remaining eggs.

*To serve: Place two slices of ham on one side of the salad per serving. Top with a poached egg. Serve with toast.*

## Rolled Omelet, *Dashimaki Tamago*

This omelet is usually a sushi topping, but is often served for breakfast. It is usually cooked in a rectangular frying pan, often made of copper. The traditional process is rather involved, with thin layers of omelet cooked successively in the pan, each layer rolled to one side, and the pan re-oiled for the next one. This recipe uses a microwave oven for convenience. For 4 servings, it is best to make another batch separately, rather than doubling the ingredients.

Yield: 2 servings

**Ingredients**
4 large eggs
4 tablespoons water
2 teaspoons powdered *dashi*
2 teaspoons mirin
1 teaspoon soy sauce
½ to 1 teaspoon sugar (optional)
1 tablespoon cooking oil
2 green *shiso* leaves to garnish

# Main Dishes

**Procedure**
1. Prepare a rectangular dish, glass or ceramic, that can be used in the microwave. Oil the bottom and sides of the dish.
2. Beat the eggs gently, without raising any bubbles, with the water, *dashi*, mirin, and soy sauce. The whites and yolks do not have to be completely mixed.
3. Pour the egg mixture into the oiled container, cover with plastic film, and microwave at 500 watts for 1 minute.
4. Remove the container from the microwave, mix the egg mixture, and put back into the microwave, again at 500 watts for 1 minute.
5. Repeat two more times, or until the omelet is done.
6. Take out the omelet and tip it onto a sheet of parchment paper.
7. Roll the omelet, enclosing it in the parchment, and twist the sides closed. Let the omelet roll rest for 5 minutes.
8. Unroll the omelet and slice crosswise into 1-inch widths.

*To serve: Place 2 slices on a serving plate, and garnish each serving with a* shisō *leaf.*

## Rikyū Tea-Flavored Rice, *Rikyū Meshi*

Sen no Rikyū, the monk who popularized the tea ceremony, lent his name to various ways of cooking: *Rikyū yaki* (grilled, roasted), *Rikyū age* (fried), *Rikyū kamaboko* (fish loaf), *Rikyū ae daikon* (dressed giant radish). Most are based on sesame seeds or sesame seed paste, allegedly due to Rikyū's predilection for them. Whether this is fact or merely apocryphal is anyone's guess. What can be ascertained is that Rikyū had a fondness for the austere pottery that came out of Shigaraki. Flecked with brown spots on a beige clay body, unglazed Shigaraki ware look as if they have been strewn with sesame seeds.

This rice dish belongs to the genre of tea-flavored dishes called *ochazuke*, usually recommended for breakfast to settle the stomach after a hangover. In the spirit of simple, unassuming meals that Rikyū preferred, the tea used here is *bancha*—an inexpensive grade of tea that includes the stems and more mature leaves. It is, of course, fine to use any type of Japanese tea.

*Yield:* 4 servings

**Ingredients**
4 tablespoons *bancha* leaves and stems, or green tea leaves
4 ½ cups boiling water
3 cups short-grain rice
4 sheets green *nori*
8 buds *myōga*, Japanese ginger flowers
8 leaves green *shisō*
4 tablespoons sesame seeds, a mix of black and white
4 cups *dashi*

**Procedure**
1. In a pan, place the *bancha* and pour the boiling water over it. Allow to steep for 10–15 minutes to get a strong brew. Allow to cool to room temperature. Pass through a sieve before using.
2. Wash the rice in two changes of water, and place the rice in the inner pot of an automatic rice cooker. Use the sieved *bancha* tea instead of water to cook the rice. Follow manufacturer's instructions for the rice cooker.
3. Meanwhile, pass the *nori* sheets over a hot plate or low flame to toast them. Snip them into short lengths. Set aside.
4. Wash the *myōga* and slice into fine julienne strips. Set aside.
5. Wash the green *shisō*, select 4 of the nicest looking ones, and set aside for garnish. Slice the rest into fine julienne strips, and set aside.
6. Dry roast the sesame seeds in a frying pan over low heat, until they start popping. Keep stirring constantly to prevent them from scorching. Set aside.
7. Once the rice is cooked, divide it into 4 warmed bowls.
8. Heat the *dashi* to just under the boiling point; pour around the rice.

*To serve: Place the sliced* nori, myōga, *and* shisō *in separate groups surrounding the rice. Garnish each bowl with a reserved* shisō *leaf.*

*Serve for breakfast with side dishes of crisp fried anchovies or grilled salted salmon.*

## Lunch

Lunch is usually a light meal for those needing to get back to work. Most working people will bring or buy a *bentō* (boxed lunch). When eating out, the most popular are one-dish meals of rice with a topping, served in deep bowls called *donburi* (shortened to "*don*"). *Katsudon* is pork cutlet (*katsu*) and egg on rice; *oyakodon* is chicken and egg on rice (*oya* means parent, *ko* mean child); *tanindon* refers to beef and egg over rice (*tanin* means

## Main Dishes

"unrelated," in witty contrast to *oyako*, the chicken-egg parent-child version). *Tendon* is tempura on rice, and *gyūdon* is beef (*gyū*) on rice. These one-dish meals come with vegetable pickles and miso soup. Fried rice (*chahan*) and fried Chinese-style noodles are also popular. These are regular offerings at Japanized Chinese-style restaurants (*chūka ryōriya*). These are, of course, also available at authentic Chinese and Taiwanese restaurants.

> Deep-fried foods, whether coated in a thin batter or breadcrumbs, are popular main dishes. Crisp-fried chicken (*kara age*) is similar to Western fried chicken on the outside, but could not be further from it in taste, having been marinated in ginger, soy sauce, and mirin beforehand. Tempura is another favorite, made from assorted seafood and seasonal vegetables, fried in a batter that has to be cold to achieve a delicate crisp crust. Since the introduction of breadcrumb-coated croquettes, other similarly coated and deep-fried dishes, such as *tonkatsu* (pork cutlet), *kaki furai* (fried oysters), and *ebi furai* (fried shrimps) have become popular main dishes.

Noodles in the form of *soba* (buckwheat), *rāmen*, *udon*, or *kishimen* are also commonly eaten for lunch. Buckwheat noodles in soup make a complete meal with toppings, such as shrimp tempura or duck and leeks (*kamo namban*). Interestingly, some set meals (*teishoku*) of noodles will also include rice. *Kishimen* are flat wheat noodles in broth that are a specialty of Nagoya. *Rāmen* is another popular dish, and three *rāmen* restaurants in Tokyo have been awarded Michelin stars. There are many regional variations of *rāmen*. Hokkaido is noted for its *rāmen* with crab or other seafood in a rich miso-flavored broth. Hakata in Fukuoka is famed for thin noodles in pork bone broth (*tonkotsu*), topped with red pickled ginger and peppery *takana* (mustard leaf) pickles. Okinawa *rāmen* is called, rather curiously, Okinawa soba, and includes slices of braised pork belly. Other *rāmen* dishes in Okinawa are *sōki soba* with pork ribs, and *tebichi soba*, with pig's trotters. A note about the use of the word *soba*: generally it refers to buckwheat, either as noodles or flour. However, there are two exceptions, the first being the dish called *yakisoba*, fried noodles, based on Chinese-style wheat noodles. The other is as mentioned earlier, Okinawa soba, which has special permission from the nationwide buckwheat association to use the word *soba* for its traditional wheat noodles.

Other options for lunch are the many chain restaurants owned by multinational and Japanese companies. These offer a gamut of Italian-style, American-style, and Japanese-style fast foods. For a light meal in summer, cold *soba* noodles are served plain on a basket (*zaru soba*) and dipped into a flavorful broth. *Soba* are the Tokyoite's preferred noodle, whereas wheat-based *udon* are preferred in the Osaka region. Fine wheat noodles (*sōmen*) in a cold broth make a refreshing summer lunch. There is also a Chinese-style version of wheat noodles called *hiyashi chūka* (chilled Chinese noodles), served with a vinegar-spiked cold broth with finely sliced cucumber, carrot, ham, shredded omelet, and canned mandarin orange slices.

## Cold Buckwheat Noodles, *Zaru Soba*

Tokyoites' favorite noodles are made of buckwheat (*soba*). Pure buckwheat dough is difficult to roll out by hand. These days, it is more usual to mix in wheat flour at about 28% of the whole to facilitate rolling, as well as reduce the price. Nevertheless, there remain purist buckwheat noodle shops that continue to make 100% buckwheat noodles (*jūwari soba*). The purist buckwheat fan prefers to eat his or her 100% soba noodles without any toppings. Cold buckwheat noodles dipped into a sauce is considered the best way to savor pure *soba*. There are special baskets for serving cold *soba*, called *seiro*, as well as special cups for serving the dipping sauce, called *soba choko*. All is not lost if you do not have these—any clean basket or a glass plate will do. Glass is commonly used to serve summer dishes, as glass imparts a feeling of coolness. For the dipping sauce, a shallow bowl wide enough to allow chopsticks and noodles to be dipped inside, and light enough to lift with one hand, will do.

*Yield:* 2 servings

**Ingredients**
1 pound *soba* noodles (preferably 100%)

*Dipping sauce*
2 ½ cups water
½ ounce kelp (*konbu*)
1 ounce bonito flakes (*katsuobushi*) and mackerel flakes (*saba bushi*)
¼ cup mirin
⅓ cup soy sauce
⅔ teaspoon sugar
½ cup green onions or chives
1 sheet *nori*
2 tablespoons prepared *wasabi* (prepared from powder or a tube)

*Main Dishes*

**Procedure**
1. Prepare the dipping sauce. First make *dashi* stock. In a saucepan over medium heat, add water and *konbu*; as soon as it boils, remove the *konbu*.
2. Add the bonito and mackerel flakes, and as soon as the flakes settle at the bottom, pass the stock through a cheesecloth-lined sieve. Set *dashi* stock aside until needed. (The *konbu* and fish flakes may be used for another dish or for secondary *dashi* stock.)
3. In a small saucepan over medium heat, put the mirin and ignite it with a match to allow the alcohol to evaporate.
4. Add soy sauce, sugar, and *dashi* stock, and simmer only until the sugar is dissolved. Turn off heat, and when the dipping sauce has cooled to room temperature, refrigerate it.
5. In a large pot over high heat, bring to a rolling boil 8 cups of water. Add the noodles, taking care to separate the strands. As soon as the water reboils, add a cup of cold water. When it reboils, add another cup of water. Take one noodle and test: it must be *al dente*.
6. Immediately scoop the noodles with a colander and plunge into ice-cold water in a large bowl to stop further cooking. Let the noodles drain until needed, covered with a damp clean cloth.
7. Slice green onions crosswise into fine rings.
8. Pass *nori* over a flame, and cut with scissors into fine strips.

*To serve: Place cold noodles on individual baskets. Mound* nori *strips in the middle of the noodles. Shape the prepared* wasabi *paste into two cones, and place one cone beside the green onions on a small saucer. Divide the chilled dipping sauce into 2 wide-mouthed cups or shallow bowls.*

## Yanakawa-Style Pork Cutlet in a Bowl, *Yanakawafū Katsudon*

"Yanakawa-style" refers to an old Edo method of cooking loach (*dōjō*, the poor man's eel) with burdock root (*gobō*), leeks, and Japanese trefoil (*mitsuba*) in soy sauce, *sake*, mirin, and beaten egg. This combination of humble vegetables in a sweet-salty sauce was a hit, and it was soon applied to other ingredients—in this instance, a pork cutlet (*tonkatsu*). It is also possible to use finely sliced pork, chicken, or beef. The eggplant can be omitted, but without the burdock root, leek, and trefoil, it would no longer deserve the name "Yanakawa-style." Having an already cooked cutlet on hand would shorten the steps involved.

*Yield:* 4 servings

**Ingredients**
4 pork cutlets
Salt
Freshly ground black pepper
1 cup all-purpose flour
1 large egg, well beaten
1 tablespoon milk
1 cup *panko* (prepared bread crumbs)
Oil for frying
4 servings of cooked white short-grain rice

*Vegetables*
½ piece burdock (*gobō*)
4 small Japanese eggplants
½ leek
1 bunch Japanese trefoil (*mitsuba*)
4 large eggs
Salt

*Braising sauce*
2 tablespoons soy sauce
2 tablespoons *sake*
4 tablespoons mirin
4 ½ cups *dashi* or water

**Preparing the Cutlets**
1. Prepare the pork cutlets. With a knife, slit the center and edges of each cutlet in 3–4 places to prevent them from curling up during frying.
2. Tenderize the cutlets by pounding them with a kitchen mallet (or a heavy bottle) on both sides. Reshape the cutlets and sprinkle lightly with salt and pepper.
3. In a clean paper or plastic bag, place 1 cup of flour. Place the cutlets, one at a time, inside and shake the bag to coat the cutlet evenly. Shake off all excess flour.
4. Mix the beaten egg with milk in a bowl, and place the breadcrumbs in another.
5. Dip the floured cutlets, one at a time, into the egg mixture, and cover them thoroughly with breadcrumbs. Repeat the dipping if necessary so that the entire cutlet is encased in breadcrumbs.

*Main Dishes*

6. Take a heavy-bottomed frying pan and place it over low-medium heat to warm up slowly. Once warm, add oil to the pan, deep enough to reach halfway up the cutlets.
7. When the oil is moderately hot, slip in the cutlets carefully. Depending on the size of your frying pan, it may be best to fry only two at a time.
8. Turn the heat down to low; otherwise the breadcrumbs will turn brown before the cutlet inside is ready. Scoop out any stray breadcrumbs on the surface of the oil while frying. Fry the cutlets until golden brown. Drain on a rack.
9. When the cutlets are cool, slice crosswise into 4–5 slices. Set aside until needed.

**Preparing the Vegetables**
1. Rub the burdock root gently to remove all soil or mud on the surface. Use a crumpled sheet of aluminum foil to scrub at the more stubborn spots. Burdock is not peeled because its distinctive aroma lies in the peel.
2. Score the burdock lengthwise in four places, then finely shave the burdock root, turning the root as you go along. This is the traditional way of slicing burdock, but it may be difficult to achieve equally fine slices in this manner. Alternatively, slice the burdock in half lengthwise, if it is fairly thick. Lay the burdock on a cutting board, and finely slice the burdock on the diagonal, keeping the slices equally thin. Soak the shaved or sliced burdock in a bowl of cold water with a tablespoon of vinegar to leach out any bitterness (*aku*), and prevent it from turning black.
3. Cut off and discard the stalk and calyx of the eggplants. Slice in half lengthwise, and slice them finely on the diagonal. Soak the sliced eggplants in a bowl of water with a pinch of salt to prevent them from oxidizing (turning brown).
4. Slice the leek finely on the diagonal, and set aside.
5. Slice the trefoil in two-inch lengths, and set aside. Reserve a few leaves for garnish.

**Preparing the sauce**
1. Combine the soy sauce, *sake*, mirin, and *dashi* stock. Taste and adjust the seasoning to your taste, balancing salty and sweet.
2. Prepare each serving individually.
3. In a small bowl, beat one egg, add a pinch of salt, and set aside until needed.
4. Divide the vegetables into 4 lots.
5. Heat the serving bowls by filling with hot water. Empty them one at a time, wipe dry, and fill halfway with hot rice.

6. In a saucepan over medium heat, place one-quarter of the sauce. As soon as it boils, add the slices from one cutlet and one quarter each of the sliced vegetables—burdock root, eggplant, and leek.
7. Stir in one beaten egg, followed by a quarter of the trefoil.
8. Once the egg is almost done, turn off the heat (the remaining heat will continue cooking the egg). Pour the sauce with cutlet and vegetables over the rice. Garnish with a leaf or two of trefoil.
9. Repeat with the remaining ingredients for each of the remaining 3 servings.

*Serve at once, accompanying each bowl with a small dish of pickled vegetables and miso soup.*

## Dinner

For young families, dinner is partaken of early in the evening, and often without the father present, particularly if he is a salaried employee (*sararīman*) in a job where overtime is the norm. The menu is often dictated by the young children's preferences: hamburger, wiener sausages, crisp-fried chicken (*chikin kara age*), or curry rice. These are usually accompanied with rice and soup, whether traditional miso or Western-style corn or other vegetable cream soup. The mother may eat together with her small children or may join the father when he gets home, if not too late. Or, as is more usual nowadays, she may have a different main dish, perhaps fish- or seafood-based or a substantial salad of fresh and cooked vegetables with some protein (tofu, fish, or chicken).

This trend of different main dishes eaten at the same table is feasible because ready-made dishes, including rice, can be purchased at convenience stores, supermarkets, or department store food sections. Varied cooked dishes are available—regional Japanese, authentic Chinese, French, German, Thai, Korean, Vietnamese, and other ethnic foods—which require only brief rewarming before serving. The fish and seafood sections also offer ready-to-serve sashimi and cooked items.

In general, dinner is a hearty meal, and if the home cook (male or female) is in full-time employment, the preference is for dishes that take mere minutes to prepare so that dinner is served within an hour. Hence, one-dish meals that combine protein and vegetables are a boon. Contemporary cooks are increasingly adventurous and more receptive to unusual flavors and ingredients and source ideas from international ethnic cuisine,

*Main Dishes*

using herbs such as cilantro or Thai basil with fish sauce, or spicy hot Korean sauces, for "one-plate" dishes.

Young adults frequently head for *izakaya* (Japanese bars) and ethnic restaurants for evening meals. *Izakaya* are the Japanese equivalent of gastro-pubs, and they often serve innovative dishes paired to the different types of *sake* or alcohol that they stock. Korean cuisine is increasingly popular with millennials for their grilled meat menus, which include unfamiliar cuts of meat, such as tripe and other internal organs. These dishes are served with a selection of Korean alcoholic drinks.

## Laghman-Style Udon Noodles, *Raguman-fū Udon*

A specialty of Central Asian cuisine, in particular Uzbekistan, is *laghman*: wheat noodles in a spicy broth served with fresh herbs. Its bold flavors transform normally bland *udon* into a zestful evening meal. Robust spicing has become popular among contemporary cooks. This dish combines vegetables, soup, and noodles that can be served in a single bowl (hence fewer dishes to wash)—an easy, satisfying meal after a long work day.

*Yield:* 4 servings

**Ingredients**
4 portions fresh or frozen *udon* noodles
3 tablespoons cooking oil
1 onion, sliced finely into half-rings
3 cloves garlic, finely chopped
2 carrots, peeled and sliced into quarter circles (ginkgo-leaf shapes)
¼ pound giant radish, peeled, and sliced similarly to the carrots
2 large tomatoes, sliced into eighths
6 cups beef broth, or water and 1 beef bouillon cube
1 ¼ pounds beef or lamb, finely sliced into bite-sized strips
1 medium zucchini, sliced into circles
4 green or Chinese cabbage leaves, sliced into bite-sized pieces
1 hot chili pepper (or to taste), sliced into rings
1 teaspoon cumin seeds (roasted and ground) or cumin powder
1 teaspoon coriander seeds (roasted and ground) or coriander powder
Mixed fresh herbs or greens—cilantro, basil (Italian or Thai), garlic chives, spring onions, green *shisō*, arugula (rocket), other herbs on hand or to individual taste
Salt and freshly ground black pepper to taste

**Procedure**
1. Prepare the noodles: follow instructions on the packet, but take out the noodles while still underdone (i.e., firmer than *al dente*, as they will undergo further cooking). Rinse noodles with cold water and set aside.
2. Prepare the sauce: in a large saucepan over medium heat, warm the oil and stir-fry the onions and garlic until softened but not brown.
3. Stir in the carrots, radish, and tomatoes.
4. Stir in the broth, and let boil. Add the zucchini and cabbage, and continue cooking until the vegetables are crisp-tender.
5. Meanwhile, in a small frying pan over low heat, toast the cumin and coriander seeds, stirring frequently to prevent burning. Turn off the heat when they give off their aroma. In a mortar and pestle, pound the seeds until fine. Set aside until needed.
6. Season to taste with salt, pepper, and half the spices.
7. Stir in the noodles, and when the broth returns to a boil, add the beef.
8. Turn off the heat while the beef is still pink.

*Serve in deep bowls.*

*Pass the fresh herbs and the remaining spices for mixing in to individual taste.*

## Okinawa Braised Pork, *Rafute*

*Rafute* is an iconic Okinawan dish that features cubes of pork braised slowly in soy sauce and *awamori* (an Okinawan alcoholic drink). A similar dish of slowly braised pork, called *kakuni*, is a Kyushu regional dish and specialty of Nagasaki and Kagoshima. *Rafute* traces its origin to Ryukyu Kingdom court cuisine. The Ryukyu Kingdom was an independent kingdom that reigned over the Okinawa islands, including the Amami islands (now part of Kagoshima Prefecture), until the Japanese Satsuma clan invaded it in 1609, and annexed the kingdom to Japan in 1879 as Okinawa Prefecture. *Rafute* and *kakuni* share a common origin in China's Hangzhou *dongpo* pork. Historically, the Ryukyu Kingdom had a long trading relationship with China, starting with the Ming Dynasty. Kyushu had similar historical trade links with Ming and Song China, resulting in a Chinese trading community settled in Nagasaki, and an equivalent Japanese community in Hangzhou.

This recipe can be prepared in a pressure cooker, which reduces cooking time by half.

*Yield:* 4 servings

**Ingredients**
2 pounds boneless pork belly, skin on (with a thin layer of fat)
4 cups water
20 g (1 ounce) *katsuobushi*
1 cup *awamori* (or *sake* or other rice-based alcohol)
½ cup dark brown sugar or Okinawa black sugar
⅓ cup soy sauce
2-inch piece fresh ginger, for garnish
Sharp Japanese- or English-style mustard

**Procedure**
1. In a large saucepan, place the pork belly, add cold water to cover, and bring to a boil. Let boil for 1–2 minutes and discard the water. Rinse the pork clean and return to the rinsed saucepan. Add just enough cold water to cover the pork. Bring to a boil, uncovered, over medium heat, skimming all scum that rises. Reduce heat to low and simmer pork for 1 hour. Take pork out of the pan and allow to thoroughly cool on a tray or large plate, covered with foil to keep it moist. Slice the pork into 1- to 2-inch slices or cubes and set aside.
2. In a small pan, bring to a boil 4 cups of water. Add the *katsuobushi*, cover, turn off heat, and let *katsuobushi* steep in the pan until needed.
3. In a heavy-bottomed stewing pot, place the pork slices. Stir in the *awamori* and black sugar. Strain the *katsuobushi* liquid directly into the stewing pot through a fine sieve. Simmer over medium-low heat for 1 hour. After 1 hour add half of the soy sauce, and continue to simmer for 30 minutes. The pork should be very tender and the skin gelatinous.
4. The braising liquid should be thick by this point. If not, transfer the pork pieces to a covered bowl to keep warm. Bring the braising liquid to a brisk boil until thick.
5. Prepare the garnish: peel the ginger and slice into fine julienne strips. Soak in cold water for 15 minutes, drain, and keep refrigerated, covered, until needed.
6. Place three slices of pork in a deep bowl, and spoon some braising liquid over them. Garnish with ginger strips and a dab of mustard.

*Serve with hot rice and vegetable side dishes, or as an accompaniment to Okinawa-style soba.*

## Kagoshima Braised Pork, *Kakuni*

*Kakuni* ("cube stew") is a Kagoshima specialty, influenced by the cooking of Chinese traders during the Tokugawa period. Belly pork is braised until very tender with Japanese leek and ginger, and allowed to rest overnight in the braising liquid. The following day it is simmered with part of the braising liquid and seasoning. Compare it with the previous Okinawa braised pork recipe (which was translated and adapted from *Katei Ryōri no Jiten*). Nowadays, this recipe is most often prepared in a pressure cooker, which halves cooking time.

Yield: 4 servings

**Ingredients**
2 pounds belly pork, in one piece
½ cup *sake*
1 stalk fat leek, white and green parts, sliced into 2-inch long pieces
2-inch piece fresh ginger, peeled and finely sliced crosswise
¼ cup *sake*
½ cup soy sauce
¼ cup sugar
4 teaspoons sharp mustard (Japanese- or English-style)

**Procedure**
1. Place the pork in a large saucepan with cold water to cover. Add ½ cup *sake*, leek, and ginger. Bring to a boil over medium heat, and simmer for 2–3 hours until a toothpick pierces the meat easily. Turn off heat and let rest in pan, covered, overnight. The following day, remove meat and rinse with water. Slice meat into 8 cubes and set aside. Strain liquid from meat through a fine sieve or cheesecloth.
2. In a heavy-bottomed stewing pot, place ½ cup of the strained liquid, ¼ cup *sake*, soy sauce, and sugar. Lay the meat cubes fat-side down, place a piece of parchment paper over the meat, and bring to a boil over medium heat. Reduce heat and gently simmer for 20 minutes. Baste meat from time to time with cooking liquid.

To serve: Transfer meat cubes to warmed bowls—2 per serving. Reduce cooking liquid to about half, and pour over meat. Spoon mustard on each cube. Serve with rice and vegetables.

# Namban-Style Salmon, *Sake no Nambanyaki*

*Namban* ("Southern Barbarian") referred to the Portuguese traders and missionaries who were the first Europeans to arrive in Japan in 1543. Although the term is no longer used to refer to contemporary Portuguese, it has remained to describe two cooking styles: a method of marinating fried ingredients, usually fish, in vinegar, leeks, and chili peppers (akin to the Spanish *escabeche*), and the liberal use of onions or leeks in a dish. The latter stems from the observation that the early Portuguese liked to eat onions for health. Another explanation of the term "Namban" for a dish with a fair amount of leeks is a mispronunciation of the place name "Namba," famous for growing leeks. *Nambanyaki* can be served hot or cold.

*Yield:* 4 servings

### Ingredients
4 salmon steaks or other firm-fleshed fish
1 tablespoon coarse salt for sprinkling
½ cup *sake*
1 teaspoon light soy sauce
¼ teaspoon salt
Freshly ground black pepper to taste
3–4 tablespoons oil for frying
2 leeks, white portion only, sliced finely on the diagonal
2 red chili peppers, sliced into fine rings, seeds removed

### Procedure
1. Lightly sprinkle salmon steaks with salt. Let rest for 30 minutes.
2. Mix seasoning mixture of *sake*, soy sauce, ¼ teaspoon salt, and black pepper, and set aside.
3. In a heavy-bottomed frying pan, heat oil over medium heat and fry the salmon. When golden brown, turn the fish steaks over.
4. Immediately add the seasoning mixture, followed by the leeks and chili pepper. Cover the pan.
5. When the leeks are slightly wilted, turn off heat. Allow salmon to rest, covered, for 15 minutes before serving, or refrigerate overnight.

*To serve:* Transfer salmon steaks to individual serving plates, and arrange leek and pepper slices separately alongside.

# Chicken Tsukudani, *Toriniku no Tsukudani*

Chicken pieces are cooked gently and slowly on low heat until the braising liquid is reduced to a thick, flavorful sauce. The original recipe uses chicken pieces no larger than 1 ½ to 2 inches, so as to be manageable with chopsticks. A contemporary method for preparing this is in a pressure cooker, which halves braising time. (Translated and adapted from *Katei Ryōri no Jiten*.)

*Yield:* 4 servings

**Ingredients**
2 pounds chicken pieces with bone (leg, back, wings), cut up into 2-inch pieces
2 quarts water
3 tablespoons oil
4 tablespoons *sake*
2 cups water
6 tablespoons soy sauce
½ cup mirin
4 tablespoons sugar
2-inch piece fresh ginger, peeled and finely minced
4 hard-boiled eggs, sliced in half crosswise
Japanese- or English-type hot mustard

**Procedure**
1. Place chicken pieces in one layer on a tray or a large colander. Bring to a boil 2 quarts of water and carefully pour it over the chicken pieces. Ensure that all sides of the chicken are exposed to the hot water. Pat chicken pieces dry with paper towels.
2. In a heavy-bottomed saucepan, heat oil over medium heat, and brown chicken pieces, a few at a time, on all sides. Set aside.
3. To the same pan (without washing), add *sake* and water. Add browned chicken pieces. Bring to a boil over medium heat. Scoop out any scum that rises to the surface.
4. Turn heat down to lowest setting. Add soy sauce, mirin, sugar, and ginger. Cover pan and simmer for 20 minutes. Turn chicken pieces over, and continue to simmer until chicken is completely cooked and tender, and only a small amount of seasoning liquid remains. Add ½ cup of water when needed. Taste and adjust the seasoning, adding more soy sauce and/or sugar to taste.
5. Distribute the chicken pieces and sauce into four deep bowls. Add 2 egg halves per bowl, cut side up, next to the chicken. Add a teaspoon of mustard (or more if liked) beside the eggs, if there is room, or in a separate small saucer.

# CHAPTER FIVE

# Desserts

## Introduction

A diner in Japan with a sweet tooth is faced with a bewildering diversity of sweets: Japanese confectionery (*wagashi*); Western confectionery (*yōgashi*), which includes European and American confections; and miscellaneous sweets from other food cultures. One can find such international sweets as Japanese-style soufflé cheesecake; New York-style cheesecake (called "rare," *re-a*, that is, "unbaked" as opposed to "baked"); ice cream in flavors such as chocolate, vanilla, and green tea (*matcha*); fruit sorbets; rice cakes in various shapes with sweet *azuki* bean fillings or toppings; French macarons; Thai-style rice-coconut confections; chestnuts embedded in sweet *azuki* bean jelly; dark brown sugar-glazed fritters (*karintō*); sweet *azuki* bean soup with tiny *mochi* dumplings; apple and other fruit pies; and many others. These comprise only a small selection of the sweets commonly sold in shops, bakeries, the food section of department stores, or available to eat with coffee or tea or as snacks in coffee shops, pastry shops, and snack shops. For those with a hearty appetite, certain snack bars offer buffets of Western-style cakes with cream or butter frosting. If your inclination is local sweets, there are shops that offer cakes and other treats made with sweet bean paste, in *tabehōdai* ("all-you-can-eat") style.

Indeed, the global influence is clearly evident in contemporary Japanese confectionery. Perhaps surprising to contemporary consumers, even the genre of what is considered today to be purely Japanese confectionery—*wagashi*—has actually absorbed elements from other food cultures. These foreign elements entered the country centuries ago and have become so thoroughly integrated into local food culture that they are no longer considered foreign. In much the same way that savory dishes such as Indian curry brought by British traders has evolved into the popular curry rice (*karē raisu*), and Chinese-style noodles in soup have undergone a metamorphosis into Japanese *rāmen*, so also have certain imported Chinese and Western sweet dishes and their manner of preparation been transformed by ingenuity and local taste and locally available ingredients, to become thoroughly Japanized.

The earliest recorded foreign food introductions to Japan, including the precursors of today's sweets, came from China. As early as the Nara period (7th century AD), the first wave of gastronomic imports accompanied the first religious and other cultural introductions from Tang China. Among the first Chinese sweets introduced were edible ritual offerings made of rice or other cereal flour and flavored with dark unrefined sugar and spices. These latter two ingredients were then unknown in Japan, and their sweet flavor and aromas were intensely attractive to the elite who were the first to taste them. The second wave of Chinese food cultural introductions arrived during the 12th century with a different branch of Buddhism (Zen) and the drinking of green powdered tea, which was partaken of with sweets. A few centuries later, Portuguese and Spanish traders in the Sengoku period (Warring States period, 16th century) brought Southern European delicacies prepared with white refined sugar and eggs. Closer to contemporary times, Western European and American confectionery were introduced during the Meiji period (from 1868), when Japan's isolationist policy was abandoned, and Japan was opened to European and American trade. These separate waves of sweet food introductions will be treated in more detail later in this chapter.

## The Concept of Sweets and Dessert (*Okashi*)

Dessert in the Western concept of the word—as a separate sweet course to end a meal—was not historically part of a traditional Japanese meal. *Kashi*, or in its polite form *okashi* (the term refers to sweet foods such as pastry, candy, rice cakes, as well as to salty foods eaten as snacks), originally referred to fresh or dried fruits and nuts. This association with fruits survives today in the term *mizukashi* (water sweets) for the final course in a formal multicourse meal called *kaiseki*. The original term *mizukashi* derives from the tea ceremony, which when it was founded by the Buddhist monk Sen no Rikyū, usually meant fruits or nuts such as persimmon or chestnuts, or, rather unusually, savory foods such as shiitake mushrooms, seaweed such as *konbu*, or roasted beans—foods that would definitely not be considered sweets today. (A passage from Rikyū's journal mentions an *okashi* consisting of a thin wafer of wheat flour, spread with a layer of miso paste flavored with herbs. This concoction would fit in with the overall definition of *okashi* as a sweet or salty food eaten outside of regular meal

# Desserts

times—in essence, snacks, or a savory. More on snacks in Chapter Eight, Street Food and Snacks.)

Dessert is called by various names in contemporary Japanese meals. A multicourse formal meal (*kaiseki*) at a specialist restaurant may refer to the sweet course as *mizumono* or *mizukashi* (water things, water sweets). Depending on the region, *mizukashi* may include different ingredients. A modern *mizukashi* course in Tokyo, for instance, will feature fresh fruits in season paired with a Western-style sweet such as cheesecake, or a Japanese-style sweet made of traditional Japanese ingredients such as rice flour, tofu, sweet bean paste (*an*), or *kuzu* flour.

Other names for dessert used are *shokugo*, *dezāto* (dessert), *suītsu* (sweets), and *wa suītsu* for a Japanese-style sweet dish. Fresh fruits were the usual ending to a family meal, but contemporary home cooks now tend to add a prepared sweet dish, and call it *dezāto* (dessert) or *suītsu* (sweets). These may be in the form of an individual cup of custard pudding (*purin*, "pudding," one of the most popular sweets for children and adults alike), flavored yogurt, ice cream or sorbet, or rice dumplings served with fresh seasonal fruits.

> Brown, unrefined sugar (*kokutō*) came to Japan from China during the Nara period (710–794). Previously, sugar was unknown, and so became highly valued: its use was confined to Buddhist rituals and medicine for aristocrats. Buddhist monks used the brown sugar to make sweet snacks called *tenshin*. It was not until the mid-1500s, when Portuguese traders brought white sugar, that sweets became widely available to common folk. Eastern Shikoku produces an artisanal sugar called *wasanbon*. Made from a temperate species of sugar cane (also called Chinese sugar cane, *Saccharum sinense*), it is used in rice cakes for the tea ceremony.

Sugar in its crystalline form was unknown in ancient Japan. Japanese monks and scholars returning from religious and cultural studies in Tang China introduced it in the 8th century as dark brown unrefined sugar. (The original process of converting sugar cane juice to solid form had come from India and spread to China, and thence to the rest of Asia. The sugar cane plant originated in Austronesia and the Southern Pacific.) Before sugar was imported, *ame* or *mizu ame* (syrup from sprouted wheat and rice) had been known as a source of sweetness since the early 8th century AD, but it was not until the Edo period that it was used to make sweets. Another source was sugarcane grown in Shikoku, called *chikutō* or *takesha* (bamboo sugar), used to produce *awasanbon* or *sanbontō*. This artisanal product, first made in the late 1770s, continues to be made and used by confectioners for exquisite *wagashi* for the tea ceremony, as well as by gourmet cooks.

In addition to the new religion, Buddhist monks also introduced other novelties from Tang Chinese culture, such as tea and the custom of tea drinking, accompanied by sweets called *kara kudamono* or *tōgashi* (both terms mean "Chinese sweets"; nowadays the word *kudamono* refers only to fruits). These early sweets were most likely fashioned from finely ground rice, millet (*awa, kibi*), barley, or other cereal grains with beans, shaped into balls or other shapes, and fried, much like traditional confections made throughout South and Southeast Asia today.

> Desserts in the form of cooked pastries were not usually part of a traditional Japanese meal. In ancient times, formal banquets at the imperial court ended with a final course called *kudamono*, consisting of fresh fruits and nuts. Nowadays the word *kudamono* refers solely to fruits. It was only with the cultural imports from China and Korea that prepared sweets became part of Japanese food culture. The first sweets were ritual offerings at Buddhist temples, made of wheat or rice flour and steamed or fried in sesame oil. Called *gūzen gashi*, they are still prepared today to celebrate Buddhist holy days.

These culinary imports from China were unlike anything made in Japan at the time, and so captivated early tasters who then set about recreating them according to local ingredients and local tastes. Associated with religious rituals, those early imported sweets survive to this day largely unchanged from their traditional form and flavor as Shinto shrine and Buddhist temple offerings called *shinsen gashi* and *gūzen gashi*. (Some of these were exotically flavored with cinnamon and cloves—spices unknown in Japan then.) These early sweets laid the first foundation for the development of traditional Japanese confectionery (*wagashi*).

## Traditional Japanese Confectionery (*Wagashi*)

Over the centuries, *wagashi* developed into a distinctive culinary art form. Shops specializing in the making of these pastries and sweets enjoyed the patronage of the elite—the aristocracy and religious establishments. These sweets were a perfect complement to the astringency of black tea in brick form, which was the type of tea initially introduced from China to Japan (the type still drunk today in Tibet and other countries in Central Asia). With the second introduction of tea from China in its green leaf form, and the development of tea drinking into the highly ritualized form of the tea ceremony (*cha no yū, sadō*, also *chadō*), the aesthetic sensibilities of tea connoisseurs influenced the further development of Japanese confectionery (*wagashi*) into the more sophisticated delicacies now called *jō wagashi* (*jo* means "superior" or "premium").

In Kyoto and Kanazawa, there are *wagashi* shops that have been in continuous operation since the early 18th century, their wares created with the same attention to detail over centuries. However, these exquisitely crafted confections, intricately shaped as seasonal flowers or fruits or auspicious symbols for special occasions, were at the time beyond the reach of common people, since tea drinking was then the exclusive pastime of the upper classes. Also, sugar, being a rare, imported ingredient, was a luxury, and priced as such, making it affordable only by the very rich. It was not until the Edo Period, when sugar began to be processed in Japan, that it became more widely available to the wider population, and traditional sweets such as *yōkan* (sweet bean jelly) and *manjū* (dumplings) also became regular accompaniments for the tea ceremony.

Confectioners developed three types of *wagashi*: fresh sweets (*nama gashi*, "raw sweets"), semi-fresh sweets (*hannama gashi*, "half-raw sweets"), and dry sweets (*hoshi gashi*). The distinction among them is the amount of moisture in the finished product. Fresh sweets contain more than 30% moisture. Semi-fresh sweets typically contain between 10% and 30%. Dry sweets usually have no more than 10% moisture. Fresh sweets traditionally were made daily, intended for immediate consumption on that day. Some *nama gashi* can be refrigerated and eaten within 3 days from purchase. However, *nama gashi* are best consumed on the day of purchase or at the latest the following day, in particular the highly elaborate artisanal premium fresh sweets (*jō nama gashi*). Semi-fresh sweets will keep for about a week at room temperature, slightly longer if refrigerated. Dry sweets will keep for about a month at room temperature. Except for the gelled sweets called *mizu yōkan*, which are intended for eating well chilled, *wagashi* are best enjoyed at room temperature.

In general, *wagashi* consist of doughs or pastry coatings made of rice (regular rice, *uruchigome*, or sticky rice, *mochi gome*, or a mixture of both), wheat flour, or *kuzu* flour. Depending on the region, millet and barley may also be mixed with rice or wheat flour, or used on their own for dough. The dough can be shaped into balls or molded into various shapes appropriate to the season, festive occasion, or reminiscent of natural forms. The resulting forms can be boiled, steamed, fried, or baked, or created through a combination of these procedures. These forms can be further elaborated with fillings such as sweet pastes made of *azuki* beans (called *an*) or green (unripe) soy beans (called *zunda*), as well as chestnuts and walnuts. The bean pastes can be smooth or chunky for added texture. Sweet *azuki* paste and green soybean paste can also be mixed with seaweed gelatin (agar-agar, *kanten*) or pectin, and pressed into molds on their own, or with the addition of chestnuts, walnuts, and other fruits or nuts. *Azuki* and green soybean paste are additionally used as outer coatings for plain dumplings. Powdered toasted soybean flour, usually a golden color (*kinako*), or pale green if made from unripe soybeans (*ao kinako*), is sprinkled over the top of some confections for texture, color, and to provide a nonstick coating to the dough, as well as for adornment. Sesame seeds, poppy seeds (*keshi no mi*), *warabi* (edible fern fronds), and *mogusa* leaf may be added to provide additional texture, color, and flavor.

---

## Chunky-Style *Azuki* Paste, *Tsubushi-An*

If you would like to try to make your own sweet *azuki* paste, the procedure is quite simple. Dry *azuki* beans can be found in Asian food shops, health food shops, and online. Cooking time can be reduced to 25 or 30 minutes, if using a pressure cooker or instant pot (a new electronic type of pressure cooker). (Follow directions given for cooking beans in your pressure cooker or instant pot.)

*Yield:* about 2 cups

**Ingredients**
1 cup dry *azuki* beans
3 cups water
¾ cup sugar, or to taste
¼ teaspoon salt

**Procedure**
1. Rinse the *azuki* beans and place in a medium-sized saucepan.
2. Add water to cover and place over medium heat. Let the water come to a boil.
3. Immediately turn off heat, drain the beans, and discard the water.
4. Return drained beans to the pan, add 3 cups water, and let beans come to a boil over medium heat.
5. Turn down heat as soon as the water boils, and let beans simmer for 45 minutes. Check the consistency: if the beans are almost cooked but still rather firm (*al dente*), take out a few tablespoonfuls and set them aside if you wish to have a bit more texture in the finished paste.

# Desserts

6. Continue to simmer the rest of the beans for 15 more minutes, or until soft enough to mash with a wooden spoon. Add more water if necessary, but there should not be more than a thin film of water remaining when the beans are done.
7. Stir in sugar and salt, adjusting sweetness to your taste. Add more sugar if necessary. Stir in the reserved beans.
8. Continue cooking sweetened beans over the lowest heat possible until sugar is completely dissolved. Watch carefully that the bean mass does not burn.
9. Turn off heat, and let the bean mass cool to room temperature. If using the beans for the Ogura Ice Cream recipe, refrigerate as soon as the bean mass has reached room temperature.

## Green Soybean (*Edamame*) Paste, *Zunda*

Green soybeans used to denote summer, until industrial freezing technology made them available all year round. Green soybean paste, *zunda* (pronounced "dzunda" in its home ground of Sendai, Miyagi Prefecture), is a regional specialty of the Tohoku (northeastern Honshu). It is historically associated with the powerful daimyo Date Masamune, who founded the city of Sendai, and ruled the region from the middle of the 16th century (Azuchi-Momoyama period) to the early 17th century (Edo period).

The traditional way to make *zunda* was with a wooden pestle against the ribbed surface of a stoneware bowl called *suribachi*. Unlike boiled *azuki* beans, boiled *edamame* cannot be passed through a sieve, and legend has it that Lord Masamune once used his sword to chop up *zunda*. Whether this account actually happened, or is simply a brilliant promotional idea for this northeastern Japanese treat is still a matter for debate.

Food processors simplify the making of this paste. After boiling the green beans in their pods, they are shelled, and the outer coat of each bean removed. Some people do not even bother, as the coats provide the right texture for an unrefined, countryside treat. However, it is worth the extra effort to create a finer texture for this sweet paste.

Once you have the paste, it can also be used as an added ingredient for ice cream, mousse, cheesecake, cookies, and cake. Its delicate green color and flavor, and—when freshly harvested—its scent reminiscent of the tropical plant *pandan* (screwpine), make the finished products very appealing.

*Yield:* about 2 cups of paste

**Ingredients**
1 ½ pounds *edamame* beans (green soybeans in their pods), fresh or frozen
¼ cup sugar, or more to taste
¼ teaspoon salt

**Procedure**
1. If fresh, wash soybean pods well. If frozen, there is no need to thaw them.
2. Fill a large pan with 8 cups of water, and let it come to a boil.
3. Add the pods and turn down the heat so that the water just simmers. Leave the pan uncovered.
4. Let pods cook for about 15 minutes. Turn off heat and transfer the pods at once to a bowl of cold water to stop them cooking further.
5. Once the pods are completely cold, shell them, and peel off the outer translucent coat from each bean. This step requires a bit of patience and effort, but it directly affects the quality of the result. The flavor of the finished paste is better and the texture is finer.
6. If you wish, reserve 2–3 tablespoons of whole peeled beans for garnish.
7. Place peeled beans, sugar, and salt in a food processor, and process until reduced to a fine paste.
8. Test paste for sweetness, and adjust sugar to your taste.

*The paste is now ready for use as a topping sauce for* mochi *balls, or as an ingredient for further elaboration into jelly, mousse, cheesecake, and other sweets.*

*Use the reserved whole beans as garnish. Alternatively, chop the beans finely and add to the finished paste for added texture and color.*

Refined red seaweed gelatin, also known as agar-agar or just agar (*kanten*) is used for gelling confections such as *mizu yōkan*, enjoyed as a cold sweet snack during the summer. The juice and rind of *yuzu* and other citrus fruits, as well as seasonal flowers, leaves, and fruits, are also used in *wagashi*. Fruit juices are sometimes used to flavor dry sweets (*hoshi gashi*), in particular *rakugan*, which are formed into diverse shapes in cherry-wood molds. *Rakugan* are traditionally given as souvenirs or favors at celebratory life events, such as weddings. They are also accompaniments for tea during a light tea ceremony (*usu cha*), as well as for gift-giving during the spring and autumn equinox festivals known as *higan*.

# Desserts

## Green Soybean Jelly, *Zunda Yōkan*

*Yōkan* is a gelled sweet most often made with *azuki* bean paste. This recipe uses *zunda* paste (sweet green soybean or *edamame* paste). Served well chilled, it is a popular summer dessert or sweet that goes well with tea, coffee, or a cold beverage.

*Yield:* 4 servings

**Ingredients**
2 teaspoons agar-agar/*kanten* powder, available at Asian food shops or online
2 ½ cups water
2 cups *zunda* paste (sweet green soybean paste)
Garnish: 2–3 tablespoons whole green soybeans

**Procedure**
1. Prepare a rectangular or square mold for the *yōkan*. Run cold water into it, drain off excess water, and refrigerate until needed.
2. In a bowl, put ½ cup water and stir in agar-agar/*kanten* powder to rehydrate. Set aside.
3. In a pan, combine *zunda* paste and the remaining water. Place pan over medium heat.
4. Stir the rehydrated agar-agar powder into the *zunda* mixture. Let the agar-agar and *zunda* mixture cook at low-medium heat for 2 minutes. The mixture does not have to boil. Remove pan from heat.
5. You may add some green soybeans, chopped or whole, to the mixture for texture and added color. Leave a few for garnish.
6. Let mixture cool slightly, then pour it into the prepared mold and set aside at room temperature. The mixture will set even without refrigeration.
8. Once thoroughly cool, transfer the *yōkan* in its mold to the refrigerator to chill thoroughly for 3–4 hours or overnight. Refrigerate the reserved beans, covered, for garnish.

*To serve: Slice into desired shapes and garnish with the reserved beans.*

Each season has its particular *wagashi*. In spring, *sakura mochi* (cherry blossom sweets) are wrapped in cherry leaves or adorned with pickled cherry blossom petals. These have a filling of sweet *azuki* bean paste enclosed in rice-based dough, tinted pink to evoke cherry blossoms. *Bota mochi* are also made in spring, when peony flowers (*botan*) are in bloom. They are oval-shaped, made of a mix of steamed regular rice and sticky rice dough, and similarly covered with *azuki* sweet bean paste. The same pastries made in autumn are known as *ohagi*, after a plant with purple flowers in bloom then, and whose flower buds are thought to resemble *azuki* beans. Summer *okashi* are predominantly made of jellied *azuki* paste (*yōkan*) and Japanese arrowroot starch (*kuzu*), as they give an impression of coolness and thus relief from the heat. In winter, *okashi* are shaped to represent snowy landscapes or molded in layers to evoke the earth awaiting the coming of spring.

The art of *wagashi*, according to one traditional confectioner whose family has created them for generations, lies in their appeal to all of the five senses. Foremost is their appeal to the eye, their exquisite forms and gentle colors always in keeping with the season. Next is their appeal to the touch: rice-based doughs are silken and soft, whereas gelled sweets are smooth as glass, especially when chilled. The aromas of *wagashi* are gentle: citrusy scents from *yuzu*, the subtle nuttiness of *azuki* beans. The use of quality ingredients (with the exception of eggs, all are from plants) ensures that *wagashi* flavors are clear—that is, the ingredients taste naturally of themselves. The final appeal is to the ear, in the poetic names given to special creations. These names often carry literary and aesthetic allusions, so that when spoken, they evoke culturally meaningful imagery.

## Portuguese-Style Confectionery (*Namban Gashi*)

The second stage in the development of confectionery in Japan came with the arrival of Portuguese and Dutch traders during the 16th century. Portuguese traders introduced the making of *kasutera* (also *kasuteira* in southern Japan; *castella*, after Castilla, the ancient name for Spain). It is a sponge-type cake, baked in a rectangular mold, and is very similar to a contemporary Spanish cake called *biscocho de azucar* (sugar cake). (Interestingly, this Spanish-style sponge cake was introduced to Italy much later and is called *pan di Spagna*, "Spanish bread.")

Castella cake, introduced and first made in Nagasaki in 1571, became its specialty, but is now widely made and eaten throughout Japan. It is one of the more popular items for guests to bring as *te omiyage* (present) when visiting someone. By the 1700s, Japanese confectioners were making castella and other Portuguese sweets, such as *bōro* (Portuguese *bolo*, "cake"), *konpeito* (Portuguese *confeito*, "sugar coated sweets"), *kaseita* (Portuguese *caixa de marmelada* or *queijada*; both terms are cited by Japanese food historians for quince-based sweets), and *hiryōzu* or *hirōsu* (Portuguese *filhós*, "fritters" or "doughnuts"). Known collectively as *namban gashi* ("Southern Barbarian confectionery"), these sweets introduced the use of eggs, milk, generous use of white (refined) sugar, wheat flour, and leavening, as well as the methods of baking and frying in oil to create sweets. Japanese confectioners adopted these ingredients, previously unused for local sweets, as well as the baking and frying methods, and adapted them to Japanese tastes and preferences, leading to the creation of diverse *okashi* today.

To this day, some of those earlier Portuguese confections live on, and have become famous specialties in southern Japan, specifically in Kyushu. *Kaseita*, for instance, whose recipe was once a secret guarded by the Hosokawa clan, historically entrusted to them by a Catholic priest, is now one of the specialties of a baker in Kumamoto City. However, instead of using paste made from the European quince (*Cydonia oblonga*), the revived modern version uses *karin*, the Japanese quince, the fruit of an altogether different plant, *Chaenomeles japonica*.

Meanwhile, the Portuguese fritters called *filhós* (*hiryōzu* or *hirōsu* in Japanese) underwent a change of flavor from sweet to savory. In the Kansai region, *hiryōzu* refers to fritters made of tofu, carrots, and other ingredients. The same dish is called *ganmodoki* ("ersatz goose") in Tokyo and surrounding areas (the Kanto region).

## Western-Style Confectionery (*Yōgashi*)

The third stage in the development of sweets came three centuries later, during the Meiji and Taisho periods (the end of the 19th to the beginning of the 20th century), with the influx of Western culture when Japan was forced to open its doors to international trade. Food businesses catering to foreign residents in Yokohama, Kobe, and other treaty ports included a French bakery in Yokohama that introduced *shū kurīmu* (choux cream, cream puffs in the United States) and eclairs. Waffles, German *Baumkuchen*, custard pudding, hot cake, chocolate, and caramel candies were also introduced, but initially did not find favor with local tastes because they contained butter (whose scent was considered unpleasant), or were too rich and strongly flavored. (Japanese nationalists disparaged anything Western as *batā kusai*, "butter stinky.")

With the establishment of cafés and an emerging, fashionable café culture, these rich, sweet Western cakes were found to go well with the bitterness of coffee. However, only the middle and upper classes could afford to frequent these cafés. In 1918, Fujiya, a major confectionery company today, created its shortcake: three layers of light sponge cake with whipped cream and fresh strawberries. This soft version of strawberry shortcake, rather than the original crisp shortbread, is still the standard today. From 1912 onward, Western food became more accessible to and affordable for the common population. The three most popular Western sweets during this era were *Baumkuchen*, chocolates, and caramel candies.

## Globalization, Sweets, and Confectionery

The final stage in the development of *okashi* and the popularization and widespread acceptance of a sweet course (dessert) began when Japan had fully recovered from the postwar period of food shortages and established its presence worldwide through international trade. Beginning in the 1970s, coffee shops boomed as coffee beans sourced from all over the world poured into Japan, and business dealings were regularly conducted in their convivial surroundings. Cheesecake, chocolate cake, and other types of cake became regular offerings at coffee shops throughout the country.

Multinational companies (mainly from the United States) introduced doughnuts of different types and flavors, varied flavors of ice cream, cheesecake with assorted fruit sauces and toppings, and other types of sweets to major Japanese cities. Department stores played a major role in introducing these foreign specialty sweets by providing space to French bakeries, such as Le Notre. Local confectionery manufacturers expanded their repertoire during Western holidays, such as Christmas, by offering cakes and sweets from different countries' Christmas traditions, such as *Stollen* from Germany and *bûche de Noël* from France. Valentine's Day created another opportunity for chocolate manufacturers, because it has become the custom (not only on leap years) for Japanese ladies to send chocolates to the object of their affection.

---

### Ogura Ice Cream

This is a quick and easy frozen dessert made with chunky-style sweetened *azuki* bean paste (*tsubu-an*), yogurt, and cream. The name *Ogura* comes from a poetic allusion to Mt. Ogura in Kyoto, and refers to dishes with whole *azuki* beans incorporated into sweetened *azuki* paste. The first use of the term allegedly was during the Edo period by a traditional Japanese confectionery shop in Tokyo called Funabashiya. The shop's confectioner used boiled *azuki* beans steeped in honey for his chunky-style *azuki* paste, and called it *Ogura-an* to distinguish it from the smooth standard *koshi-an*. Another reason is that the best quality *azuki* beans—the larger and better-tasting Dainagon *azuki* beans—are grown in the area of Mt. Ogura.

As mentioned previously, *wagashi* are often given names with classic literary allusions, and *Ogura-an* is no exception. Mt. Ogura is famous for deer, and dark whole beans amongst the smooth paste reminded Funabashiya's confectioner of mottled deer skins. Yet another literary allusion is that Mt. Ogura was the site of Heian poetry gatherings, so that it is locally referred to as The Poets' Mountain.

## Desserts

If you wish to make a quick and easy version of this recipe, just add whole sweetened *azuki* beans, as much as you like, to plain vanilla ice cream. Mix thoroughly and refreeze. Alternatively, you can serve sweetened *azuki* beans as a topping over scoops of vanilla ice cream.

The same procedure detailed here can be used to make green soybean ice cream. Simply substitute *zunda* (sweet green soybean) paste for the *azuki* beans or paste.

*Yield:* 4–6 servings

**Ingredients**

1 cup plain unsweetened, unflavored yogurt (10% Greek-type, preferably)
1 cup thick cream (30%–35%) or whipping cream
1 ½ to 2 cups whole sweetened *azuki* beans, canned or in a sealed pack (labeled *tsubu-an*, *tsubushi-an*, or *yude azuki* (boiled *azuki* beans), available from Asian food shops or online. Alternatively, prepare your own (see the recipe for Chunky-Style Azuki Paste).
¼ cup sugar, or to taste

**Procedure**

1. In a large bowl, mix thoroughly the yogurt, cream, and *azuki* beans.
2. Taste for sweetness before adding sugar, as the beans may provide enough sweetness.
3. Add sugar to taste, if needed. Mix well until sugar is thoroughly incorporated.
4. Transfer to a sealable container and freeze for 2 hours.
5. Remove from freezer and mix well, incorporating as much air as possible.
6. Return to freezer and freeze for another hour.
7. Let stand at room temperature for 10–15 minutes, or in the refrigerator for 20–25 minutes, to soften before serving.

*Alternatively, transfer the unfrozen mixture to an ice cream maker, and follow the manufacturer's instructions for use.*

With widespread prosperity as Japan's economic boom continued, more Japanese could afford worldwide travel, and exposure to foreign food cultures created a desire among many to experiment with making these foods at home, as well as to study abroad to learn patisserie in France and return with their expertise to open their own confectionery shops. Weekly or monthly journals were and continue to be instrumental in promoting innovative ways of eating and preparing novel foods. The first Japanese cookbook specializing in *okashi*, *Kokon Meibutsu Gozen Gashi*

*Hidenshō* ("Secrets to Famous Sweets, Ancient and Modern") was published in 1718 with 105 recipes, most of Portuguese provenance. These days, a specialist cookbook publisher, Shibata Shoten, carries a monthly magazine, *Cafe Sweets*, in hardcover and online versions, presenting novel pastry recipes to accompany coffee, as well as reporting on international trends in confectionery. Books by the renowned patisserie maker Hidemi Sugino lead this publisher's dessert section. Sugino says his *okashi* recipes are intended as desserts. In comparison to previous decades' menus, women's journals now include dessert recipes. A few examples from *H2O*, a women's journal, include peeled and ready-to-eat grapefruit slices, baked cherry flan made with canned cherries, and a sweet cream cheese and yogurt base for fresh fruits. Blogs and online recipe websites (for example, Cookpad Japan) are increasingly featuring Japanese-style desserts. These are often based on traditional Japanese *okashi* ingredients such as rice, *kuzu* flour, or agar gelatin, combined with cream or cream cheese, ingredients not customarily used for *wagashi*.

It is interesting to speculate when traditional Japanese *okashi* ingredients such as *kuzu* (Japanese arrowroot) flour, *kinako* (toasted soybean powder), and sweet *azuki* paste will find their way into European and American desserts and sweets. With the rapid dissemination of trends worldwide through the internet and social media such as Instagram, Flickr, Twitter, and Facebook, it may not take too long. Miso, for instance, has already been used in an award-winning ice cream submitted to an international competition.

*Matcha* (powdered green tea) has become ubiquitous worldwide in latte, cupcakes and other pastry, mousse, and ice cream. Powdered chocolate or coffee can be replaced by *matcha* in many recipes. The health benefits of green tea (noted for its antioxidants) as a drink are already well known, and *matcha* is a convenient way of adding those benefits to baked goods and other sweet and savory concoctions.

## *Matcha* Milk Jelly

*Matcha*, powdered green leaf tea, has become a popular food ingredient, not only in Japan, but worldwide, particularly among consumers who wish to increase their intake of antioxidants. *Matcha* is made from green tea leaves that have been shaded from direct sunlight for about three weeks, which makes their chlorophyll content higher, and the leaves greener, with a more concentrated amount of health-preserving phytonutrients. Due to its powder form, it is easy to incorporate it into recipes for pastry and other

# Desserts

baked goods that originally call for cocoa powder. Its fresh green color, which is retained after baking or heating, is another factor in its current popularity as an added ingredient to sweets and desserts. *Kanten* powder (food-grade agar or agar-agar powder) is sold in Asian food shops. Most Japanese brands of *kanten* powder contain 4 sachets, and each sachet is 4 grams (2 teaspoons), which is sufficient to gel the liquid in this recipe (or follow the proportions given on the packet if using other brands.)

*Yield:* 4 servings

**Ingredients**
1 tablespoon *matcha* (powdered green leaf tea)
2 cups milk
3 tablespoons sugar, or to taste
2 teaspoons *kanten* (agar, also agar-agar) powder, sold in Asian food shops or Japanese/Asian food shops online
1 cup whipping cream or thick cream (30%–35% fat content)
Garnish: 2 tablespoons black sesame seeds or 4 sprigs of mint

**Procedure**
1. First prepare the *matcha* paste. In a big bowl, pass the *matcha* powder through a sieve to remove lumps.
2. Using a wire whisk, gradually stir in 2 tablespoons milk to make a smooth paste. If necessary, add a tablespoon or more of milk until a moist paste is achieved. Set *matcha* paste aside.
3. Prepare a rectangular mold for the jelly. Rinse the mold with cold water and drain off the excess. Refrigerate mold until needed.
4. Next, prepare the milk and agar-agar mixture. In a pan, put the rest of the milk, sugar, and agar-agar. Using a wire whisk, stir until well combined.
5. Place the pan over medium heat, and continue to stir the milk mixture until it starts to boil.
6. Turn down heat immediately, and let mixture continue to cook, stirring all the while, or until all sugar and agar-agar powder have dissolved. Turn off heat.
7. Slowly add the hot milk and agar-agar mixture to the bowl with the *matcha* paste.
8. Whisk the mixture to incorporate air.
9. Take the mold out of the refrigerator, and pour in the *matcha*-agar-agar mixture. Let stand at room temperature until the mold is no longer hot to the touch.
10. Refrigerate the mold with *matcha*-agar-agar mixture for 2–3 hours or overnight, until firm. Because agar-agar powder is used, the mixture will set even without refrigeration, but it is best served and eaten cold.

> *To serve: Chill 4 dessert bowls, preferably glass. Just before serving, whip the cream into soft peaks, and distribute among the chilled bowls. Slice the matcha jelly neatly into small pieces—squares, diamonds, rectangles—according to personal preference. Place the matcha jelly slices in a mound over the cream. Scatter a few black sesame seeds, or place a mint sprig over the jelly as garnish.*

With the current trend toward veganism—that is, a diet without animal-sourced foods—there may be a place for classic *wagashi*, as well as the individual ingredients used in traditional *wagashi*. Prior to the introduction of eggs, as influenced by Southern European sweets, traditional Japanese sweets contained only plant-based ingredients: rice and other cereal grains and *azuki* beans, sweetened with rice malt syrup (*ame*). No eggs or dairy products were used. *Mochi* is currently being used as a soft pastry shell for fruit-flavored ice creams in Spain and France. These can be found in the frozen section together with ice creams in major supermarkets. The ice cream flavors include mango, coconut, *yuzu*, raspberry, and other more familiar flavors such as salted caramel and espresso.

# CHAPTER SIX

# Beverages

## The Tea Ceremony: A Model for Eating, Preparing, Serving, and Enjoying Food and Drinks

One cannot speak of Japanese beverages without mentioning tea and the tea ceremony (*sado*, also *chado*, the way of tea), known informally as *cha no yu* (water for tea). Created in the 15th century at a time when Japan was in the throes of civil war, the tea ceremony provided a haven of calm and an escape from the chaos of daily life. The drinking of powdered green tea had come from Song dynasty China in the 12th century, with Japanese monks who had undertaken Buddhist studies there. Interestingly, drinking powdered tea is no longer practiced in China, but survived through millennia in Japan as an established art form and meditative perspective, in the same manner as *karatedō*, *aikidō*, *kyūdō* (archery), and *kadō* (flower arrangement). The aesthetic principles espoused by the tea master Ochoo, most notably practiced and disseminated by his disciple Sen no Rikyū, have touched every artistic sphere—architecture, interior design, garden design, flower arrangement, among many others—and directly established how food, tea, and *sake* are best enjoyed. These principles apply to their preparation and presentation, and to the responsibilities and behavior of host and guest. These principles relating to all aspects of food and drink are embodied in *cha kaiseki*—the formal meal that precedes a full tea ceremony—and apply as well, with suitable modifications and without the stricture of ritualistic rules, to Japanese fine dining and other food events.

In contrast to the ostentation and rowdiness that characterized tea gatherings at the time, Rikyū created a simple, restrained way of enjoying tea, which he called *wabi cha* ("impoverished tea"). Tea drinking has its roots in Zen Buddhist meditation. Monks brought heated stones tucked into their robes to enable them to better withstand the cold and discomfort of sitting during long meditative sessions. This practice gradually evolved into tea ceremony guests bringing small, easily transported foods. However, the strength of *koicha* (thick tea), the first tea served, was found not to sit well on lightly filled stomachs; hence the idea of a full meal before drinking thick tea (akin to an after-dinner espresso).

The tea gatherings of Rikyū's time were the setting of cultural events: *renga* and *waka* poetry composition and readings, music and dance performances, and tea tastings (like today's wine tastings). These were occasions for elaborate feasts with abundant food and *sake*, most of which went to waste. The dishes served were cold and far from tasty, as each diner had to season his or her food from the salt, *sake*, vinegar, and *hishio* (fermented seasoning) dishes at each food tray. Most food was for display and not for actual eating. The waste of food and the rowdiness did not accord with Rikyū's ideas nor with the contemplative nature of tea drinking associated with Zen meditation.

The original format of *cha kaiseki* as one soup-three dishes (*ichijū sansai*) was set by Rikyū to cut down on food waste by limiting the number of dishes served, and by serving them sequentially. This ensured that guests ate everything before them, as the next course was not served until the previous one had been eaten. Contemporary *cha kaiseki* meals have added other dishes, called *azuke bachi* and *shiizakana*, contradictory to Rikyū's original intent of constraint. These additional dishes call for specialist cooking skills, rather than the home cooking style on which the simpler soup-and-three-dishes format was based. These supplementary dishes have also become the focus of competition among tea practitioners for extraordinary vessels on which to present them, contrary to Rikyū's dictum to avoid ostentation and needless expense.

The basic principles for a *cha kaiseki* are as follows.

1. Ingredients must be fresh and of good quality. This rule essentially means that to be a good cook, it is not sufficient to have the right cooking skills: one must know how to identify freshness and quality in choosing ingredients. Ingredients do not have to be luxurious or expensive; the best-tasting are those in season.
2. The food must be freshly cooked. Hot foods must be served hot, cold foods must be served cold. *Miso shiru* and *sumashi jiru* are to be served at just below boiling point, the best temperature for these dishes. Plates and bowls for hot dishes must be warmed with hot water before use. Similarly, serving dishes for cold food must be chilled.
3. The food should look good; the eyes are served first. Food that is beautiful to the eyes will also taste delicious. The dishes used must be appropriate to

the season. In summer, a sense of coolness is desirable, and in winter, comforting warmth. This applies equally to the garnishes and decor on the food.
4. The best way to appreciate food is to eat with a grateful heart. Any food, eaten with gratitude for the host's efforts, will be delicious. It is also incumbent upon the host to prepare the meal with care and from a genuine desire to please his or her guest/s. Any food prepared with the guest's pleasure and well-being in mind will be delicious.

Graciousness and consideration for a guest's enjoyment and comfort are at the heart of the term *omotenashi* (Japanese hospitality), which is an intrinsic characteristic of almost all dining events in Japan, found not only in the tea ceremony but in all eating events.

Rikyū is additionally credited with laying the foundation of true Japanese cooking by featuring *nimono*, stewed or braised dishes, as the main course in *cha kaiseki*. By making it the highlight of the meal, Rikyū also brought attention to this homely dish, and perfection to this manner of cooking. Additionally, he emphasized proper seasoning of food by the cook, not by the diner, as an extension of the cook's responsibilities to prepare food that was tasty. Having been given the starring role as the tastiest dish, *nimono* deserves to have *ichiban dashi*, the first infusion from *katsuobushi* flakes, to flavor it. The second infusion, *niban dashi*, can flavor the *miso shiru* served before it.

## The Structure of Cha Kaiseki

There are seven types of *cha ji*—tea drinking events. Each has its own set of rules for drinking, eating, and the responsibilities of the host and guest, but the most complex is the midday *cha kaiseki*, *shōgo kaiseki*.

### *Shōgo Kaiseki*, The Midday *Kaiseki*

This event usually lasts around four to five hours, depending on the number of guests. Around 20 minutes are devoted to waiting and welcoming guests. The *kaiseki* meal itself takes about 1 hour and 20 minutes. This is followed by a 20-minute break for the host to clear away and prepare for the thick tea ritual, which takes about 30 minutes. Another break of 20 minutes follows for the host to prepare for the light tea ritual, and this includes picking flowers from the garden to make a floral arrangement to place at the *tokonoma* (alcove for decorations). The light tea ritual and final tidying-up take place during the final hour.

The first course of rice, miso soup, and *mukōzuke* (raw seafood) signals that this meal is not to be solely a *sake*-drinking event. The rice is no more than two bites, shaped as a bar, the ideograph "one." Similarly, the soup is also a half serving. This restrained first course ensures that the guest is warmed by the hot rice and soup, and gently eased into the forthcoming dishes. It also ensures that the guest will not become inebriated with the first round of *sake*. The rice is eaten first. When the guest takes a sip of the soup, it signals the host to bring out the *sake*. This signifies that *sake* is complementary to the meal, and that forthcoming dishes have been chosen specifically for their affinity to *sake*.

Next, the guest eats the *mukōzuke*, usually a sashimi or *namasu*, a raw seafood dish dressed with vinegar. Raw seafood goes well with *sake*, and it is appropriate to start a meal with the lightest-tasting dish. As the meal progresses, subsequent dishes display a corresponding complexity of flavor. "Raw" is also one of the five traditional methods of preparation; the others are steaming (*musu*); boiling or stewing (*niru*); frying (*ageru*); and grilling or roasting (*yaku*).

The first course is served on lacquer, on a tray called *oshiki*, and the rice bowl and soup bowl are similarly of lacquer, usually black and plain. The *oshiki* is a flat tray (that is, without feet), in contrast to the footed, elaborately patterned trays called *zen* for elite banquets. The *oshiki* may be any shape—completely round or two-thirds round, hexagonal—but it is most commonly a square. Lacquerware is appropriate for serving rice and soup at all seasons, for its quality of keeping hot foods hot. The placement of the three dishes for the first course forms a triangle: rice bowl to the left, soup bowl to the right, the *mukōzuke* behind and centered (from the guest's perspective). The material of the *mukōzuke* bowl denotes the season: fine ceramic or stoneware in winter, glass or blue-and-white ceramic in summer.

Next comes the main dish: *nimono*, in a covered lacquer bowl (lacquer is a good insulator, and it will have been warmed with hot water beforehand). The *nimono* bowl is larger than that used for rice and soup, and may have a different color and seasonal motif. The main ingredients of the *nimono* are in odd numbers—1, 3, 5, 7—and are chosen from seasonal foodstuffs, with an eye to their combination of colors, textures, and flavors.

Besides the five cooking methods, there are other five-based elements of a meal: the colors red, yellow, white, green (also blue), and black; and the flavors salty, sour, sweet, spicy, and bitter. Additionally, the five senses are addressed: sight, hearing, smell, touch, and taste. The garnish—perhaps fine slivered ginger, a sprig of *sanshō*, a dab of mustard, or a tiny disk of *yuzu* zest—addresses the sense of smell. Hearing is addressed by the sounds generated by the ingredients' textures (crisp, crunchy). The sense of touch is stimulated by the textures and temperature of tableware.

> *Yuzu* (*Citrus junos*) is a small citrus fruit that has become popular around the world. Most of the *yuzu* in Japan is grown in southern Japan, in Kochi, Tokushima, and Ehime Prefectures. It is highly valued, used sparingly as a garnish and to provide its aroma to delicate foods such as steamed custards and soups. The juice is mixed with soy sauce to make a dipping sauce called *ponzu*. However, it is the perfumed rind that is the most appreciated part of the *yuzu*. *Yuzu* is now being more widely used in jams and jellies, as well as to flavor beverages and alcoholic drinks.

Another round of *sake* follows, and next comes a roasted or grilled dish (*yakimono*), served in a large dish, so that guests may help themselves, according to individual appetite, to one or more pieces. The serving dish may be a basket in summer, or stoneware or porcelain in winter. This eclectic mix of serving dishes reflects Rikyū's taste. He encouraged the use of pottery from local kilns and ordinary household utensils combined with the fashionable imported Chinese lacquerware and ceramics of his time. He also improvised with natural materials, such as leaves or split bamboo culms. Rikyū's aesthetic taste in mixed tableware has prevailed to this day.

More rice is offered from a large covered lacquer container. Another round of *sake* follows. The classic one soup-three dishes meal format (*ichijū sansai*) ends here.

A further course called *shiizakana, susumi zakana*, or *azuke bachi*, which used to be the host's prerogative to add or not, has now become standard. This may consist of mixed steamed (*takiawase*) or parboiled vegetables (*hitashi*), or a vinegar-based dish (*sunomono*).

Next is a thin soup called *hashi arai* ("chopstick rinse," to clear the palate and rinse the tips of the chopsticks in preparation for the next course, *hassun* [literally, 8 *sun* (a unit of measurement)], named after the dimension of the serving dish (24 centimeters or 9 inches). On these are two dishes, one from the land and the other from the sea, to go with a further round of *sake*. Assorted pickles follow along with a final helping of rice, usually including the crisp layer at the bottom of the cooking pot, over which salted hot water (*yutō*) is poured.

Thereafter come fresh sweets (*nama okashi*) before the serving of thick tea (*koi cha*), and dry sweets before the serving of thin tea (*usu cha*). These conclude the tea ceremony.

## Green Tea

The hot beverage most drunk in Japan is, unsurprisingly, green tea. A recent survey of 1,000 people revealed that green tea drinkers were the majority, and preferred their tea brewed from leaves. However, they were not averse to drinking it from sachets or from cans or PET bottles when out on a picnic or traveling. The next most popular tea is wheat tea (*mugi cha*), followed by black tea ["English-type" tea, called "red tea" (*kōcha*)], and last, Oolong or Chinese-type tea.

Why is green tea still the most popular hot drink today? One reason is that green tea goes best with Japanese food, especially sushi. Green tea and sushi fans say that the slight astringency of green tea enhances the sweetness of rice, balancing bitter and sweet. Drinking green tea while eating sushi is considered relaxing and calming. Another reason is that green tea is a link with home and family, because it was the hot drink most grew up with, and drinking green tea evokes memories of mother brewing tea leaves in a teapot, and pouring it out for each family member. Yet another reason given is health: one young mother attributed her and her children's good health to daily drinking of green tea brewed from leaves.

Tea arrived during the Heian period from China as fermented brick tea, the type of tea still drunk in Tibet, Mongolia, and Central Asia. Although this was welcomed by the Japanese elite of the time, it did not really catch on. It was not until tea was re-introduced much later as green leaves that it became widely accepted. Its appealing color and finer flavor were found to be more suited to the Japanese taste. In 1985, green tea began to be packaged in cans and in 1991 in PET resin bottles. These were convenient for people on the go and for vending machines, which could serve them hot or cold. Green tea is the usual accompaniment to a Japanese-style breakfast with rice, traditional sweets, such as rice cakes (*okashi*), and salty snacks (*oyatsu*) such as rice crackers (*senbei*).

All tea—green and black—is made from the leaves of the tea plant, *Camellia sinensis*. Green tea results when the leaves are steamed to prevent oxidation (blackening) and the ensuing fermentation that produces black tea. In Japan, green tea is graded from low to high: *bancha, sencha, gyokurō*. *Bancha* is ordinary tea, usually the leaves picked during the third and fourth flushes of growth. The leaves from the first and second flushes of growth go into the higher grades of tea (*sencha* and *gyokurō*). The leaves from the third and fourth flushes are more astringent and bitter than the top two grades. *Gyokurō*, the name of which translates to "dew jewel" or "dew jade," is shaded for 20 days or at least a week before harvest: a labor-intensive procedure, thus its higher price. *Gyokurō* tea must be brewed at a lower temperature and for slightly longer than *sencha* and *bancha*.

Other parts of the tea plant, such as the leaf stalks and stems, which are not as astringent, are used to make *kuki* (stem) *cha*, and it is chilled for summer drinking. *Hōjicha*, another chilled summer tea, consists of roasted *bancha* and *kukicha*, its brown, roasted leaves imparting a caramel-like flavor. The roasting process makes for a milder brew, suitable even for children. Another summer drink is chilled barley tea (*mugi cha*). Although it is called *cha*, it does not contain leaves from the tea plant. Rather, barley grains are roasted, packed in sachets (bags), steeped, and chilled.

## Matcha Latte

Green tea powder (*matcha*) has gone global, incorporated into cakes, ice cream, chocolate bars, noodles, and frozen yogurt, among many other applications. Its high caffeine content makes it suitable for making the same drinks usually made with coffee.

*Yield:* 2 servings

**Ingredients**
2 teaspoons good quality green tea powder (*matcha*)
6 teaspoons hot water
2 cups hot milk, or cold milk (if cold latte is desired)
Sugar to taste

**Procedure**
1. Prepare cups for serving: warm 2 cups with very hot water. Discard water and dry the cups.
2. Place one teaspoon of *matcha* in each cup.
3. With a small whisk or teaspoon, gradually stir in 3 teaspoons of hot water to dissolve the *matcha* into a smooth paste.
4. Continue to whisk or stir the *matcha* paste while slowly adding hot milk.
5. Add sugar to taste.
6. Repeat procedure for the second cup.

*Garnish: Put a small pinch of* matcha *powder in a small fine sieve. Tap the sieve over the matcha latte.*

The tea ceremony uses special ground or stone-milled leaves called *matcha* (literally, "rubbed tea"). The leaves intended for *matcha* are shaded, as for high-grade *gyokurō* tea, to enable the tea plant to manufacture more chlorophyll, giving *matcha* a more vivid green color. The Uji area in Kyoto is famous for the quality of its *matcha*. Shizuoka Prefecture produces the most tea, followed by Kagoshima and Mie Prefectures.

## Coffee

Coffee's initial appearance in Japan was on the island of Dejima, Nagasaki, where the Dutch had a trading post during the 18th century. However, it was not until the Meiji period (19th century), when Japan was opened to trade, that coffee shops for the foreign community were established. Decades later, coffee shops became a popular meeting place for the Japanese elite and intelligentsia. From 1912 on, coffee became more reasonably priced and within the reach of the average Japanese. However, it was not until Japan had fully recovered from World War II that coffee shops (*kissaten*) really came into vogue, as a way of socializing and meeting up with friends, listening to music (often live and of diverse types, from classical to jazz), or just relaxing, having time and space to oneself, and reading. Coffee shops also served as venues for discussing business with colleagues, as most urban homes did not have the space for entertaining guests.

From the late 1960s until the 1990s, coffee shops featured coffee varieties from different countries—Brazil, Colombia, Jamaica, etc.—wherever coffee beans could be imported. The ambience of each coffee shop, usually run as a small business, depended on the owner's taste, and coffee beans were often roasted on the premises, releasing enticing aromas, and ground directly before use. The focus was on the coffee beans' qualities and characteristics. Daily or weekly specials, posted on a board, introduced customers to coffee varieties worldwide. Coffee shops-cum-roasters had spider charts illustrating the taste profile of coffee varieties, aimed at educating the customer.

The high price of each cup was warranted by the individual attention to the slow, manual brewing of each cup, using a siphon, and by the tasteful tableware, usually artisanal, in which the coffee was served. The making of coffee at a specialist coffee shop in that era was almost a ritual, paralleling the tea ceremony, except in more relaxed fashion.

The coffee that captured the Japanese coffee drinker's heart was Jamaican Blue Mountain coffee, an Arabica-type coffee full of flavor and aroma, with little bitterness. It is also one of the most expensive coffees in the world. Japan buys between 80% to more than 90% of the crop years in advance. Coffee has since become a preferred drink for breakfast, rivaling green tea, especially for working people. Coffee shops also offer a "morning service"—a Western-style full breakfast with a cup of coffee. Coffee is the preferred drink with a Western-style pastry or cake.

## Soft Drinks

The world of soft drinks in Japan is vast—fizzy soda drinks from multinational and local companies, familiar and exotic fruit juices and blends, shakes, fermented milk drinks, vitamin-packed drinks, sports drinks, vegetable drinks—all available in cans and plastic bottles from ubiquitous vending machines, supermarkets, convenience stores, shops, and eating places. There are two classic Japanese soda drinks from the late 19th century still drunk today: *ramune* (lemonade) and *saidā* (cider). *Ramune* is a fizzy lemonade created in 1872 in Kobe and bottled in an eccentric bottle, called a Codd-neck bottle, sealed with a glass marble. It is still sold in the original bottle, now a collectible item. *Saidā* came out in 1884 and is similar to ginger ale. Besides the original flavor of lemonade soda, *ramune* currently comes in 17 other flavors, including lychee, bubble gum, and, curiously, coconut curry. *Saidā*, still made by the original company, Mitsuya, has mango, acerola, Fuji apple, muscat grape, and *ume* (Japanese plum) flavors.

Another classic Japanese soft drink is Calpis, a dairy drink concentrate made from low-fat fermented milk. It was adapted from a Mongolian fermented milk drink called *airag* in 1919, and is a traditional summer drink diluted with cold water. In the United States it is called Calpico. Besides the traditional citrusy yogurt flavor, it comes in mango, lychee, strawberry, and peach. The same company also produces other yogurt and dairy-based drinks. Nata de coco yogurt drink is based on a Philippine coconut jelly dessert that became a fad some decades ago due to its low calorie content and chewy texture. Milk-based drinks made by the Calpis parent company feature caramel and five mixed fruits (apple, banana, pineapple, peach, and orange), aimed at the children's market and to satisfy the health recommendation to eat five fruits daily.

---

### Calpis Strawberry Soda

Calpis is a fermented milk concentrate that is added to cold water or soda for a refreshing summer drink. It can be mixed with fruits to make milkshakes or with *shōchu* or vodka for cocktails. For a warming drink, it can also be mixed with hot water.

*Yield:* 4 servings

**Ingredients**
1 ½ pounds fresh strawberries
8 tablespoons Calpis, or to taste
4 cups sparkling water
Ice cubes

**Procedure**
1. Wash strawberries, and set four berries aside for garnish.
2. Trim and hull strawberries, slice into quarters, and place into a large mixing bowl to mash them, or into a food processor or blender.
3. Add Calpis and sparkling water.
4. Taste and adjust to your taste, adding more Calpis or water.
5. Pour over ice cubes into tall glasses.

*Garnish with reserved berries.*

Health drinks usually contain supplements such as arginine, taurine, niacin, leucine, and other vitamins. These are sold in vending machines, in single-serving bottles and cans. They are often drunk by those who have overindulged in alcohol, in the belief that they protect the liver and kidney from damage. These health drinks may also contain exotic ingredients such as guarana, maté, ginseng, and other foodstuffs rich in antioxidants such as acerola and açai berry.

Green and black tea and herbal teas, in various blends with or without milk, combined with various fruit juices, come ready to drink in cans or plastic bottles. Hot natural lemon juice and honey drink (with or without black tea) is a welcome drink on cold days. Coffee and cocoa, likewise in diverse permutations, including fancy latte and cappuccino, are also sold in cans or plastic bottles. These drinks are available, hot or cold, at vending machines that can be found everywhere, including train station platforms.

Natural juices and smoothies, made from local fruits, such as Hokkaido's haskap, *yuzu*, Okinawa's *shikwasa*, the Japanese plum (*ume*), pomegranate, and exotic fruits such as mango, açai berry, and guava are widely available in cans or bottles from shops and vending machines.

*Beverages*

---

### *Yuzu* Avocado Yogurt Smoothie

*Yield*: 4 servings

**Ingredients**
1 avocado
4 tablespoons *yuzu* syrup, or more to taste (available from Asian food shops)
2 cups unflavored, unsweetened yogurt
Ice cubes
Mint sprigs to garnish

**Procedure**
1. Halve avocado, remove the pit, and scoop out the flesh into a blender.
2. Add *yuzu* syrup, yogurt, and ice cubes.
3. Blend all until smooth.
4. Taste and add more *yuzu* syrup if needed.

*To serve: Pour into chilled glasses and garnish with mint sprigs.*

---

## Alcoholic Drinks

### *Sake*

The first written mention of *sake* is in the *Nihon Shoki* (Japan Chronicles). The Shinto god of the sea and storms, Susano-o, asks his future parents-in-law to brew *sake* so that he can confront the giant serpent that has eaten all of their seven daughters except the one remaining, whom Susano-o rescues and takes for his wife. The dreaded serpent comes, drinks the *sake*, and falls asleep, enabling Susano-o to chop it up and get a sword from its tail. This sword later became the sacred sword of Japan's imperial regalia.

> *Sake* is called rice wine, though technically it is made using a two-stage fermentation process similar to that for making beer. (Wine is made from fruits, and rice is not a fruit.) *Sake* was customarily drunk warm when served to accompany food, and cold when passed around among well-wishers and participants during festivals, especially in the summer. However, since the 1990s, craft or regional *sake* (*jizake*) are being enjoyed as cool drinks to accompany all types of cooking, not only Japanese. Specialist *sake* bars typically serve *sake* from cool to cold, depending on each regional *sake*'s individual character.

Since then, *sake* has enjoyed an intimate association with the *kami* (deities), and is offered to a Shinto shrine for a festival, special event, or personal supplication. *Sake* is also considered therapeutic on account of this divine connection. The *sake* offerings are later shared with the immediate community at a ritual meal called *naorai*. All who partake of the *omiki* (*sake*'s name changes to *omiki* once blessed) are assured of well-being and protection from illness and other calamities. *Sake* is indispensable at a Shinto wedding: the bride and groom sip *sake* three times from three ceremonial cups formally binding the marriage, in a ritual called *sansankudō* ("three times three").

*Sake* is enjoying a revival, transformed from its former image as an unsophisticated drink into quality regional craft *sake*. These new types of *sake* can be drunk with both Japanese and non-Japanese food. Depending on the season and type of *sake*, it can be drunk from barely warm to hot, as well as slightly chilled and cold. However, *sake* specialists recommend drinking regional craft *sake* chilled, much like white wine. *Sake* consists of water, rice, and a fermenting agent called *kōji* (*Aspergillus oryzae*). Some grades of *sake* will contain added distilled alcohol. *Sake* alcohol content ranges from 10% to 16%, similar to wine. The taste and quality of *sake* are determined by the quality of rice, water, and the environment in which it is made; for example, *sake* made in northern Japan from rice grown there and local water will taste different from *sake* made from local ingredients in southern or other regions of Japan. As with wines, there are dry *sake* (*kara kuchi*) types that are crisp and refreshing, and "sweet" *sake* types (*ama kuchi*) with a deep, richer taste. Contemporary types of craft *sake* include a sparkling *sake*, produced through in-bottle fermentation that produces carbonic gas; *sake* types for drinking before or after dinner, for eating with chocolate or dried fruit (such as figs) or other dessert.

Certain regions are famed for their *sake*, though each region brews to its inhabitants' taste preference. Regional *sake*s are known as *jizake*, and they are brewed using locally grown *sake* rice. Rice used for making *sake* is not the same variety as that for eating. Special varieties of *sake* rice (*sakamai*) are bred to have a low protein, low fat, and high starch content. These can also be milled as low as 35% and still produce excellent *sake*. Yamadanishiki is regarded as the king of all *sake* rice varieties and has been around since 1936. Other specially bred *sake* rice varieties are Gohyakumangoku from Niigata, which yields a fruity *sake*, and Hanafubuki from Akita, a rice variety especially resistant to cold weather.

Five *sake* breweries in Kobe (called the *Nada Gogo*) produce almost 25% of all *sake* in Japan, and are renowned for their quality, attributed to using Yamadanishiki rice, hard (alkaline) water, highly experienced brew masters, and cold temperatures that slow down fermentation. Niigata

*Beverages*

attributes the quality of its *sake* to its snow-bound landscape. Niigata *sake* is noted for its handcrafted individuality and the scientific support of the Niigata *Sake* Research Institute.

*Amazake* (sweet *sake*) comes in two types: the alcoholic version made with the lees (solids) that remain after *sake* is filtered, and the nonalcoholic version made with *kōji* (*Aspergillus oryzae*). Freeze-dried *amazake*, four packs to a bag, is available online and from Asian food shops.

*Shirozake* (literally, white *sake*) is an unfiltered rice wine with 7%–9% alcohol that is drunk mostly by mothers during the *Hina Matsuri* (Doll Festival) on Girls' Day in March. Young girls themselves drink nonalcoholic *amazake*. Nonalcoholic *amazake* supplies vitamins and minerals, and is highly recommended for gut health. The smoothie recipes that follow use nonalcoholic amazake. *Amazake* is available at Asian food shops and in freeze-dried form online. To use *amazake* for the following drinks, follow the instructions on the *amazake* package.

---

### Banana Yogurt *Amazake* Smoothie

*Yield:* 4 servings

**Ingredients**
2 ripe bananas
1 cup unflavored, unsweetened yogurt
1 cup *amazake*
Ice cubes

**Procedure**
1. In a blender, put bananas, yogurt, and *amazake*.
2. Add 6 ice cubes.
3. Blend until smooth.

*Pour into cold glasses and serve.*

---

### Avocado Pineapple *Amazake* Smoothie

*Yield:* 4 servings

**Ingredients**
1 ripe avocado
½ ripe pineapple
2 cups *amazake*

Ice cubes

**Procedure**
1. Prepare the fruits. Remove pit from the avocado and scoop the flesh into a blender.
2. Peel the pineapple and cut off the hard central core. Slice into large pieces and add to blender.
3. Pour in the *amazake*, add ice, and blend all until smooth.

*Pour into cold glasses and serve.*

## Strawberry Tomato *Amazake* Smoothie

Yield: 4 servings

**Ingredients**
½ pound strawberries
1 cup tomato juice
1 cup *amazake*
Ice cubes

**Procedure**
1. Hull and trim strawberries.
2. Place strawberries in a blender together with tomato juice, *amazake*, and ice cubes.
3. Blend until smooth.

*Pour into cold glasses and serve.*

*Namazake* (literally, raw *sake*) is *sake* that has not been pasteurized. For this reason, it continues to ferment unless it is kept refrigerated.

*Doburoku* is an unfiltered, unpasteurized alcoholic drink that cannot technically be called *sake*. Though made from the same ingredients, the process of fermentation is different. Its alcohol content is lower than that of *sake* and thus it is considered milder.

*Shōchū* is a spirit between 25%–35% alcohol by volume, distilled from various base materials (sweet potato, buckwheat, barley, rice, or brown sugar). It was regarded as an old-fashioned man's drink, but has become more widely drunk by the younger generation, including women, as a cocktail with lemon, orange, *yuzu*, and other fruit juices, soda, and ice, called *chūhai* (from "*shōchū* highball"). *Shisō-* (perilla) and *ume-* (Japanese plum) flavored *shōchū*, slightly sour and sweet, are being produced to widen *shōchū*'s appeal. *Shikwasa*, Okinawa's native citrus, is also popularly used in *shōchū* cocktails.

---

### *Yuzu Shōchū* Cocktail

*Yield:* 4 servings

**Ingredients**
4 tablespoons *yuzu* syrup, or more to taste (available in Asian food shops or specialist liquor shops)
1 cup *shōchū* (available in Asian food shops or specialist liquor shops)
4 cups sparkling water
Ice cubes
4 fresh *yuzu* zest or lemon slices, to garnish

**Procedure**
1. Into 4 tall, chilled glasses, distribute the *yuzu* syrup.
2. Add about ¼ cup (or according to preference) of *shōchū* to each glass.
3. Stir in sparkling water, and taste, adding more syrup or water, as necessary.
4. Add ice cubes.

*Garnish with* yuzu *zest or lemon slices.*

---

## Other Alcoholic Drinks

Japan grows many grape varieties for eating and wine making. Yamanashi, Yamagata, and Nagano Prefectures, along with Hokkaido, are the main wine-producing regions. The Japanese climate and soil are not ideal for growing Southern European wine grapes, because of the high humidity and rainfall, insufficient sun, and lack of space for extensive vineyards. However, locally hybridized varieties such as Koshu (for white wines) and Muscat Bailey A (for red wines) produce wines that pair well with Japanese food. Besides these wines for casual dining, small family wineries produce outstanding wines from their own hybrids of native grapes, and these have won international and national prizes and are priced accordingly (more than US$100 a bottle).

Japan also produces whisky, using imported barley grain. Whisky is a popular bar drink, often as a highball (*mizuwari*). Eight Japanese distilleries currently produce 5% of the world's whisky. Single malt whisky from Scotland is highly regarded in Japan, and the taste of Japanese-made whisky is reminiscent of Scottish whisky. Although Japan has produced whisky since 1924, the products from local distilleries did not attract international attention until Suntory and Nikka, Japan's two major distillers, began producing award-winning single malts and blended whiskies. Though whisky is not traditional to Japan, Japanese whiskies—both the blended and single malt types—are now world-famous for their quality and complexity of flavors, as a result of the continuous search for excellence that underlies many Japanese endeavors. Their prices match their high acclaim.

Some Japanese companies are producing whisky from rice. These new products are reported to have a complex taste, with flavors reminiscent of citrus and various fruits, including herbs. Lemon grass, lychee, green apple, melon, clementine, pear, and nectarine are some flavors described. A similar complex flavor profile comprising floral, fruity, and herbal scents is found in a newly released Japanese gin. It is said to contain cherry blossoms, *sanshō* spice, and two kinds of choice tea—*gyokurō* and *sencha*.

Rum is produced from sugar cane grown in Okinawa, and like Japanese whisky it is aged in oak barrels that have previously held sherry or bourbon. Additionally, Japanese whiskies may also be matured in oak casks that have held wine, port, and, rather interestingly, *umeshū* (Japanese plum liqueur).

### Plum Liqueur, *Umeshū*

When the rainy season begins sometime between May and June, the unripe fruits of the Japanese plum (also known as Japanese apricot) start appearing at greengrocers' shops—a reminder to make your own *umeshū* (plum liqueur). *Ume* fruits rarely ripen properly, due to excessive humidity from incessant rain, and what better way to stop the fruits going to waste than to turn them into a refreshing alcoholic drink? Although it is very simple to make and takes no more than a few minutes of your time, *umeshū* needs some time to rest and mature before it is ready to drink (from six months to a year). It gets even better with age. *Umeshū* has a lovely fruity aroma and sweet-sour flavor, and aside from drinking it neat, it can also be mixed with cold sparkling water, or even hot water for *umeshū* tea. It is mixed with *shōchū* or vodka for cocktails. It can be used to flavor fruit cakes and fruit salad, or as a sauce over ice cream. After a year, most of the alcohol will have evaporated, and the remaining fruits can be eaten as they are, used to adorn a chilled glass of *umeshū*, or chopped up and added to a fruit salad.

*Beverages*

## Japanese Plum Liqueur, *Umeshū*

*Yield:* about 6 cups

**Ingredients**

2 ¼ pounds unripe Japanese plums (*ume*), or substitute small unripe plums or apricots
2 quarts (or 60 fluid ounces) *shōchū*, vodka, or other unflavored, uncolored spirit, between 35%–40% alcohol
1–1 ½ pounds rock sugar or white sugar (use the greater quantity if you wish a sweeter result)

**Procedure**

1. Prepare a glass preserving jar that holds 4 quarts: wash well with hot soapy water, and sterilize by placing it in a 210°F oven until thoroughly dry, about 20 minutes. The lid, if plastic, should be sterilized in boiling water.
2. Wash *ume* well, and remove any stalks. Discard discolored or bruised fruits.
3. Place fruits in the sterilized jar in two layers, alternating with the rock sugar.
4. Add *shōchū* to completely cover.
5. Close the jar, and place in a cool and dark place.

*The* umeshū *will be drinkable after 6 months, but it will taste better after a year.*

## *Umeshū* Sparkling Drink

*Yield:* 4 servings

**Ingredients**

4 tablespoons *umeshū*, or more to taste
4 cups cold sparkling water
Ice cubes
4 whole *ume* or 4 slices of lemon for garnish

**Procedure**

1. Into 4 tall, chilled glasses, distribute the *umeshū*.
2. Add sparkling water, and taste, adding more *umeshū* if needed.
3. Add ice cubes, and garnish with *ume* or lemon.

## *Umeshū* Warmer

This is a hot drink for chilly evenings, with or without an additional tot of your favorite tipple.

*Yield:* 4 servings

**Ingredients**
4 tablespoons *umeshū*, or more to taste
4 cups hot water
Brandy, whisky, or other liqueur, optional
4 cinnamon sticks, for garnish

**Procedure**
1. Into 4 warmed cups or mugs, distribute the *umeshū*.
2. Pour hot water over and stir. Taste and add more *umeshū*, if needed.
3. Stir in as much brandy or whisky as you like.

*Garnish with the cinnamon sticks.*

# CHAPTER SEVEN

# Holidays and Special Occasions

## Introduction

The yearly cycle of celebrations begins on New Year (called *shōgatsu*, also *oshōgatsu*) on the first day of the first month (January). Each succeeding month on the same cipher as the month—the second of February, the third of March and so on—has a special event to be observed according to the Shinto or Buddhist calendar of celebrations. Most monthly special events were adopted during the Nara and Heian periods together with other Chinese cultural practices, and adapted to Japanese circumstances. The common aim of these festivals is to ensure good health, long life, and good fortune, and to ward off illnesses and other misfortunes. Also, because of the ancient belief that evil spirits cause illness and miscellaneous unpleasantnesses to happen, celebrations and timely temple and shrine offerings ensured that good spirits would continue to protect the celebrants and neutralize the power of evil spirits.

From ancient times, *sekihan* (red rice) has been a constant at celebrations and special occasions. *Sekihan* is *mochi* (glutinous) rice, or a mix of *uruchi* (regular) rice and *mochi* rice, steamed together with *azuki* beans. The resulting color is not quite bright red: more a reddish purple. The origin of *sekihan* is *kowa ii* (strong rice), or simply *okowa*, served in ancient aristocratic meals. Today, it is served to celebrate birth, coming of age, marriage, the completion of a house, roof-raising, or other significant family event and celebration. It is also served during a *matsuri* (festival) at a neighborhood shrine, and also for Buddhist rituals and celebrations, such as the Bon Festival. It is served during sad occasions as well. In parts of northeastern Honshu (Tōhoku), Hokkaido, and regions close to Tokyo such as Ibaraki, *sekihan* is served after a funeral and the first seven days after burial. However, black, rather than red, beans are more commonly cooked with *mochi* rice on sad occasions, or when someone has fully recovered from grave illness.

# Red Rice, *Sekihan*

No celebration goes by without *sekihan*, red rice. The rice used is not the regular rice for daily meals, but glutinous or sticky rice, called *mochi gome*, which is stickier than normal rice. It is also known as sweet rice, used for New Year and other celebrations, as well as traditional pastries. *Mochi* rice cannot be cooked as regular rice is—it must be steamed.

*Azuki* beans are used to dye the *mochi* rice red. You will need four days to prepare red rice: two days to soak and partially cook the *azuki* beans, another day to soak *mochi* rice in the *azuki* cooking water to dye it, and the fourth day to steam the beans and rice together.

*Yield:* 10–12 servings

**Ingredients**
1 cup dry *azuki* beans
5 cups glutinous rice (*mochi gome*)
Light brine (1 teaspoon salt to 1 cup water) for sprinkling
1 cup black sesame seeds, toasted
Salt

**Procedure**
Day 1. Prepare the beans. Soak beans in water to cover for at least 4 hours or overnight. Rinse thoroughly and drain.
Day 2. In a heavy-bottomed pan over medium heat, place beans with enough water to cover, and bring to a boil. Do not cover the pot. Let beans boil briskly for 8–10 minutes, or until scum rises to the surface. Turn off heat. Discard the water and rinse beans thoroughly.
Return rinsed beans to the pan. Cover with 4–5 cups water, and bring to a rolling boil over high heat. As soon as water boils and beans are rising to the surface, turn down heat and let beans simmer for about 15–20 minutes, or until water has taken on a reddish color.
Test the beans. They should still be somewhat raw because they will be cooked further (another 35–40 minutes) with the *mochi* rice. Turn off heat. Leave beans and water in the pan to cool down to room temperature.
Drain beans, but reserve the cooking water. Once cool, refrigerate the beans, covering them with plastic wrap. The water can stay, covered, at room temperature.
Day 3. Wash *mochi* rice in two to three changes of water, until the rinse water is not so cloudy. (Tip: A good way to reuse this perfectly clean rinse water is to water your house plants or garden.)

## Holidays and Special Occasions

Place *mochi* rice in a large bowl with the water from cooking the beans. Leave to stand at room temperature, covered with plastic wrap, overnight or for 24 hours.

Day 4. Drain the *mochi* rice, which should have absorbed the reddish color of the *azuki* water. If you have a large enough steamer in which all the rice and *azuki* beans can fit into a thin layer of about 1 inch, mix the *mochi* rice evenly with the *azuki* beans. Line the steamer with cheesecloth and distribute the *mochi* rice and *azuki* bean mixture evenly on it.

If not, divide the *mochi* rice and *azuki* beans equally into two or three portions to be steamed separately.

Wrap the cover of the steamer with a clean kitchen towel to absorb steam and prevent moisture dropping onto the rice and bean mixture.

Over high heat, steam the *mochi* rice and *azuki* bean mixture for a total of 35 to 45 minutes. Halfway through, sprinkle brine lightly over the mixture. Replace the steamer cover and continue steaming until the *mochi* rice and *azuki* bean mixture is completely cooked. Leave *sekihan* to cool to room temperature.

*To serve: Place a mound of* sekihan *in individual bowls and sprinkle with toasted sesame seeds and salt.*

*Azuki* beans partnered with root vegetables, such as sweet potatoes, or squash in a stew called *itokoni* ("cousins stew") are a traditional offering on the *kamidana* (god/deity shelf in the home) and at Buddhist temples for New Year, Obon, and other festive occasions. Each region has its own version with different ingredients: sweet potato with *azuki* beans, taro with giant radish, carrot with burdock, root vegetables with *konnyaku* (devil's tongue) or tofu. This pairing of root vegetables, with or without red beans, has its roots in temple offerings of the Jōd sect of Buddhism and in vegetarian cuisine (*shōjin ryōri*).

The small red bean called *azuki* is a constant ingredient in foods for special occasions. It is mixed with sticky or glutinous rice (*mochi*) to make the celebratory rice dish called *sekihan* (red rice). Mixed with squash and braised, it becomes another special dish called *itokoni* that is eaten during the winter solstice (December 21–22) to ward off illness and other calamities and promote well-being and good fortune. Roasted *azuki* beans are used to throw at demons and keep them (and the misfortunes they cause) away during the festival called *Setsubun*, with the words *fuku wa uchi, oni wa soto* (good fortune in, demons out!).

The combination of squash and red beans is called *tōji nankin* ("winter solstice squash," *nankin* being a former name for squash) in the snowbound Hokuriku region and Hokkaido. Traditional knowledge advised nutrient-rich foods such as squash and *azuki* beans to fortify the body against colds, frostbite, and strokes. Additionally, the red color of *azuki* beans assures protection from all ills and calamities. Eating *itokoni* and taking a *yuzu* (*Citrus junos*) bath on the winter solstice (21–22 of December) is a traditional custom to ward off colds, strokes, and ill health. (*Yuzu* fruits are floated in some public baths at this time.)

## Cousins Stew (Braised Squash and *Azuki* Beans), *Kabocha to Azuki no Itokoni*

How did this dish get the name "Cousins Stew"? First of all, squash and *azuki* are cooked separately, since they require different cooking times. To braise or stew separately is *meimei niru*. The squash and beans are also cooked one after the other, as expressed by the phrase *oioi niru*. *Mei* incidentally is the word for "niece," and *oi* for "nephew." A niece and nephew together are cousins, hence *itokoni*: "cousins stew."

The seasoning for *itokoni* varies—some regions make it sweet, mashing the *azuki* beans with sugar and adding *mochi* balls. The savory *itokoni* version in Sakai, Yamaguchi Prefecture, includes *kamaboko* (fish loaf) and *shiitake* mushrooms flavored with soy sauce and just a hint of sugar. The following recipe is rather on the sweet side, but flavoring can be adjusted to your personal taste.

*Yield:* 4–5 servings

### Ingredients
2 cups dry *azuki* beans
1 pound winter squash (a Japanese variety such as *uchiki kuri*, or Hubbard)
5 cups *dashi* (kelp or *shiitake dashi* for a vegetarian dish, bonito and kelp for a regular dish)
4 tablespoons sugar
1 tablespoon soy sauce
½ teaspoon salt
Maple leaves or other red (nontoxic) leaves for garnish

### Procedure
1. The day before, soak *azuki* beans in water to cover. The next day, rinse them and place in a heavy-bottomed pan. Over medium heat, simmer

# Holidays and Special Occasions

with fresh water to cover until tender, but not falling apart, as they will be cooked further. Add more water to the pan as needed. *Azuki* beans can also be cooked in less time in a pressure cooker or automatic hot pot (follow manufacturer's instructions for use). Drain beans and set aside.
2. Discard seeds and central fibers of the squash, and slice into 2-inch cubes. Do not peel if using a Japanese variety. Set aside.
3. In a heavy-bottomed pan, place squash with 5 cups of dashi and bring to a boil.
4. Add drained *azuki* beans, lower the heat, and stir in sugar, soy sauce, and salt.
5. Simmer until squash is tender and braising liquid has been reduced to half. Taste and adjust seasoning to your taste. Depending on the sweetness of the squash, you may wish to add more salt or sugar. Turn off heat.

*To serve: In individual bowls, mound the squash cubes and surround with azuki beans. Garnish with red maple leaves or other red (nontoxic) leaves. Serve warm or cold.*

Foods associated with celebrations are called *medetai sakana* (celebratory dishes), and sea bream (*tai*) and carp (*koi*) top the list. The sea bream is auspicious because of its red color and pleasing shape, taste, and texture. Additionally, the syllable or sound *tai* forms part of the word *medetai* (meaning "felicitous"). The carp is noted for its extraordinary ability to climb waterfalls, and the same ability to surmount obstacles and succeed at one's goals is wished for the celebrant(s) and attendees. It also happens to be a tasty fish. A whole sea bream or carp may be the centerpiece of a celebratory occasion, though carp is not served at a wedding feast.

## Salt-Grilled Sea Bream, *Tai no Shioyaki*

For all festive occasions, a whole fish with head and tail intact is the centerpiece. The red bream, *tai*, is regarded as the most auspicious because its sound is included within the word *medetai*, meaning "felicitous." In other regions, the preferred festive fish are those whose names change as they grow, such as the *buri*.

Traditionally, a newborn child was given a name only on the seventh day after birth. Child mortality in ancient times was extremely high, and the first seven days after birth were rather fraught. It was thought prudent to wait to make sure that the child would survive before giving her or him a name. The name-giving ceremony is called *oshichiya*, "seventh night."

Complementing whole grilled fish is *sekihan*, red rice, the celebratory dish for all festive occasions.

*Yield:* 4–6 servings

**Ingredients**
1 whole red bream, 1 ½ to 2 pounds
½ cup salt, or more as needed
1 cup *sake*, or more as needed
1 lemon
Bamboo leaves, a small pine branch, or red maple leaves for garnish

**Procedure**
1. Scale and gut the fish, but leave the head, fins, and tail intact. Rinse the fish inside and out thoroughly. With a sharp knife, slit the thickest part of the bream's body with 2 strokes to create an X. Slit the other side likewise. Sprinkle the fish inside and out with salt, including the cut areas, not forgetting the head and tail. Take care that the tail and head are not damaged.
2. Pour the *sake* over all sides and parts of the fish, inside and out. Leave the fish on a tray to stand at room temperature for about half an hour, covered with plastic wrap.
3. Meanwhile, preheat the oven to 400°F.
4. Gently pat the fish with a paper towel to absorb excess moisture. Do the same for the fish's belly. Apply salt to the fins and tail (to protect these parts from scorching and as embellishment called *keshōjio*, "cosmetic salt").
5. Lay the bream on a grid on a roasting or baking tray in the middle rack of the oven, head facing left.
6. Bake for 20 minutes at 400°F, then lower the temperature to 350°F, and bake for another 15 minutes. If the fins and tail are scorching, cover them with foil.
7. Carefully, so as not to break the fins and tail, transfer the fish to a serving platter. Keep the head facing left.

*Garnish with bamboo leaves and lemon halves.*

---

Red is an auspicious color, and red foods are favored for special occasions, in particular the red *azuki* bean. Shrimp, lobster, and crab, which turn red when cooked, are natural celebratory foods. The red sea bream (*tai*) is valued for celebrations, not only for its color, but also for its pleasing shape and excellent texture and flavor. As well, the word *tai* evokes *medetai*, meaning "felicitations." Red applies also to the dishes and containers in which celebration foods are served—red lacquer tiered boxes (*jūbako*) for New Year foods called *osechi*—as well as decorative garnishes of red leaves.

*Holidays and Special Occasions*

The color red is auspicious. Besides sea bream, other marine foodstuffs that turn red when cooked, such as shrimps, crayfish, and lobster, are indispensable at any celebration, as are red vegetables such as carrots and red radishes. Additionally, the bodies of shrimps, crayfish, and lobster curl up when cooked, evoking the curved backs that come with ripe old age, and thus these crustaceans signify wishes for longevity. Other signifiers of longevity are cranes and turtles, and their shapes are often carved from vegetables such as giant radish to garnish celebratory dishes. Bamboo, pine, and Japanese plum are felicitous plants, and besides the use of fresh material from these three plants to garnish serving dishes, they are frequent motifs used to adorn tableware. The red leaves of the *nanten* (*Nandina domestica*) are especially regarded as felicitous. (Its common name in English is sacred bamboo, but it is not a bamboo relative.)

## New Year

Of all the holidays, New Year, *oshōgatsu*, is the most important. Celebrations begin on the 31st of December and last to the 3rd of January. It is traditional not to cook during this time; thus, food that keeps without refrigeration is prepared no later than the 28th of December, which is when, traditionally, all shops close for the holiday. On the 31st, year-end noodles (*toshikoshi soba*) are eaten to welcome the coming year. This tradition is said to come from Kyoto merchants who used to end each month's accounting with noodles, hoping that the next would be profitable.

On New Year morning, the household gathers to drink spiced *sake*, called *toso* (also *otoso*). This is a tradition originally from China that came into practice during the Heian period, and is drunk for health, because the five spices—which include cinnamon bark, Japanese mountain pepper (*sanshō*), and other ingredients from traditional Japanese/Chinese medicine (*byakujutsu*, the rhizome *Atractylodes japonica*; windflower root, *Platycodon grandiflorus*; *chinpi*, dried mandarin orange peel)—are effective against colds and respiratory ailments. The ground spices come in a sachet to be steeped in the first water drawn (traditionally from a well) on the first day of January. The spiced water is mixed with mirin (sweet *sake*) or *sake*, and poured into shallow lacquer bowls that are passed around for each family member to drink.

Celebratory foods for New Year, called *osechi*, are placed in lacquer boxes called *jūbako*, usually in five tiers, but two or three tiers are becoming more common. The boxes can be square, round, hexagonal, or diamond-shaped. Lacquer prevents the food inside from drying out. (Incidentally, *jūbako* are also used to pack picnics for cherry blossom viewing.) Modern *jūbako* are also made of porcelain.

By tradition, the topmost tier contains foodstuffs traditionally auspicious for New Year: black beans (*kuro mame*), seasoned dried anchovies (*gomame*, also called *tazukuri*), herring roe, and in the Kansai region, also burdock (*tataki gobō*). The word *mame* means "bean," evoking the adjective *mame*, meaning "honest," "faithful," "devoted." Similarly, herring roe, *kazunoko*, sounds like the words for "plentiful children," and thus signifies wealth and plenty. *Konbu* (laver) is auspicious, and not only for New Year, because it calls to mind the word *yorokobu*, "to rejoice."

The second tier from the top contains dishes called *kuchitori* (literally "mouth take") that are traditionally part of life-cycle celebration banquets, to be eaten with soup. Five to nine dishes are traditional, combining different colors, textures, and flavors. They may include sweet chestnut paste (*kinton*), slices of pink and white fish loaf (*kamaboko*), and other seasonal foods from fish, seafood, poultry, vegetables—essentially a mix of foodstuffs from land and sea. The third tier contains grilled, pan-fried, or roasted foods (*yakimono*); the fourth tier, stewed or braised dishes (*nimono*); and the fifth tier, vinegared dishes (*sunomono*). For two- or three-tiered *jubako*, the contents may be mixed, though strong-flavored items are bordered with cut leaves of aspidistra (*haran*). These days the tendency is to cook a few favorite items, or buy ready-made *osechi*. Specialist food companies and department stores now offer a wide choice of *osechi* menus, ranging from traditional Japanese to international (Chinese, European, Thai, other ethnic) dishes.

Two more dishes are traditional for New Year: seven-herb gruel and *zōni* (also *ozōni*), a soup with *mochi* and assorted vegetables. The seven-herb gruel, like spiced *sake*, ensures health throughout the year. *Zōni* is eaten during the first three days of the New Year. The origin of *zōni* is a traditional food-sharing ritual called *naorai*, during which the offerings of *mochi* and vegetables at a Shinto shrine at year-end were cooked and shared among the community. Each region (and each family, too) has its version of *zōni*. In the Kanto region, square *mochi* is grilled first, and added with chicken, *kamaboko* (fish loaf), and greens to a clear soup. In the Kansai region, the *mochi* are round, and vegetables are usually taro and giant radish in a miso base. Hokkaido *zōni* contains salmon (and often salmon roe), and *zōni* in the Hokuriku region includes *buri* (yellowtail).

## Gosekku

The *Gosekku* (Five Seasonal Festivals) hark back to ancient imperial court celebrations, originally adopted from China. They are observed on the odd-numbered months of the year—1, 3, 5, 7, and 9 (January, March, May, July, and September)—and called *Jinjitsu, Joshi, Tango, Tanabata*, and

*Holidays and Special Occasions*

*Choyo*, held on the seventh of January, third of March, fifth of May, seventh of July, and ninth of September. *Jinjitsu* observance in certain regions has been combined with New Year. The third of March is celebrated as *Hina Matsuri* (Doll Festival) or Girls' Day (see details following), and the fifth of May is celebrated as Boys' Day (see details below).

The third of March (the fourth of April in certain regions), Girls' Day, was traditionally called *Hina Matsuri*, the Doll Festival, when a set of dolls dressed in ancient aristocratic robes is displayed in the main room of the house (the dolls are not played with). The dolls represent the emperor and empress, and other members of the imperial court: ministers of the left and right, ladies-in-waiting, and musicians and their instruments. Many families have a set passed down from mother to daughter over generations; other parents buy a new set for their daughter. A little gathering of girls and their mothers is usually held on this day. Traditional foods eaten are *hishi mochi* (three-colored diamond-shaped rice cakes), bite-size multicolored rice crackers (*hina arare*), clam soup, and *chirashizushi*, sushi rice topped with seafood and vegetables. Unfiltered rice wine (7%–9% alcohol content) called *shirozake* ("white *sake*") is for the mothers, and the girls get nonalcoholic *amazake* (sweet *sake*) during the celebratory meal. The colors of *hishi mochi* evoke early spring—green for newly growing plants, white for remaining snow, and pink for blossom. These festive foods invoke long life and a good future for girls.

## Smoked Salmon Scattered Sushi, *Smōku Sāmon no Chirashizushi*

Unlike the Edo-style hand-pressed sushi, this scattered-type (*chirashi*) sushi is easier to make. This dish resembles a cold rice salad mixed with smoked salmon and colorful vegetables. You are welcome to substitute any vegetables in season; just ensure a nice variety of colors and textures. Keep sushi rice covered with a damp kitchen towel until needed to prevent it drying out. Likewise, keep the other ingredients covered with plastic wrap until assembly. Fresh lotus root is available at Asian food shops.

*Yield:* 4 servings

**Ingredients**
4 cups sushi rice
½ pound smoked salmon slices
4 eggs

¼ teaspoon salt
1 tablespoon cooking oil or more
1 bunch (about 1 cup) watercress
1 medium fresh lotus root
Rice vinegar
1 cup frozen tender green peas, thawed
1 carrot
1 small head Roma lettuce or several leaves of iceberg lettuce

**Procedure**
1. Prepare sushi rice according to the Sushi Rice recipe.
2. Slice smoked salmon into bite-size pieces and refrigerate until needed.
3. Beat eggs and season with salt. Heat a small frying pan over medium heat, brush the pan with oil, and make several crepe-thin omelets. Drain omelets on paper towels, and slice into fine strips.
4. Wash watercress very well, trim off any roots, and slice into bite-size pieces. Set aside.
5. Wash and peel lotus root, and slice crosswise into fine rings. Immediately after slicing, keep immersed in a bowlful of water with 2 teaspoons vinegar to stop them oxidizing (turning brown). Drain before using. Place in a pan with new water to cover and 2 teaspoons of rice vinegar. Simmer briefly over medium heat until translucent. Do not cook too long, as their best feature is crispness. Set aside and let cool in the cooking water.
6. Place green peas in a pan with water to cover. Over medium heat, bring peas to a boil. If very tender and young, the peas do not need more than a few minutes' cooking. Turn off heat at once, and leave peas to cool in the cooking water. If taken out immediately, the peas will shrivel, and will not look appetizing. Drain peas from their cooking water only when you are ready to mix.
7. Peel and slice the carrot crosswise into thin disks or fine julienne strips. You may wish to make the carrots more decorative by slicing them into flower shapes, as follows. Cut the peeled carrot crosswise into 3 cylinders. Make 4 or 5 shallow triangular cuts around the diameter of the carrot cylinder. The cuts should run all along the length of the cylinder. Discard the cut-out pieces, and slice the cylinder crosswise into disks. The sliced disks will look like "flowers" with 4 or 5 "petals." Set aside.
8. Wash and pat dry the lettuce leaves, and set aside.

**Assembly**
1. In a large mixing bowl, mix sushi rice with peas and carrots.
2. Line 4 small soup or glass salad bowls with lettuce leaves.
3. Place one cup of sushi rice over the lettuce leaves.

*Holidays and Special Occasions* 139

> 4. Distribute watercress and lotus root over the rice, but leave the summit free.
> 5. Arrange salmon pieces between the watercress and lotus root.
> 6. Arrange a mound of omelet shreds at the summit.
>
> *Serve at once.*

The fifth of May is celebrated as Children's Day, and traditionally known as the Boys' Festival or *Tango no Sekku*. A set of wind streamers in the shape of carp (*koinobori*) in decreasing sizes is flown from a house window or from a tall pole in the garden. These signify the family members. The carp, as mentioned earlier, symbolizes resilience and determination to surmount barriers. Boys are bathed with iris leaves, symbolic of swords. Indoors, miniature weapons and armor are displayed, symbolizing bravery. Celebratory foods are rice cakes wrapped in bamboo leaves (*chimaki*) and oak leaves (*kashiwa mochi*). *Kashiwa mochi* have two types of fillings, sweet bean and miso.

## Other Festivals and Special Occasions

Immediately after a child is born, a rice dish called *ubumeshi* ("birth rice") is prepared, together with other dishes, to be shared with relatives, friends, and neighbors to ensure the infant's good health and growth. Two heaped bowls of rice are prepared and placed at the home's family altar in gratitude for the safe delivery and the mother and child's continuing health. Heaped rice bowls are also offered at the local shrine to thank the *kami* (deities). For the new mother, a carp dish called *koikoku* is prepared. The carp, as mentioned previously, is a festive fish.

> ### Braised Carp, *Koikoku*
>
> This stew was very popular during the Edo period, especially in places far from the sea, where freshwater fish such as carp were the most common fresh fish. It was traditional to cook this for mothers who had just given birth. The long and gentle simmering draws out calcium and other minerals from the carp, and the accompanying vegetables provided additional nutrients to nourish the new mother and help her recover her strength, and to stimulate milk production. The head of the carp enhances the flavor of the broth and increases the amount of gelatin that enriches this stew.

*Yield:* 4 servings

**Ingredients**
1 medium whole carp, cut into 4 portions plus the head
2-inch piece ginger, peeled and sliced into fine julienne strips
1 leek, finely sliced diagonally (reserve a few for garnish)
4 tablespoons *sake*
3 tablespoons mirin
2 tablespoons miso
1 cup finely shredded burdock root (*gobō*)
1 carrot, sliced into fine julienne strips
1 cup giant radish, sliced into bite-size cubes
1 block firm tofu (cotton-filtered *momen dōfu*)

**Procedure**
1. Wash the carp pieces well, and place into a heavy-bottomed pan with ginger. Add 4–5 cups of water.
2. Bring to a boil over medium heat, skimming off all scum that arises.
3. Reduce heat to the lowest possible, and add leek, *sake*, mirin, miso, burdock, carrot, and radish. Simmer gently until the carp and radish are tender enough to be pulled apart with chopsticks.
4. Add the cubed tofu, and continue simmering until the tofu is heated through. Turn off heat.

*To serve: Place one fillet in a deep bowl, and garnish with the reserved leek slices, sliced into fine shreds.*

Hatsumiyamōde is the first visit made by a newborn child to the neighborhood shrine, usually when a newborn boy is 30 days old, and 33 days old for a girl. In some regions, this may be on the seventh day or a hundred days after birth. The visit introduces the newborn to the local shrine *kami*. After the child's return home, rice cakes are offered to neighborhood children. In ancient times, child mortality was high, and it was believed that the ages of 3, 5, and 7 were critical years. Thus, girls and boys at 3, boys at 5, and girls at 7 years old are taken to the neighborhood shrine to be blessed on the 15th of November. They are dressed in traditional robes, and after being blessed by the Shinto priest, they receive a large triangular gift bag containing ten-thousand-year candy (*chitose ame*), symbolizing long life, to be shared with family and other well-wishers. At major shrines in Tokyo, such as Meiji Jingu, celebrities such as sumo wrestlers are often invited to present the gifts.

*Holidays and Special Occasions*

Coming of Age day, *Seijin no Hi*, is observed on the 15th of January for young people who have turned 20 and are thus legally allowed to drink alcohol. Young ladies wear kimono to visit the shrine and have formal portraits taken.

The second of February is *Setsubun*, and this month is considered the coldest of the year, making people more susceptible to illness, calamity, and other evils brought by demons. It is customary to throw roasted beans at invisible demons lurking outdoors while saying, *"fuku wa uchi, oni wa soto!"* (good fortune in; demons out!).

The eighth of April is Buddha's birthday, which is celebrated by pouring sweet tea (*ama cha*) over Buddha's statue at Buddhist temples. It is customary to eat sweets.

*Hanami*, cherry blossom viewing, in spring is popular, and peak viewing time for each region is well publicized, starting from late March in the south. *Hanami* is an occasion to enjoy a picnic outdoors with family and friends for the first time after winter. It was traditional to take a picnic in tiered lacquered boxes. *Sake*, beer, and other drinks are liberally partaken of at these events, especially at night when the cherry blossoms are lit up.

## Higan

*Higan* is a Buddhist custom of paying respect to departed family members by visiting graves. It is observed twice—during the spring equinox and the fall equinox—for seven days each time, and these are official public holidays. It is customary for people to return to their family homes, and help tidy up the graves of relatives and home altars. It is also a time for bringing together all family members. The traditional practice is to eat only vegetarian food for the three days preceding, during, and three days after the festival. Strong spices and onions, garlic, leeks are avoided. Sweet *botamochi* is the celebratory food during spring *higan*, and *ohagi* for fall. (These rice cakes are identical, except *botamochi* is pink.) The customary dishes are soba noodles, vegetarian tempura (*shōjin age*, that is, without seafood), and tofu dishes, such as *ganmodoki* (also known as *hiryōzu*). The stock for these vegetarian dishes is made only from dried mushrooms or kelp (*konbu*).

### Vegetarian Tempura, *Shōjin Age*

Vegetarian tempura is one of the dishes traditionally eaten during *higan* that takes place twice a year, during the spring and autumn equinox. This festival marks the return of many people to their ancestral homes to pay their respects to departed family members. Tempura is actually Southern European in origin, introduced to Japan by Portuguese traders in the 16th century. The Japanese word tempura is derived from the Portuguese word *têmporas*, which refers to days of fasting and abstinence (from meat, in particular) formerly required of Catholics; hence, shellfish and fish have traditionally been the central ingredients of tempura. A classic tempura restaurant in Tokyo with a history that dates back to the Edo period only has fish and seafood—no vegetables—in its tempura, being faithful to the original recipe. The reason being that at that time there already existed a Buddhist vegetarian dish of fried vegetables called *shōjin age* ("vegetarian fry"). (Vegans, please note that the following recipe uses eggs.)

The most important requirement for good tempura is that the batter should be cold. Pat dry all surfaces of the vegetables, and dust with cornstarch. Dusting with cornstarch has a dual purpose: to seal in moisture and to enable the batter to adhere better. Do not overmix the batter; the secret to a light, crunchy coating is to leave it lumpy. The batter should also be mixed just minutes before frying. Left standing, it becomes gluey. Take care to fry at the correct temperature and not crowd the frying surface. Finally, serve and eat immediately, while everything is piping hot. If this is not possible, keep tempura hot in a low-temperature oven.

The vegetables listed in this recipe are simply suggestions. Use whatever is fresh and in season. If you find Asian greens such as green *shisō*, Japanese trefoil (*mitsuba*), chrysanthemum greens (*shungiku*), and other Asian vegetables, such as fresh lotus root or fresh bamboo shoot, use them. Edible flowers, such as squash or zucchini, are also excellent.

An alternative for the following batter recipe is tempura batter mix, available at Asian food shops and online. Simply follow the directions on the package.

The ideal frying temperature for vegetables is between 320°F and 340°F.

*Yield:* 4 servings

**Ingredients**
8 fresh medium *shiitake* or other mushroom caps (set aside stalks, see below)
8 stalks green asparagus, sliced in half
1 sweet potato, unpeeled, sliced crosswise into ⅛-inch disks
1 zucchini, unpeeled and sliced into equal-sized strips
1 carrot, peeled and sliced into julienne strips
1 bunch watercress, trimmed and roughly chopped
8 mushroom stalks (reserved from caps above), trimmed and chopped

*Holidays and Special Occasions* 143

**Batter**

½ cup all-purpose flour plus ½ cup cornstarch, plus extra cornstarch for dredging ingredients
¼ teaspoon baking soda
1 large egg
1 cup ice-cold water
Oil for deep frying
¼ cup sesame oil

**Dipping Sauce**

1 cup vegetable-based (*konbu*) *dashi* (see recipe for Konbu Dashi)
4 tablespoons mirin or *sake*
¼ cup soy sauce, or to taste
1 cup finely grated radish
¼ cup finely grated fresh ginger root

**Procedure**

1. Pat dry all vegetable ingredients.
2. Prepare dipping sauce. In a small pan, heat *dashi*, and stir in mirin and soy sauce. Adjust seasoning, adding more soy sauce, if needed. Set aside.
3. Have ready 4 serving dishes, preferably small wooden trays or baskets. Line serving dishes with white paper folded in half asymmetrically—that is, with the edge of the upper half covering the edge of the bottom half (the reverse of the usual custom where the bottom half's edge is visible). This reversal is done only for *higan* or other sad occasion, such as a funeral).
4. Organize your cooking space so that everything is handy and ready to go into the frying pan in sequence. Prepare a draining rack over a tray where fried vegetables can drain.
5. Dredge vegetables with cornstarch, except the chopped watercress and mushroom stalks.
6. Over low-medium heat, slowly bring the frying oil and sesame oil up to 320°F.
7. In a bowl, mix thoroughly the flour, cornstarch, and baking soda. Sift the mixture. In another larger bowl, mix the egg and cold water.
8. Immediately stir flour mixture into the egg-water mixture, just until combined. It does not matter if there are unmixed flour portions around the bowl. The mixture will be lumpy—this is as it should be.
9. Test the temperature of the oil with a frying thermometer.
10. Once 320°F is reached, begin frying. Dip the mushroom caps one at a time into the batter and slide them gently into the oil. Do not crowd the pan. Vegetables should start a bubbling sound as soon as they hit the oil.
11. Take care not to splash hot oil on yourself.

12. Once the bubbling sound has ceased, the vegetables are done. Transfer them to the draining rack. Once drained, transfer them to an oven on low heat.
13. Continue frying the remaining vegetables a few at a time until the first batch of batter is used up. Mix another batch of batter, if needed, and continue frying the remaining vegetables.

*To serve: Distribute vegetables among the individual dishes, arranging them nicely. Place a cone of grated radish topped with grated ginger to one side. Divide dipping sauce into 4 small bowls.*

*To eat: With chopsticks, add a bit of radish and ginger to the surface of a vegetable, or (as is more commonly done) add the condiments to the dipping sauce. Dip each vegetable into the dipping sauce and eat.*

## Tofu Fritters, *Ganmodoki, Hiryōzu*

Tofu and other vegetarian dishes are central to commemoratory meals during *higan*. These tofu fritters are known by two different names: *hiryōzu* in the Kansai region, and *ganmodoki* ("ersatz goose") in the Kanto region. The word *hiryōzu* is from the Portuguese word *filhós*, which refers to sweet fritters. Interestingly, a few years after the recipe for the sweet version was published, a savory version was created, and both types of fritters co-existed for some time. It appears that the savory version was preferred, and survives to carry the name *hiryōzu* or *ganmodoki* today. Ingredients are available at Asian food shops.

Yield: 4 servings

**Ingredients**
1 block cotton-filtered firm tofu (*momen dōfu*)
2 tablespoons oil for frying
2 tablespoons finely shredded burdock root (*gobō*)
2 tablespoons finely shredded carrot
2 dried *shiitake* mushrooms, rehydrated, squeezed dry and chopped finely
¼ cup ginkgo nuts, finely sliced
3 tablespoons poppy seeds (*keshi no mi*)
¼ teaspoon salt, or to taste
3 tablespoons Dioscorea yam (*yama imo*), pureed
1 large egg white, beaten to soft peaks
¼ cup cornstarch, or more as needed
Oil for deep frying

**Procedure**
1. Drain tofu of excess water by wrapping it in cheesecloth and placing it between 2 cutting boards or 2 flat plates. Place a weight on top, such as a couple of heavy food cans, and leave the tofu to drain for 20 minutes to half an hour. It does not have to be bone-dry; just not sopping wet.
2. Meanwhile, in a frying pan over medium heat, place 2 tablespoons oil and when hot, briefly stir-fry the burdock, carrot, mushrooms, ginkgo nuts, and poppy seeds. Sprinkle with salt, and allow to cool to room temperature.
3. Mash drained tofu in a food processor or with a potato masher. Transfer to a large bowl, add stir-fried ingredients, and combine well with the pureed Dioscorea yam and egg white. Add cornstarch to the mixture to firm it up if too moist.
4. Dust your hands with cornstarch, and form patties with the tofu mixture. Place finished patties on a parchment-covered tray while making patties with the rest of the tofu mixture.
5. In a frying pan at medium heat (320°F), deep-fry the patties, a few at a time so as not to crowd the pan. Turn them over to get them evenly browned. Drain them on paper towels or on a wire rack.

*Serve with Japanese mustard and soy sauce.*

# CHAPTER EIGHT

# Street Food and Snacks

## Street Food and Festivals

A *matsuri* (festival) is the place to see and taste street food, when many kinds are prepared and sold at the festival venue. In most cases, the *matsuri* celebrates the *kami* (deities) of the neighborhood shrine or a Buddhist holy day, and food stalls are set up a few days before, all around the shrine or temple precincts. There will be sweets familiar to children around the world: cotton candy or candy floss (*wata gashi*), though packed in a bag in Japan, and candy-coated red apples. There are crepes filled with vanilla cream or chocolate, hot dogs (often coated in a batter and deep fried), and caramel popcorn.

Other street foods may not be so familiar: pancakes filled with sweet red bean paste (*dorayaki*), *yakisoba* (wheat noodles fried on a griddle), small "meatballs" of chopped octopus (*tako yaki*), grilled whole cuttlefish, *yakitori* (grilled chicken on skewers), *okonomiyaki* ("as you like it" crepe), and a recent introduction, grilled skewered beef (*gyū kushi*). To drink, there are familiar and unfamiliar choices: international fizzy cola and lemon-flavored drinks, as well as Japanese lemonade soda (*ramune*) in its classic quaint, collector's-item bottle, stoppered with a glass marble. There will be fresh fruit juices and *kaki gōri* (shaved ice topped with syrup in assorted flavors—strawberry, melon, blue Hawaii apple, cola). In winter, festival offerings include hot sweet *sake* (*amazake*), which is a nonalcoholic semi-sweet rice "soup" (or very thin gruel) slightly fermented with *kōji* (rice yeast), and sweet red bean soup with tiny rice balls (*oshiruko* or *zenzai*).

### Sweet Bean-Filled Cakes, *Dorayaki*

*Dorayaki* are palm-sized pancakes sandwiched around a sweet bean filling. Other fillings are vanilla cream, chocolate cream, or hazelnut chocolate cream.

*Yield:* 10–12 filled cakes

**Ingredients**
1 ⅔ cup cake flour
1 ¾ teaspoons baking powder
¼ teaspoon baking soda
⅔ cup sugar
3 large eggs
1 tablespoon mirin
1 tablespoon honey
1 teaspoon soy sauce
¼ cup water, or more as needed
2 cups prepared sweet bean paste (*anko*)
Oil for brushing the pan

**Procedure**
1. In a bowl, combine cake flour, baking powder, baking soda, and sugar.
2. In a larger bowl, add eggs, and beat well with mirin, honey, soy sauce, and water, until thoroughly incorporated and the mixture is smooth.
3. Add the flour mixture in three batches, mixing well after each addition.
4. The consistency of the batter should be similar to that for pancakes. Add a bit of water if it is too thick.
5. Over medium heat, heat a heavy-bottomed griddle or frying pan. Brush griddle with a thin film of oil.
6. Use a ladle or small cup to pour the batter to about 2–3 inches diameter. (Try to get a uniform size for the cakes.)
7. If your pan is wide, you can cook two or three at the same time, but be sure to leave a fair amount of space between the cakes, as the batter will spread.
8. Once the surface of the cakes is full of bubbles, and it has lost its moist sheen, use the tip of your turner to check that the bottom is golden. Flip the cake over, and cook the other side. It will not take as long to cook as the first side, nor will it be as golden.
9. At once put the cakes onto a tray and cover with plastic film, so that they do not dry out.
10. Continue cooking the remaining batter.
11. Once cakes have cooled to room temperature, they can be filled.
12. Divide sweet bean paste into 10–12 portions.
13. Take a cake and spread the bean paste on the side that is less golden, stopping just ¼ inch from the edge of the cake.
14. Top with another cake, making sure that the more golden side faces outward.
15. Press cakes together to form a sweet bean paste "sandwich."

*Street Food and Snacks* 149

16. Wrap the "sandwich" securely with plastic wrap, molding the two cakes together around the filling, so that the cakes have a chance to better adhere to the filling.
17. Keep other cakes under plastic film while filling, to keep them from drying out.
18. Repeat filling the other cakes in the same manner, and wrapping the finished bean paste sandwiches in plastic film.
19. Let the "sandwiches" rest for 30 minutes, before serving.

*To serve: Remove plastic film, slice cakes in half, and arrange two halves, one half leaning slightly on the other, on a dessert plate.*

*Serve with green tea, or cold milk.*

## Fried Noodles, *Yakisoba*

*Yakisoba* is one of the most common street foods. It is ubiquitous at all neighborhood festivals and school and university events. It may sometimes be offered at temporary food stalls set up in the evening at the exit of train stations. A robustly flavored dish with its combined seasoning of Japanese-style sweet Worcestershire sauce and Chinese oyster sauce and topping of red pickled ginger, it is customary to sprinkle it with *katsuobushi* flakes and green *nori*. Nowadays, many diners season it further with Japanese mayonnaise. A word about Japanese sauces: in Japan, Worcestershire sauce is thicker and sweeter than the British original. The leading brands of mayonnaise in Japan have taste-enhancing amino acids or MSG (monosodium glutamate) added, and use milder rice vinegar than non-Japanese brands which use apple cider vinegar, wine vinegar, or other types of distilled vinegar. Japanese sauces and other ingredients are available at Asian food stores or online.

*Yield:* 4 servings

**Ingredients**
1 pound pork belly
8 cabbage leaves
4 fresh *shiitake* mushrooms
1 medium onion, washed and peeled
2 carrots, washed and trimmed
4 stalks green onion
1 package (containing 3–4 "nests") of yakisoba noodles
Oil, as needed

**Yakisoba sauce**
4 tablespoons Japanese Worcestershire sauce or Okonomiyaki sauce or Tonkatsu sauce
4 teaspoons oyster sauce
2 teaspoons instant *dashi* (*katsuobushi* stock) powder, optional
Salt and pepper to taste
Garnish (any or all of the following): pickled red ginger (*beni shoga*), *katsuobushi* flakes, green *nori* strips or flakes
Table sauce: Japanese-style mayonnaise

**Procedure**
1. Slice pork belly into thin, bite-size pieces.
2. Wash cabbage leaves; remove central vein and discard. Slice cabbage into bite-size pieces.
3. Trim and discard the bottoms of *shiitake* stalks. Finely slice the cap and remaining stalks.
4. Peel the onion, cut in half, and slice finely.
5. Peel the carrots, and slice into fine julienne strips.
6. Slice the green onions into 2-inch lengths.
7. Loosen the strands of the yakisoba noodle "nests."
8. In a small bowl, combine Japanese-style Worcestershire sauce, oyster sauce, and instant *dashi* powder, if using. Taste and adjust seasoning.
9. Take a large frying pan, wok, or sauté pan, and heat it slowly over medium heat. Once hot, add pork belly slices, evenly spaced, and cook them on both sides until golden and releasing fat. If there is insufficient oil in the pan, add 2–3 tablespoons and let the oil warm up again before continuing.
10. Stir-fry the onion for 2–3 minutes, then add cabbage and carrot.
11. Turn up heat to high, and season with salt and pepper.
12. Once the cabbage leaves are almost done but still crisp, add the *shiitake* and green onions, and stir-fry them for 2–3 minutes, until *shiitake* have turned soft and released their juices.
13. Add noodles, followed by the sauce. Turn down heat to medium. Keep stirring until all ingredients are coated with sauce.
14. Check seasoning, and adjust to your taste. Turn off heat, and serve noodles *al dente*. (The residual heat will continue to cook the noodles.)

*To serve: Garnish with red pickled ginger,* katsuobushi *flakes, and green* nori. *Pass around the Japanese-style mayonnaise.*

# Japanese-Style Mayonnaise

The mayonnaise commercially available in Japan is milder, sweeter, and, because it may contain glutamic acid, amino acid, or monosodium glutamate (MSG), has a pronounced umami flavor. To approximate the taste of Japanese-style mayonnaise at home, this recipe uses a combination of lemon juice and mild rice vinegar, *hondashi* powder or MSG, and sugar. You may leave out the sugar if you prefer, and there are brands of *hondashi* powder that do not contain MSG. Rice vinegar, Japanese-style mustard, and *hondashi*, as well as MSG powder, are available at Asian food stores or online.

*Yield:* 1 cup

**Ingredients**
1 very fresh large egg yolk at room temperature
1 teaspoon Dijon or Japanese-style mustard
1 tablespoon freshly squeezed lemon juice
1 tablespoon rice vinegar
½ teaspoon salt
¼ teaspoon freshly ground white pepper
¼ teaspoon *hondashi* powder or MSG
1 teaspoon sugar (optional)
1 cup mild-tasting oil

**Procedure**
1. Into the bowl of a food processor, put the egg yolk, mustard, lemon juice, rice vinegar, salt, pepper, *hondashi* powder, and sugar (if using).
2. Check that the plunger in your food processor feeder has a tiny hole at the bottom. Add as much oil (from the total of 1 cup) as will fit into the plunger.
3. Turn on the food processor, starting at low speed to incorporate the initial ingredients. Gradually build up to medium speed as the oil dribbles in and the mixture starts to emulsify.
4. Add remaining oil to the plunger, once the first lot has been added.
5. Turn off processor once all the oil has been added.
6. Mix the mayonnaise and test the seasoning. Add more salt, pepper, lemon juice, rice vinegar, *hondashi* or MSG, or sugar to your taste.
7. Store in an airtight container in the refrigerator, and use within a week.

> ### Quick Japanese-Style Mayonnaise
>
> If you are concerned about the use of raw egg yolk in mayonnaise, you might like to modify commercial mayonnaise with rice vinegar and *hondashi* powder or MSG.
>
> *Yield:* 1 cup
>
> **Ingredients**
> 1 cup American-style mayonnaise (any brand)
> 1 tablespoon rice vinegar
> ½ tablespoon freshly squeezed lemon juice
> ¼ teaspoon *hondashi* powder or ⅛ teaspoon MSG
> 1 teaspoon sugar, optional
>
> **Procedure**
> 1. In a bowl, combine mayonnaise, rice vinegar, lemon juice, *hondashi* powder, and sugar (if using) until smooth.
> 2. Check the seasoning, and add more rice vinegar, lemon juice, *hondashi* powder, and sugar to your taste.
> 3. Store in an airtight container in the refrigerator, and use within a week.

Eating while walking (called *tabe aruki*) is normally considered bad manners, but during a festival—and note, only within the festival grounds—the rules for good manners are relaxed, and *tabe aruki* (of foods that can be held in one hand, such as an ice cream cone) and *nomi aruki* (drinking while walking) are permissible. The men and women balancing a *mikoshi* (shrine palanquin) on their shoulders will be swigging *sake* (often to semi-inebriation) straight from the bottle, and offering some to onlookers and festival well-wishers. Often the *sake* is distributed to the crowd from newly opened barrels and ladled into square cups of cedar wood, its resinous scent rising as *sake* is poured in.

> The place to sample street foods is at festivals (*matsuri*) and open-air markets, such as flea or antique markets and *tori no ichi* (market on the days of the rooster in November and December). These usually take place within the grounds of a Buddhist temple or Shinto shrine. Stalls line temple or shrine grounds offering grilled corn cobs, *tako yaki* (octopus balls), *yakisoba* (fried noodles), *oden* (a hodgepodge stew of fish paste products), *yakitori* (grilled chicken bits on bamboo skewers), candy floss, candy-coated apples or apricots, steamed buns filled with meat and vegetables (*niku man*), and other quickly prepared foods.

## As You Like It Crepes, *Okonomiyaki*

Literally "cook to your own taste," *okonomiyaki* combines meat and/or seafood and assorted vegetables with a crepe-like batter. There are regional variations—Tokyo, Osaka, Hiroshima, and possibly more—with devoted fans of each style. Whereas the Tokyo and Osaka versions mix all the ingredients together during cooking, the Hiroshima version presents the ingredients in separate layers. All are usually prepared in front of the customer on a large metal hotplate and provide an entertaining performance, especially if the chef is a rather chatty type who likes exchanging banter with customers. Some restaurants feature *okonomiyaki* as a do-it-yourself dining event, with hotplates built into each table, though restaurant staff members are around to assist.

Hiroshima-style *okonomiyaki* makes for a more spectacular dish, as the chef builds up layer after layer of ingredients during cooking, and the whole towering assembly is then flipped over several times with great agility and control. The process takes a considerable amount of time, so while waiting, customers usually have a drink or two and a light appetizer. However, be warned: *okonomiyaki* is far from being a light meal—it is a whole meal in itself.

Although the Tokyo- or Osaka-style *okonomiyaki* can be prepared at home on one large, wide, heavy-bottomed frying pan or wok, the Hiroshima-style version requires more cooking space. Ideally, have a rectangular hotplate, either set on a stove, or preferably an electric one, with temperature control. Failing that, improvise with two frying pans. Two frying turners or wide metal spatulas are also needed to flip the multiple layers conveniently during cooking.

As the name of the dish suggests, this is prepared as you like it. This can be made for vegetarians if the meat is omitted, and other preferred vegetables can be added. For seafood lovers, substitute the meat with fresh squid or shrimp, or perhaps imitation crab's legs, or shellfish such as mussels or, if your budget can afford it, oysters, a Hiroshima specialty. Aromatic herbs, such as green *shisō* (perilla) or *mitsuba* (trefoil), or a few scented leaves of *shungiku* (spring chrysanthemum leaves) may also be added on top of, or instead of, the bean sprout layer.

*Okonomiyaki* sauce and Japanese-style mayonnaise are available at Asian food shops or online. *Okonomiyaki* sauce is basically a mix of Japanese-style Worcestershire sauce and oyster sauce. You may wish to mix your own and adjust the result to your own taste. (For reference, YouTube features videos of Hiroshima-style, as well as Osaka- and Tokyo-style, *okonomiyaki* being made.)

*Yield:* 4 servings

**Ingredients**
½ head medium cabbage
2 cups bean sprouts
4 stalks spring onions
2 cups flour
1 teaspoon baking powder
¼ teaspoon salt
2 eggs, well beaten
1 cup water
2 teaspoons *hondashi* stock powder
1 pound belly pork, sliced into long, thin rashers like bacon
4 servings fresh *yakisoba* noodles
4 eggs
Oil (any neutral flavored) for cooking
Salt and freshly ground pepper to taste

**Sauces and garnishes**
*Okonomiyaki* sauce
Japanese mayonnaise
Powdered *aonori* (green seaweed)
4 tablespoons *katsuobushi* (dried bonito) flakes, or more as needed
4 teaspoons pickled ginger

**Procedure**
1. Prepare the vegetables, and keep them in separate bowls.
2. Remove the hard central core and thick veins of the cabbage; slice or shred finely (the finer, the better).
3. Wash bean sprouts well, and trim any discolored roots.
4. Trim green onions and slice as finely as possible.
5. In a large bowl, combine flour, baking powder, and salt. Make a well in the center of the flour mixture, and add the 2 eggs and water. Begin mixing from the center, bringing in the flour, until all the flour has been incorporated into the egg mixture, and you have a smooth batter. If the batter is too thick, add a bit more water. The batter should be as thick as pancake batter, but still pourable. Let batter rest for 30 minutes.
6. Prepare *okonomiyaki* sauce and Japanese mayonnaise if making them from scratch.
7. Over medium heat, put a heavy-bottomed rectangular griddle to heat up. If you have an electric hotplate, set it to medium or 350°F.
8. Once griddle is hot, brush it with a thin film of oil.
9. Using a ladle or cup, take a quarter of the batter and place it on one side of the griddle, leaving space for cooking other ingredients later. Immediately spread the batter to form a crepe about 6–7 inches in diameter. Try

*Street Food and Snacks*

not to get the crepe wider than this, to make it easier to flip the assembly later. Sprinkle batter with 2 teaspoons of *hondashi* (stock powder).
10. Let crepe cook undisturbed for about 2 minutes, then add a quarter of the cabbage in a loose heap over it. Sprinkle cabbage with salt, pepper, and *hondashi*.
11. Place a quarter of the bean sprouts loosely over the cabbage; season as before.
12. Place a quarter of the belly pork rashers, side by side in one layer, over the bean sprouts. Season as before.
13. Drizzle a few spoonfuls of the batter over the meat, to help it adhere to the previous layers.
14. Let these layers of the *okonomiyaki* cook for about 10–12 minutes. Press down lightly over the meat to reduce the bulk of the vegetables.
15. Lift an edge of the crepe at the bottom with the cooking turner to check if it is done. If it has turned golden, or is showing random brown spots, then flip the assembly, with the help of two cooking turners on either side, so that the crepe is now on top, and the meat is at the bottom.
16. Meanwhile, parboil a serving of *yakisoba* noodles, and drain it.
17. On the other side of the hotplate or griddle, brush a thin layer of oil and set the parboiled and drained *yakisoba* noodles on it. Drizzle the noodles with a bit of oil, then season with salt, pepper, and *hondashi* powder. Loosen the noodles and slice them in half with the edge of the turner, so that all strands are exposed to the cooking surface. Let the noodles cook for about 4–5 minutes.
18. Next, with the help of the cooking turners, lift the entire layered assembly and place it over the noodles. Press down lightly on the crepe to further reduce the height of the okonomiyaki.
19. On the space cleared on the griddle, scrape off any bits that have stuck to the surface.
20. Brush a thin layer of oil, and crack an egg on it. Break the yolk and spread it around the egg white, to get a marbled yellow and white effect.
21. Next, using the two cooking turners, move the layered *okonomiyaki* and place it over the egg. Let the egg cook for 2–3 minutes, or until done.
22. Next, flip the layered assembly of okonomiyaki over, so that the egg is now on top.
23. Brush the egg's surface generously with *okonomiyaki* sauce.
24. Sprinkle green seaweed powder over, and top with the chopped spring onions, bonito flakes, and pickled ginger.
25. Pipe parallel lines of mayonnaise lengthwise and crosswise, and serve.
26. Repeat with the remaining ingredients.

*Serve at once.*

# Beef Skewers, *Gyū Kushi*

This is a recent addition to the genre of grilled skewered street foods. Beef slices are marinated in soy sauce, mirin, vinegar, ginger, and sugar (optional). Alternate the beef with leek slices or tiny sweet peppers, or both.

*Yield:* 4 servings

**Ingredients**
1 ½ to 2 pounds beef round or London broil
1 leek, white part only, sliced into 1 ½- to 2-inch pieces, or 12–20 small green (sweet) peppers (*shishitō*).

**Marinade**
½ cup soy sauce
¼ cup mirin
4 tablespoons rice vinegar
2 tablespoons sugar (optional)
2 tablespoons grated ginger
bamboo skewers
3–4 tablespoons cooking oil (preferably neutral tasting), or more as needed
Garnish: 1 teaspoon powdered *sanshō* or *shichimi tōgarashi*, or to taste

**Procedure**
1. Slice beef into bite-size pieces, and place in a large bowl.
2. In a small bowl, combine soy sauce, mirin, rice vinegar, sugar (if using), and grated ginger. Pour over beef and mix well, ensuring that all pieces are coated with marinade. Cover with plastic film, and refrigerate for 20 minutes to 1 hour.
3. Meanwhile, soak bamboo skewers in water, so that they do not catch fire during grilling.
4. Thread beef pieces onto skewers, alternating each piece of beef with a slice of leek. Brush skewered beef and leeks on both sides with oil.
5. Grill briefly on both sides over hot coals outdoors, taking care not to overcook the beef. The beef pieces should still be pink in the center.
6. Alternatively, to cook indoors: place skewers evenly spaced on a wire grill over a baking pan. Place pan on the topmost oven shelf, and set the oven to broil. Keep a close watch so that they do not burn. Broil the skewers for 2–3 minutes on each side, or until done to your liking.

*To serve:* Sprinkle with sanshō *or* shichimi tōgarashi.

*Street Food and Snacks*

## Snacks

Snacks are called *oyatsu*, and there are salty and sweet types, traditional Japanese and Western styles. Traditional Japanese snacks are served with green tea or cold barley tea (*mugicha*) in summer. In the countryside, where teatime is always a welcome opportunity for a break from ever-pressing farm chores, the initial snack offerings are usually salty, especially when the neighborhood young mothers or grandmothers get together briefly at mid-morning or mid-afternoon. During snowbound winters, teatime becomes a whole-morning or whole-afternoon affair. In summer, often the first "course" will be a dish of homemade quick pickles—fresh cucumbers or small white turnips, or whichever vegetable is in season, just picked from the garden, or bought from a farm lady making the rounds. The vegetables are sliced into chunks and briefly marinated in brine with no loss of crispness. In winter, the pickles will be more elaborate and are often matured in slightly alcoholic *sake* lees (the rice mass that remains after all liquid is pressed) or miso for several months, up to a year. These long pickles are often works of art—for instance, winter melons stuffed with whirlpools of colorful chrysanthemum petals or carrots—and are much admired during tea drinking. After the savory pickles, and more tea drinking, may come rice crackers: *arare* and *senbei*.

*Arare* means "hailstone," but has lent its name to rice crackers of roughly the same size, shape, and color. Traditionally, *arare* crackers were made from the stacked *mochi*, called mirror *mochi* (*kagami mochi*), that were offered to the neighborhood shrine just before New Year. Some of the offered *mochi* was formed into balls or squares and added to the New Year soup called *ozōni*. Invariably there was always a lot of *mochi* left over, and thus the idea was to repurpose them. After several days, if not weeks, of exposure to cold air and indoor heating over the year-end and New Year holidays, the *mochi* become hard and dehydrated. They will not recover their original texture and flavor. The idea of frying or toasting small pieces of dried *mochi* and flavoring them came from Tang China, during the period of flourishing trade between the Chinese and the Japanese imperial courts. Trade negotiations and deals were usually sealed over *arare*, and *arare* has been regarded as a luxury, upper-class snack ever since.

*Okaki* is a rice cracker made of the same ingredient as *arare*, that is, dried *mochi*. In contrast to the rarefied history of *arare*, however, *okaki* has always been more oriented to common taste. It was considered a discourtesy to the *kami* (shrine god or gods) to use a metal instrument to slice or cut into the hard and dehydrated *mochi* that had been offered to the shrine god. Thus, a wooden hammer called *tsuchi* was used to chip off pieces from the large *mochi* disks. The act of chipping is *kaku*, and the pieces chipped off were known as *kaki*, or in polite language, *okaki*. *Okaki* are much larger than bite-size *arare*, and in the past were randomly shaped by the chipping process. Nowadays *okaki* are often in the form of narrow strips with unusual flavors such as *nattō* (fermented soybeans) with green onions or sesame. Other contemporary *okaki* are aimed at the younger generation, flavored with cheese, or cheese and almond.

In the past, *arare* were flavored exclusively with soy sauce, and some were further wrapped in seasoned *nori*. These days *arare* may be flavored with light soy sauce or plain salt. Contemporary *arare* may also come flavored with cheese, mayonnaise, or shrimp.

> Traditional snacks called *wagashi* (Japanese pastries) are made from two types of rice: the regular type cooked for meals (*uruchimai*) and the sticky or glutinous type made for celebratory dishes (*mochi*). Rice cakes made of soft dough with a filling of white or red bean paste are made from *mochi*, or a mix of *mochi* and *uruchimai*. These soft rice cakes, called *nama gashi* (raw or fresh pastries), are best eaten on the same day they are made. *Nama gashi* come in exquisite shapes and colors that evoke seasonal themes, and are made for the tea ceremony.

*Senbei* are another type of rice cracker. It is said that the first *senbei* were made from unsold rice dumplings in teahouses. These days, however, *senbei* are made of flour from nonglutinous rice (*uruchigome*, also *uruchimai*; the flour itself is called *jōshinko*). In contrast, *arare* and *okaki* are made from *mochi* or glutinous rice, or from glutinous rice flour (*shiratamako*). *Senbei* are industrially produced in diverse flavors and shapes, and every year manufacturers come up with innovations—fried disks with a crackled surface brushed with a honey glaze (*age ichiban*), white sugar-glazed (*yuki no shuku*), and the very popular salty-sweet *potapota yaki*, from one of Japan's largest manufacturers of rice-based snacks. The packaging of *potapota yaki* has a nostalgic image of a sweet grandmother making snacks for her grandchildren. On the back of each wrapper is a snippet of countryside wisdom and traditional lore.

*Karintō* are traditional glazed fritters that many people of a certain age wax nostalgic about, because these humble sweets remind them of their postwar childhood. They are homely and simple, one of the *dagashi*—unsophisticated sweets—unlike the fine pastries created for the tea ceremony.

# Glazed Fritters, *Karintō*

*Karintō* are well-liked for their crunchy texture, and their caramel-flavored glaze.

*Yield:* about 25 pieces

**Ingredients**

*Dough*
1 ¾ cups flour, plus extra for rolling dough
1 ½ teaspoons baking powder
¼ teaspoon salt
1 egg, beaten
¼ cup milk
Oil for deep frying

*Glaze*
¾ cup brown sugar
¼ cup water

**Procedure**
1. Prepare the dough. In a food processor, combine flour, baking powder, and salt.
2. Add beaten egg and milk, and process just until all come together. Take care not to over-process.
3. With lightly floured hands, remove dough from the processor, and let it rest at room temperature, covered with a clean, moist kitchen towel, for 20–30 minutes.
4. On a lightly floured surface, roll out dough to a rectangle ¼-inch thick.
5. Divide rectangle into strips 2 inches wide. Slice strips into bars ¼ inch wide.
6. Lay bars on lightly floured parchment paper or cookie sheets until ready to fry.
7. Over medium heat, deep-fry the bars (without crowding the pan) at 350°F, until they are fully expanded, crisp and golden. Drain fried bars on a wire rack or paper towels.
8. Prepare the glaze. In a wide frying pan over medium heat, combine brown sugar and water until the sugar melts.
9. Lower heat when large bubbles start to form on the sugar syrup.
10. Continue cooking until the large bubbles turn into smaller ones and the syrup becomes thicker.

11. Add the fried bars. With a large cooking turner or ladle, mix thoroughly until all are coated with syrup.
12. Turn off heat, but continue mixing until all the syrup has been absorbed, and the syrup becomes crystallized.
13. Lay glazed *karintō* on a wire rack until the glaze is completely firm and dry.
14. Serve with green tea, black tea, or other hot drink. *Karintō* also go nicely with cold milk and other cold beverages.

Sweet potatoes are often roasted over hot stones and peddled by street vendors as a late night snack in the cold months. The street vendor calling out *Ishi yaki imo! Yaki tate!* (Stone roasted sweet potatoes! Just roasted!) around Tokyo neighborhoods used to be a regular winter evening event. These days it is rare to come across a sweet potato peddler, and his call is now a recording from a small van where the roasting is done. Now that ovens are becoming common in Japanese homes, sweet potatoes can be roasted at home, but they never taste as good as those roasted over hot coals and stones by an itinerant vendor.

## Glazed Sweet Potatoes, *Daigaku Imo*

Sweet potatoes are often prepared glazed with caramel syrup. The name *daigaku imo* ("university tuber") derives from its history as a favorite snack among university students in the 1900s. To this day, it is a regular offering at food stands during university festivals. An alternative to frying is tossing the sweet potatoes in 2 teaspoons oil and roasting them in a hot (400°F) oven for 20–30 minutes, or until tender, golden, and crisp.

*Yield:* 3–4 servings

**Ingredients**
1 pound sweet potatoes
oil for deep frying

**Caramel Syrup**
2 tablespoons oil (optional, to keep the syrup from burning)
¼ cup sugar
½ teaspoon soy sauce
1 teaspoon lemon juice (or rice vinegar, to keep the syrup liquid)
About 2 tablespoons black sesame seeds for garnish

**Procedure**
1. Wash potatoes well, as they will not be peeled.
2. Trim the ends and make the first slice diagonally. This slice will be triangular.
3. Thereafter rotate the sweet potato a half turn, and make another diagonal cut, resulting in a rhomboid slice. Make the slices equal so that they cook at the same time.
4. This type of slicing is called *rangiri*, and is generally used for sweet potatoes, carrots, and similar solid-fleshed vegetables. The numerous rhomboidal angles created by this type of slicing expose more surfaces to cooking, ensuring even cooking and shorter cooking time. Otherwise, slice the sweet potatoes into cubes of about 1 ½ inches.
5. Place the sweet potato slices in a large bowl with enough cold water to cover; this is to remove excess starch.
6. After 15 minutes, drain the sweet potatoes and wipe dry.
7. In a frying pan over medium heat, heat an inch of oil between 340°F and 350°F. If you don't have a cooking thermometer, put the end of a wooden chopstick or wooden spoon into the oil. If small bubbles form around it, the oil is hot enough for frying.
8. Do not crowd the pan. Deep-fry the potatoes until golden brown and crisp.
9. To test for doneness, insert a toothpick through a slice: if it goes in smoothly with no resistance, the sweet potato is cooked.
10. Place the fried sweet potatoes on a rack or kitchen towel to drain off excess oil.

To prepare the syrup:
1. In a frying pan over low heat, combine 2 tablespoons oil, sugar, soy sauce, and lemon juice. Keep a close watch as soon as the sugar starts to melt. Do not stir. (Stirring will make the syrup crystallize.)
2. Agitate the frying pan to keep the sugar melting evenly and turning into caramel.
3. Turn off heat when the sugar has become a light brown syrup. The residual heat in the pan will continue to cook the syrup, turning it darker. Set aside.
4. In another, small frying pan over low heat, briefly toast the sesame seeds. Keep stirring frequently, as sesame seeds burn quickly. Once the sesame seeds start giving off their characteristic aroma, turn off heat, and allow the seeds to cool.
5. To assemble: add fried sweet potatoes to the caramel glaze. Mix thoroughly to ensure that each sweet potato is coated.
6. Let caramel-coated sweet potato slices cool on a rack or parchment paper, well-spaced, so that they do not stick together.

*To serve: Sprinkle with the toasted sesame seeds.*

## *Otsumami*

Snacks that accompany soft or alcoholic drinks are called *otsumami*. *Tsumamu* means "to pinch"; hence, *otsumami* are finger food. One of the most popular is *kaki no tane* (persimmon seeds), crescent-shaped rice crackers. A traditional homemade snack in Niigata Prefecture, *kaki no tane* were first produced commercially in the 1920s. The original molds got distorted, but the producer was reluctant to replace them. A customer said the distorted crackers resembled persimmon seeds, and that's what they've been called since. In no time at all, they became popular nationwide. The tiny crackers taste slightly peppery from a glaze of soy sauce and hot chili pepper sauce, but because they are small, the chili flavor is rarely overwhelming. In the 1960s, peanuts were added, and the novel combination boosted sales. There are various stories of how peanuts got into the mix. Apparently the idea had come from the popularity of peanuts among international customers at a Tokyo hotel bar; thus, peanuts gave *kaki no tane* a cosmopolitan aura and a touch of luxury, as peanuts in the 1960s were expensive. Another story is that the peanuts kept the crackers (which absorbed moisture) from going stale too quickly. Yet another version is that originally the crackers and peanuts were sold separately by weight, and some peanuts somehow got mixed in with the crackers, and the accidental combination became a hit, because the peanuts' creamy taste balanced the crackers' spiciness. Today *kaki no tane* are combined with roasted peanuts in a proportion of 60% rice crackers to 40% peanuts per package. Invariably the peanuts get finished first. There was a request for a 50–50 proportion of peanuts to crackers, but oddly enough, this did not prove as popular as the original 70–30, so a compromise was made to 60–40. *Kaki no tane* are ever-present at all drinking parties, whether student gatherings or company *kompa* (drinking get-togethers). They have even crossed the ocean, and are now manufactured in the United States and conform to American taste preferences. Labeled as savory rice snacks, they are more strongly flavored than those produced in Japan. Current U.S. flavors are wasabi and chili. (The same company also produces soft *senbei* for the American market, labeled frosted rice crackers, in two versions: sweet-salty and ginger-flavored.)

In Japan, *kaki no tane* have become sophisticated and have flavors beyond the original soy sauce and chili: chocolate-coated, *ume shisō* (Japanese plum and purple perilla), *wasabi* (horseradish), sesame and black pepper, bacon and black pepper, seven-spice (*shichimi*) mayonnaise, and low-salt for the health-conscious. Some versions feature premium ingredients such as *uni hotate* (sea urchin and scallop) and truffle salt. Some do not include peanuts, but rather mix in wasabi- or cheese-flavored beans. With the boom in outdoor activities, individual packs, rather than the original packs for sharing, make them convenient to take as snacks on a hike.

Beef jerky in various flavors—teriyaki, wasabi, hot chili pepper—is a common accompaniment to beer, *sake*, *shōchū*, and other alcoholic drinks. A specialty *otsumami* of Hiroshima is *senjigara*: deep-fried pork intestines, pork cheek, and chicken gizzards. There are also dried *horumon* ("innards"): dried pork heart and stomach. From Hokkaido comes salmon jerky. Tuna and whale also come in jerky form, and dice-sized dried bonito—the same fish used for fish stock (*dashi*)—is seasoned and wrapped individually as *otsumami*.

## Western-Style Snacks

Western-style snacks, such as potato chips from multinational companies, are widely eaten. Japanese manufacturers also make them, but the flavors are given a local spin—pizza-flavored potato chips, or flavored with hot chili peppers or wasabi. For the health-conscious, there are chips from assorted vegetables such as beets.

The iconic Parisian pastries known as *macaron* have also been given a Japanese makeover. Rather than the original powdered nut and meringue base, shrimp-flavored *senbei*, commonly known as *ebisen*, are used to sandwich savory fillings. The fillings are based on cheese: mozzarella and basil, gorgonzola and honey, camembert and black pepper, and cheddar and parmesan. Other Japanese-style macaron (in Japanese called *wafu makaron*, wittily shortened to *wakaron*) flavors include *matcha* (green tea powder), black tea, *yuzu* citrus, *sudachi* citrus, Japanese chestnut, and roasted sweet potato.

Sweet snacks, such as caramels and chocolate candy, have been continuously popular since their introduction almost a hundred years ago during the Meiji period. Multinational branded candies of all kinds are widely eaten, as well as locally manufactured versions that are less sweet to cater to local taste. As with salty snacks, local sweets feature unusual flavor combinations: *matcha* (Kit Kat) chocolate bars, strawberry cream-dipped pretzel sticks. The same goes for ice cream and other frozen foodstuffs, with local flavors such as fermented milk (Calpis) in semi-frozen drinks in squeezable packs. The same fermented milk flavor can be found in ice cream as well. *Mochi* (glutinous rice) balls can come with sweet red beans in vanilla ice cream, or with assorted fruits in a fruit-salad ice cream.

# CHAPTER NINE

# Dining Out

## Introduction

Eating out is the second most popular leisure-time activity among contemporary Japanese, with around 670,000 eating establishments throughout the country. With Japan's population in 2019 at 126.8 million, that works out to one restaurant per 189 diners. In comparison, the United States has almost the same number of restaurants (660,000) for about 2.5 times the number of people. (The U.S. population in 2019 was about 329 million). Tokyo alone has 160,000 restaurants, about 25% of the country's total, and 230 of these have one Michelin star or more. (Compare this with New York's 71 and Paris's 113 Michelin-starred restaurants.) Way before Japan's gastronomic scene appeared on Michelin's radar, Tokyo had already acquired a reputation as a mecca for foodies. Osaka too has long been renowned for its cuisine, now confirmed with 203 restaurants receiving Michelin stars in 2019. In fact, it is Osaka, rather than Tokyo, that historically had been a gourmet paradise. This is attested to by the often-quoted expression *Osaka no kuidaore, Edo no nomidaore, Kyoto no kidaore*: Osaka gourmets go bankrupt from eating to excess, Edo (Tokyo) people lose their money to alcohol, and Kyoto people spend all their money on fashionable clothing.

Japan's eating places range from fine dining and specialist/specialty restaurants (*ryōtei*), to casual restaurants, fast-food places serving Western-style or Japanese-style food, family-style restaurants with Western- or Japanese-style offerings, noodle shops, sushi restaurants, grilled meat restaurants, pubs/bars with light meals (*izakaya*), cafés, and ethnic restaurants serving miscellaneous international cuisines that do not fall into the European-Western-style category. Japan does not lack for fast food from major American multinational chains: burgers, pizza, doughnuts, ice cream, cheesecake, and pies are widely available in major cities.

MacDonald's, Subway, and Burger King are well represented, with their Japanese competitors offering similar menus. In addition to established restaurants, there are also nonpermanent, impromptu eating places. At night, one can find food stalls set up with marquees and stools near train stations. These offer hot noodles or other light snacks and drinks such as beer, *shōchu*, and *sake*. Come daylight, these will be gone, only to reappear again at nightfall. In Tokyo and Osaka, even now in the 21st century, one can still find, in certain areas that retain an atmosphere of the previous century, food carts serving *oden*, a homely simmering hodgepodge of vegetables and fish-meal patties eaten with sharp Japanese mustard and warm *sake*.

For the average Japanese, a meal at a specialist restaurant (*ryōtei*), unless paid for by a business expense account, is a rare event. Dinner at any of these exclusive restaurants would cost well over $200–$300 per person, and some of the more exclusive places, especially in Kyoto, post no exterior signs indicating that they are restaurants. They do not advertise; to gain entry, one needs an introduction from someone known to the restaurant, somewhat like a members-only club. Nevertheless, despite their high prices for dinner, some of these offer the general public a chance to sample their fare. At lunchtime, they may offer set meals below $25 that include soup (miso soup usually), a main dish, rice, and pickles. Tea and water are free.

Even in restaurants that have not been recognized with Michelin stars, dining out is a satisfying experience, because in general, it is not only the good taste of their food offerings, but also the warm service and welcome (*omotenashi*) that most eating places provide. Despite Japan's reputation as an expensive place for eating out, there are eating places to suit every level of budget and taste. As mentioned earlier, midday is a good time for a hearty meal, as most restaurants have special menus at prices reasonable enough to attract workers during their lunch hour. It helps to be able to read Japanese, of course, because these special lunch deals are often written on a chalk board just outside the restaurant, and may not be posted on the restaurant's website or online food forums. These may even take the form of *tabehōdai*—all you can eat—within a set time period, usually two hours.

In 2018, the average Tokyo resident ate out 90 times during the year; oftener than once a week. She or he would have spent more than 100,000 yen (almost US$1,000) on these meals spread over the year. These figures most likely underestimate the number of times that young single working people (who still live at home) and young families eat out during the year, as well as the amount they spend. Most employed people eat out during lunch—quite often a simple meal of *rāmen* or *soba* noodles or curry rice. Many will also stop for a drink and something light to eat with colleagues for a *choi-nomi* ("one for the road") before heading home. Families with young children, with both parents employed, will probably eat out two or three times a week, especially on weekends. In terms of expenditure, *sushi* accounts for the largest share of a family or a person's eating-out budget, followed by *rāmen* and soba noodles. Hamburger accounts for the lowest share.

Cooking at home, specifically cooking from scratch, is noticeably on the decline. In a recent survey of 10 million households in which both husband and wife were employed, only 20% of wives in their twenties cooked three times a day. Compared to a decade or so earlier, when the traditional meal consisting of miso soup and three side dishes was cooked at least three times a week, these days most families prepare this type of traditional meal, if at all, only once a week, usually on the weekend. In another survey conducted in 2016 by the Japan Broadcasting Corporation (NHK), of 1,519 respondents aged from 16 to over 70 years old, 28% ate out when they could not be bothered to cook. In another set of 1,787 respondents, 27.2% said they hardly did any cooking.

The lockdowns imposed nationwide since March 2020 because of the novel coronavirus pandemic has negatively impacted dining-out culture. With restaurants and bars closed, and people isolating themselves and working from home, fast-food, take-out, drive-through, and delivery food services are increasing their business. Cooking and baking at home are becoming popular. The lockdowns have caused widespread bankruptcies and unemployment in the food industry. Innovative alternatives for unemployed chefs include cooking meals in people's home kitchens, the menu set by clients' preferences, or setting up in virtual kitchens (also known as ghost or cloud kitchens) or food trucks in major urban areas. Virtual kitchens are a new food business model in which facilities are rented by chefs who are spared the expense of waiting staff, dining space, and other associated expenses, which enable minimal start-up business investment. Virtual kitchens, such as **Shoku no Mori** ("Food Forest"), are usually tied in with third-party online food delivery services, such as Uber Eats. Although introduced to Japan before the pandemic, virtual kitchens have become more prevalent since the first nationwide lockdown in 2020.

In a survey of 10,007 informants aged above 20 conducted by the Tokyo-based market research company Values in September 2020 on changes in dietary habits and food awareness, 70% of the women (total 4945) and 60% of the men (total 5062) reported decreased dining out.

Cooking and baking at home from scratch increased by 36% among the women and 23% among the men.

At home, the most popular foods for most people are, in order of preference: sushi, curry rice (an all-time favorite among children and adults), rāmen (especially among men), grilled meat (yakiniku), crisp-fried chicken (chikin kara age), and gyōza. By way of comparison, when dining out, a recent survey revealed that the top-ten kinds of eating places preferred by women and men aged between 20 and 60 are: sushi restaurants, including conveyor-belt shops; pubs/bars (izakaya) or beer halls; grilled meat/yakiniku or Korean-style restaurants; Italian-style restaurants; Japanese-style restaurants serving traditional meals; Chinese-style restaurants; yakitori places; rāmen/soba noodle places; family-style restaurants; and (lastly) Western-style restaurants. When only women were surveyed, their first five preferences mirrored those of the general survey; however, rāmen and soba noodle shops were replaced by buffet-style restaurants. These all-you-can-eat restaurants are called tabehōdai or baiking ("Viking," smorgasbord-type buffets). In contrast, men put izakaya or beer halls as their first choice, and included set-meal restaurants (teishokuya) in their top-ten preferences.

## Pan-Fried Dumplings, Gyōza

These are the Japanese equivalent of the Chinese dumplings called pot stickers in the United States. The filling may taste different from what Americans are used to, as is only natural, because these dumplings have been adapted to the Japanese taste. They are filled with ground pork, cabbage, Chinese cabbage, garlic, garlic chives (nira), and dipped in a sauce of vinegar, soy sauce, sesame oil, and hot mustard or hot chili oil at the table.

Gyōza are popular for lunch eaten out, as well as for otsumami (appetizers to go with a cold soft or alcoholic drink). They are also often eaten at home, quickly and conveniently prepared from frozen or chilled packages.

Making gyōza at home from scratch is not that difficult—it is the wrapping process that takes time. A group of friends or all the family wrapping gyōza together makes it fun, with everyone getting to enjoy the delicious just-cooked dumplings afterward as a treat.

Yield: about 50 pieces

**Ingredients**
12-ounce package of round dumpling (pot sticker) wrappers

**Filling**
¼ cup finely chopped onion
¼ cup finely chopped cabbage
¼ cup finely chopped Chinese cabbage
½ pound ground pork
2 tablespoons finely chopped garlic chives
2 tablespoons finely chopped Japanese leek or green onions
1 tablespoon finely grated garlic
1 tablespoon finely grated fresh ginger

**Seasoning**
1 teaspoon sesame oil
2 teaspoons honey
1 teaspoon chicken bouillon powder
½ teaspoon salt
Freshly ground black pepper to taste

**For wrapping the** gyōza
1 small bowl of water for moistening the fingers

**For cooking the** gyōza
2 tablespoons sesame oil
⅓ cup hot water

**Dipping sauce**
2 teaspoons soy sauce, or more as needed
½ teaspoon sesame oil, or more as needed
1 teaspoon vinegar, or more as needed
1 teaspoon hot mustard
½ teaspoon hot chili oil

**Procedure**
1. Prepare the filling. Take a clean, dry kitchen towel, and place the chopped onion, chopped cabbage, and chopped Chinese cabbage in the middle. Bring the ends of the towel together and wring the towel, squeezing out as much liquid as possible from the vegetables.
2. Into a large bowl, place the squeezed onion, cabbage, and Chinese cabbage and combine with the ground pork and the garlic chives, Japanese leek, garlic, and fresh ginger.
3. Stir in sesame oil, honey, chicken bouillon powder, salt, and freshly ground pepper.
4. Using your hands, thoroughly mix the seasoning and the filling, kneading the seasoning in well.

**Fill the *gyōza* wrappers:**
1. With clean dry hands, take a *gyōza* wrapper in one hand, and put about ⅔ to ¾ tablespoon of filling in the center. Do not overfill the wrapper.
2. Fold the wrapper over to enclose the filling, creating a crescent (half-moon). Do not press the wrapper shut yet at this point.
3. Moisten the fingers of your other hand with water, and make 3 or 4 pleats (folds) on the back side of the wrapper (the side away from you), and press the wrapper edges together.
4. The pleats create a pucker, enabling the dumpling to stand upright.
5. Repeat the wrapping process with the rest of the filling and wrappers.
6. Cook the *gyōza*. Take a heavy-bottomed frying pan and spread sesame oil evenly on its surface.
7. On the oil, place the dumplings close together, standing up.
8. Turn on the heat to medium for 4–5 minutes, or until the bottoms of the dumplings have turned a pale golden color. Check that they have done so by lifting a dumpling. Keep a close watch, as the dumplings are liable to scorch.
9. Pour hot water around the dumplings, and cover. Let the dumplings cook for about 10 minutes, or until all the water has been absorbed, and the dumplings are done.
10. Turn off the heat. The dumplings will continue to cook in the residual heat.
11. Remove the dumplings to a serving plate. Keep in a low oven to keep warm while you continue to cook the rest of the dumplings.
12. Mix the dipping sauce. In a small bowl, mix the soy sauce, sesame oil, and vinegar.

*To serve: Put dipping sauce in small saucers next to each diner. Diners help themselves to mustard or hot chili oil to mix with the dipping sauce.*

## Korean-Style Grilled Meat, *Kankoku-fū Yakiniku*

The current generation of young Japanese eats more meat than fish. Besides burgers and steaks, a popular way of eating meat when dining out is Korean-style barbecue. It is well-liked in Japan, especially among the younger generation, because of its intense flavor and aroma from its marinade of garlic, leeks, and sesame seeds, as well as the conviviality generated by everyone taking turns cooking while sitting around the table. While the meat is cooking, everyone helps themselves to various types of *kimchi* (spicy pickled Chinese cabbage and other vegetables), and mixed vegetable salads with glass noodles (*chapchae*, also spelled *japchae*, pronounced "chapuche" in Japanese), and drinks, either soft drinks or alcoholic drinks such as beer

*Dining Out*

or *sake*. There is a Korean equivalent to *sake*, called *makgeolli* (pronounced "makori" in Japanese) that contains about 1%–2% less alcohol than *sake*. It is coarsely filtered, milky white, and resembles the Japanese drinks *nigori zake* (cloudy *sake*) and *doburoku* (unfiltered Japanese *sake*).

The kiwifruit or Japanese pear (*nashi*) for the marinade functions as a meat tenderizer. The traditional way of cooking Korean-style grilled meat is at the table, on a clay stove with glowing coals with an iron pan or a metal grid above. These days, yakiniku restaurants tables have inset gas grills with overhead ventilators that efficiently suck up the smoke. At home, a charcoal barbecue outdoors or an electric hotplate on the table is an alternative. *Kimchi* and other Korean-style vegetable dishes, as well as the ingredients for this recipe, are available at Asian food shops.

*Yield:* 4 servings

**Ingredients**
1 ½ pounds beef (round, London broil, boneless short-rib, or for sukiyaki), thinly sliced into 1 ½- to 2-inch pieces
5 leeks, trimmed, white only; 4 sliced crosswise into bite-size pieces; 1 chopped to add to the marinade
4 green bell peppers, seeded and quartered lengthwise
1 head Chinese cabbage, washed and sliced into 2-inch pieces crosswise.
Cooking oil

**Marinade**
1 green kiwifruit, peeled and finely chopped, or Japanese pear (*nashi*), peeled, cored, and finely chopped
2-inch knob of ginger, peeled and finely grated
3 cloves garlic, finely chopped
2 red chili peppers, sliced into rings (discard the seeds for a milder heat), or 1 teaspoon red chili flakes
4 tablespoons sesame seeds
2 tablespoons soy sauce
2 tablespoons *sake* or mirin
2 tablespoons sesame oil

**Dipping sauce**
4 tablespoons soy sauce, or more as needed
4 tablespoons mirin, or more as needed
1 tablespoon sesame oil, or more as needed
2 teaspoons sesame seeds, or more as needed
2 tablespoons green onions, finely chopped, or more as needed

**Procedure**
1. First, dry-roast the sesame seeds. Place a dry frying pan over medium heat and when hot, place the sesame seeds in it. Turn down the heat to low, and keep stirring the sesame seeds so that they do not scorch. As soon as the seeds start popping, turn off the heat. Set the sesame seeds aside.
2. Mix the marinade ingredients, including the chopped leek. Combine thoroughly with the beef. Cover and marinate for 30 minutes to 1 hour, refrigerated.
3. Mix the dipping sauce ingredients, and distribute among 4 sauce bowls. Set a bowl and chopsticks for each diner.
4. Heat a tabletop griddle over medium heat, and when thoroughly hot, spread a thin film of oil evenly on the surface. Place an assortment of pieces of beef, leeks, peppers, and Chinese cabbage in one layer, well spaced, to cook.
5. Each diner takes a piece as soon as done to his or her liking (rare, medium, or well-done), and dips it in the dipping sauce. Each diner adds more meat, leeks, peppers, or Chinese cabbage to the griddle.
6. Have hot plain rice on hand, assorted *kimchi* pickles, and salads.

*Drink with your preferred soft drinks or beer.*

## Grilled Skewered Chicken, *Yakitori*

*Yakitori* are small pieces of chicken meat on bamboo skewers grilled over charcoal. Slices of leek or small green peppers are usually interspersed between the meat. After grilling, the whole skewer is dipped into a sweet-salty sauce or simply sprinkled with Japanese mountain pepper (*sanshō*) or seven-spice mix (*shichimi tōgarashi*).

Yield: 4 servings

**Ingredients**
1 ½ pounds chicken, boneless breast meat or thigh meat
1 leek, white part only, sliced into 1 ½- to 2-inch pieces, or small green sweet peppers (*shishitō*).

**Marinade**
½ cup soy sauce
¼ cup mirin
4 tablespoons rice vinegar

*Dining Out*

2 tablespoons sugar (optional)
2 tablespoons grated ginger
bamboo skewers
3–4 tablespoons cooking oil (preferably neutral tasting), or more as needed
Garnish: 1 teaspoon powdered *sanshō* or *shichimi tōgarashi*, or to taste

**Procedure**
1. Slice the chicken into bite-size pieces, and place in a large bowl.
2. In a small bowl, combine the soy sauce, mirin, rice vinegar, sugar (if using), and grated ginger. Pour over the chicken and mix well, ensuring that all pieces are coated with the marinade. Cover with plastic film and refrigerate for 20–30 minutes.
3. Meanwhile, soak the bamboo skewers in water. (This ensures that they do not ignite during grilling.)
4. Thread the chicken pieces onto the bamboo skewers, alternating each piece of chicken with a slice of leek or green pepper. Brush the skewered chicken and vegetables on both sides with oil.
5. Grill briefly on both sides over hot coals outdoors.
6. Alternatively, to cook indoors: place the skewers evenly spaced on a wire grill over a baking pan. Place the pan on the topmost oven shelf, and set the oven to broil. Keep a close watch, and broil the skewers for 5–8 minutes on each side, or until done.

*To serve:* Sprinkle with sanshō *or* shichimi tōgarashi.

## Sushi

Clearly, the most desirable food for almost everyone, whether eating at home or out, is sushi. Why is sushi such a preferred food? The first two reasons given by most Japanese are that it is delicious (*oishii*) and beautiful (*utsukushii*). Absolute freshness in any food ingredient—be it fish, seafood, meat, or vegetable—makes food delicious, and this quality is unmistakable. It is this clear, undisguised natural flavor of foods that is prized by discerning diners in Japan. Sushi, and by extension sashimi, provide the best examples of the natural, undiluted taste of fish and seafood. The innate flavors of fish and seafood are complemented by the slight acidity and texture of the vinegar-flavored rice base, and sharpened by the surprising bite of *wasabi* (horseradish). Texture is another factor that affects the flavor of sushi and sashimi. Fish and seafood are chosen for their varied textures and their mouth-feel, but the way they are sliced influences the textures they present to the diner's tongue and teeth. This is clearly illustrated by the way scallops are cut, for example. When sliced horizontally, they do not taste as good as when they are sliced vertically. Another factor in the deliciousness perceived by diners is the variety of fish and seafood toppings. There is such an ever-changing variety of marine food, depending on the season. The diner is at liberty to freely choose, and the tongue and taste buds do not have a chance to get bored. Because servings are small—at most two or four bites per portion—a diner's taste buds are constantly being stimulated with each succeeding choice of fish or seafood.

The origin of the word sushi is *sumeshi*: *su* means "vinegar" and *meshi* means "rice." In time, the syllable *me* was dropped. The toppings and other ingredients for the vinegar-flavored rice are not all raw. Steamed, simmered, and pickled ingredients, as well as fried (egg omelet), crisp-fried, and smoked (such as salmon) ingredients are just as frequently used. These days, innovative toppings include meat such as beef and chicken, raw and cooked.

The origin of sushi was fish, shellfish, even meat (wild boar) and various vegetables preserved in cooked rice, leading to lactic acid fermentation. The result was a preserved or pickled dish known as *narezushi*, characterized by a sour taste and a strong smell. The process preserved the food for long periods—not merely days or months but also years. The fermented rice, having done its job of preservation and pickling, was discarded. Only the fish, shellfish, and other ingredients were eaten.

Lactic acid fermentation continues to be a common food preserving process, seen in Hokkaido's winter specialty dish of seafood, rice, and vegetables, called *izushi*, and in sauerkraut and kimchi. Because of the risk of botulism poisoning, vinegar was substituted for the cooked rice to provide the desired sour taste. Furthermore, vinegar also served as a preservative. *Narezushi* then evolved from a long-term pickled dish (where the rice was not eaten) into *nama nare* (raw pickled), a short-term pickle of a few days where the rice was eaten. From there, it developed over time into the popular Edo-style sushi known and eaten worldwide today. *Narezushi* using whole small river fish such as *ayu* (sweetfish) survives today as a regional specialty in several prefectures.

The original Edo-style sushi used fish and shellfish from the bay around Edo (now Tokyo). They were sold from mobile carts called *yatai*. Two of the original *yatai* became restaurants and are still around today, one in Nihonbashi and the other in Kudanshita in Chiyoda ward. Both make sushi rice to the same age-old recipe used for the original Edo-style sushi rice—which is red vinegar. Moreover, neither restaurant uses sugar, which is a usual ingredient in contemporary sushi rice. The following recipe is a modern one, but the sugar is optional.

# Sushi Rice, *Sushi Meshi*

*Yield:* 4 servings

**Ingredients**
4 cups short-grain rice
4 cups water
3 tablespoons *sake* (optional)
4-inch piece *dashi konbu* (kelp for making stock, available at Japanese and other Asian food shops or health food shops)
8 tablespoons rice vinegar (available at Japanese and other Asian food shops or health food shops)
1 tablespoon sugar or more to taste (optional)
2 teaspoons salt or to taste

**Procedure**
1. An hour before cooking, wash the rice twice or three times until the rinse water is no longer cloudy. Note that the rinse water will not become completely clear. Soak the rice for 30 minutes, then drain the rice on a sieve, and let it air-dry at room temperature until needed.
   (If using an automatic rice cooker, follow instructions for the appliance. Use the measuring cup that comes with the automatic rice cooker, and add water according to the markings on the rice cooker's inner pan.)
2. In a heavy-bottomed pot, place the drained rice and 4 cups of water, *sake*, and *dashi konbu*. Cover and let it come to a boil over medium-high heat. As soon as it boils, remove the *dashi konbu* and discard.
3. Cover the pot, turn down heat to low, and continue cooking the rice for 18–20 minutes, or until all the water has been absorbed. Do not uncover the pot at any time during the 18–20 minute period.
4. Turn off the heat. Leave the rice, still covered, in its pot for 5–10 minutes.
5. While the rice is cooking, mix the seasoning vinegar.
6. In a small pan over low heat, warm the rice vinegar, sugar (if using), and salt until the sugar and salt are dissolved. Taste, and adjust the sugar and salt to your liking. Allow to cool, and set aside until needed.
7. In a wide bowl, spread the just-cooked rice, and distribute the seasoning vinegar all over the rice.
8. Using a flat rice scoop or wide spatula, mix the seasoning vinegar mixture all over the rice using a light slicing motion, as if cutting into the rice layer, taking care not to mash the rice grains. Turn over the rice with the scoop, and repeat the slicing motion to mix and cool the rice. In

Japan it is customary to use a hand fan to quickly cool the rice. Rapid cooling of the rice by using a fan and slicing strokes during mixing bring out the gloss of the rice grains.
9. This rice is now ready to be used for various sushi recipes, such as *Kani Hosomaki* (Crab Sushi Rolls, recipe follows) and the Smoked Salmon Chirashizushi recipe in Chapter Seven: Holidays and Special Occasions.

## Crab Sushi Rolls, *Kani Hosomaki*

Rolled sushi (*norimaki*) are considered one of the tests of a sushi chef's skills, especially one filled with red meat tuna (*maguro*), called *tekka maki*. The other test is egg omelet. Sushi aficionados consider the flavor of egg omelet an indication of the chef's expertise. This is the reason that some sushi diners begin with egg omelet.

*Hosomaki* means "thin roll." This recipe uses widely available "crab legs," which are actually made of fish paste (*surimi*) shaped and dyed with food coloring to approximate real crab-leg meat. If you are fortunate enough to have real crab legs on hand, by all means use them. Alternatively, instead of ersatz crab legs, you may use canned tuna meat or even fresh raw tuna slices, thinly sliced roast beef, or even boneless crisp-fried chicken slices. For added color, use finely sliced cucumber or avocado.

Vegetarians may leave out the fish or meat filling altogether, and use fresh champignon mushrooms. Other fillings are simmered *shiitake* mushrooms, as well as fresh spinach leaves on their own or mixed together with chrysanthemum greens (*shungiku*), quickly parboiled. These are traditional fillings for vegetarian sushi rolls at Buddhist monasteries and nunneries. Colorful fillings may also include parboiled edible chrysanthemum petals, or, if unavailable, other edible flowers that are more easily sourced outside of Japan. Think of what you would like to put in a sandwich—only instead of using bread slices, you are using flavored rice.

*Yield:* 4 servings

**Ingredients**
4 cups sushi rice
2 sheets *nori*
½ medium cucumber
1 teaspoon salt
12 sticks "crab legs"

*Dining Out*

1 tube of prepared *wasabi* paste
Sushi rolling mat
Japanese soy sauce for dipping
Small tub of sweet pickled ginger (available at Asian food shops or major supermarkets)

**Vinegar and water mixture for moistening hands**
¼ cup water
1 teaspoon rice vinegar

**Procedure**
1. Prepare the sushi rice as in the preceding recipe. Cover the rice with a damp clean kitchen towel to keep the rice from drying out while assembling the rolls.
2. Prepare the *nori*. Over medium heat, quickly pass the shiny surface of the *nori* sheets to toast them. Do not let the *nori* stay over the flame or burner too long, as it may scorch.
3. With kitchen scissors, cut the *nori* sheets in half. Set aside.
4. Wash the cucumber and peel. Discard the central pulp with seeds, and slice the remaining flesh into fine julienne strips. Sprinkle with a bit of salt and when the strips wilt, pat them dry with paper towels. Set aside.
5. In a small bowl, mix the water and vinegar, and place close to your working surface.
6. Prepare for rolling. Set the sushi mat on a wide cutting board.
7. Lay one *nori* half sheet in the center of the mat.
8. Moisten your fingers with the vinegar and water mixture to prevent the rice from sticking to your fingers.
9. Leaving about ¼ of the *nori* sheet farthest away from you uncovered (free of sushi rice), using your fingers, spread sushi rice to cover the *nori* to an even layer about ⅛ of an inch thick.
10. With your finger, spread a thin line of wasabi across the rice layer, placing it at around the bottom quarter of the rice.
11. Place three sticks of "crab legs," end to end, directly on top of the wasabi, all across the rice.
12. Next place a layer of julienned cucumber, surrounding the "crab leg" layer, at around half the thickness of the "crab legs."
13. Now draw the sushi mat up and over the *nori*, rice, and "crab-leg"-cucumber filling, keeping your fingers lightly supporting the rice and filling, and keeping them from sliding away.
14. Continue rolling to the end of the *nori*. Tighten the mat as you reach the farthest edge; this will seal the *nori* to the filled rice layer. Set aside.

> 15. Repeat with the rest of the *nori* sheets and filling.
> 16. Using a sharp knife, slice the long rolls crosswise into bite-size pieces.
>
> *Serve with small saucers of soy sauce for dipping. Diners may help themselves to additional wasabi if desired.*
>
> *Serve with pickled ginger. Accompany the sushi with green tea, beer, or a soft drink of your choice.*

Wasabi is an important component of sushi and sashimi: it has a function beyond its value as a taste-shocker. (Some diners who take too much at once report their hair standing on end, or their noses and ears feeling ready to burst.) *Wasabi* also acts as an antibacterial agent and serves to prevent minor stomach upsets that result from eating raw marine products. Additionally, according to a sushi professional, *wasabi* serves to bond the topping to its rice base.

The first sight that greets a diner upon entry into a sushi restaurant is the colorful diversity of the day's offerings arrayed in the chiller shelves in front of the sushi chef's preparation area. Seeing the sea's bounty spread in that manner never fails to impress the eyes and tempt the taste buds. This initial visual attraction *in macro* is followed up by the diner's choices *in micro*. The beauty of sushi, especially Edo-mae sushi (that is the hand-pressed variety rather than the rolled *maki*), lies in the aesthetic presentation of each individual serving. The natural colors and textures of seafood—red, gray, white, and orange—are enhanced by being framed in the diminutive space provided by the bite-size rice layer beneath. When adorned with the contrasting colors of spring onions, green or red *shisō* leaves, young radish sprouts, *shisō* flower spikes, and other plant materials used as *ashirai* (accompanying condiment and garnish), their presentation serves to "feed" the diner's eyes first, heightening the expectation of tasting and eating such tempting morsels.

One sushi fan prefers to sit at the counter rather than at the tables. A major part of the fun of eating sushi, according to him, is not just the taste and looks of the food itself, but in watching the process of it being made, observing the expertise of the chef as he prepares each serving calmly and confidently, and then laying the glistening pair of gem-like bites in front of the diner with "*hai, toro desu*" ["Here's the *toro*" (the choicest part of Atlantic blue-fin tuna)] or whatever item it is the diner has just requested. There is also the added pleasure of conversation with the sushi chef. Making sushi is an art that takes years to master, and the process of its making, in front of diners, is quite a performing art, accomplished with economy of movement and grace. The less contact the fresh ingredients have with the chef's hands, the less chance they have of having their chilled temperature—and thus their taste, texture, and appearance—altered.

> Sushi and tempura were the first fast foods, served from carts called *yatai*, during the Edo period. The population of Edo (now Tokyo) at the time was heavily skewed toward single male workers who flocked to the *yatai*. The *yatai* eventually developed into restaurants; a few are still around today. One venerable sushi restaurant was the first to offer the belly of the Atlantic blue-fin tuna, *toro*, as a topping. This part used to be discarded because it was considered rather greasy. One customer inspired the name *toro* by his comment that its texture was *torotto shite iru* (meltingly soft).

Yet another important factor given by Japanese diners for preferring sushi is that it is safe to eat, despite being based on mostly raw ingredients. The attention paid to hygiene and cleanliness—not only regarding the food, but also to every single aspect of the kitchen and eating area—is impeccable. With mere seconds to create each small serving, and equally seconds to eat it as well, sushi is also a fast food—one of the original fast foods, created during the Edo period, as what was then Edo was already beginning to expand. For many busy people taking a break from work, eating sushi does not take too much time, as long as one is served immediately.

The first "Edo-mae sushi," as the hand-formed bite-sized sushi are called, in contrast to those formed in a wooden mold, were sold from carts called *yatai*. One of the oldest sushi restaurants in Tokyo traces its origin to just such a food cart parked by the riverbank in Nihonbashi district. The sushi served there has remained true to its original recipe: the rice base is flavored only with *sake* vinegar, called red vinegar, with no addition of sugar. The seasoning is boiled-down soy sauce, painted on the surface of the fish with a fine brush, and therefore there is no need to dip the topping in soy sauce. The current chef-owner, who is the ninth generation to take over the restaurant, majored in economics at university, but before he could take over, he had to undergo the required years of training. Unlike other sushi restaurants, he does not accept *omakase* orders (*omakase* means the chef's choice). He only makes sushi to each diner's choice. An evening meal of sushi, perhaps with a side dish of sashimi and clear soup, at such a specialist restaurant would set a diner back a good US$200–300. However, it is possible for anyone to experience a meal at such historical restaurants during lunchtime, when a more affordable set menu is offered.

At the other end of the scale from these specialist shops are the conveyor-belt sushi places called *kaiten zushi* (revolving sushi). Even these are not without their charms, according to one fan, who takes pleasure in watching the small dishes laden with a variety of offerings as they travel along the moving rail, much as model train enthusiasts are fascinated by them even long past their childhood. *Kaiten zushi* have become more like family restaurants, especially in rural areas, as they offer not only sushi and sashimi, but also other fish- and seafood-based dishes, as well as desserts.

## Varieties of Toppings

The long-established sushi restaurant mentioned earlier has kept to the family's traditional offerings. It does not offer salmon, for instance, a very popular topping among contemporary diners. Because of its attractive color and texture, salmon is offered by most sushi restaurants, but it was not so popular half a century ago. Interestingly, another popular topping today and one of the most expensive—*toro*, the fatty belly of the blue-fin tuna—was not acceptable as sushi or sashimi in the past either, because it was considered too fatty and rich. It was the great-grandfather of this long-established sushi restaurant who pioneered serving it. It was a most unusual *tane* ("seed," sushi insider terminology for topping, often syllabically reversed into *neta* by sushi professionals) for that time. And that nonconformist use of *toro* made the restaurant so famous that it became known as *the* toro restaurant. The word "toro" for that part of the tuna did not exist at the time, either. It was a customer who described the sensation of eating it as "melting in the mouth"—*torotte shite*—who provided the name *toro*.

The most popular toppings for conveyor-belt sushi in 2018 were: salmon; *maguro* (red meat Atlantic blue-fin tuna); *hamachi*, also known as *buri*; *maguro chū toro* (medium fatty belly of the Atlantic blue-fin tuna); shrimp; squid; *negi toro* (green onions with *toro*); *engawa*, the chewy-textured fin muscle of flatfish such as flounder and plaice; and scallop, tied with *ikura* (salmon roe). In contrast, the favored toppings at high-end sushi restaurants were *toro*; abalone; sea urchin; rock fish (*nodoguro*); *ikura*; and milt (*shirako*).

How should one eat sushi? A famous food critic recommends eating with the fingers—the traditional and perfectly correct way to eat it. You may use chopsticks to pick up the pickled ginger, however. Hold the sushi piece right side up with the short end facing you, the thumb and forefinger supporting the long edges of the topping, and the rice base supported by the middle finger. Now invert the sushi piece, so that the topping is at the bottom and the rice layer is now on top. Dip one edge of the topping—just the topping, and only briefly and lightly, into the soy sauce. Do not ever let the topping swim in the soy sauce. As food critics say, you have not come to a sushi restaurant to eat soy sauce. This light dipping ensures that the natural taste of the fish—which is, after all, the main attraction—is not obscured by that of the soy sauce. Bring the seasoned sushi to your mouth, still in inverted position, so that the seasoned topping touches your tongue first before anything else. This recommended way of eating takes some getting used to.

Another important point in eating sushi is not to dilute the *wasabi* into the soy sauce. Doing so results in a muddy appearance—not a pretty sight! Also, by being diluted in liquid, the *wasabi* loses its fieriness. Usually the sushi chef has already smeared *wasabi* between the topping and the base, but if you want more heat, take the tip of your chopsticks and dip it into the *wasabi*, then place as much or as little as you like between the topping and the rice.

In what order should sushi be eaten? If you are seated at the counter, you do not have to start with sushi immediately. You can begin with an appetizer (*otsumami*) or *sashimi* (slices of raw fish or seafood). This can be accompanied by beer or *sake*. After this, you can place your order. How does one order at the counter? In theory, one proceeds from the light-flavored toppings to the more robustly flavored ones, then to the fat-rich ones, and finally to the rolled items (*nori maki*). Examples of mild-tasting fish are sea bream (*tai*), flounder (*hirame*), plaice (*karei*), and sea bass (*suzuki*). These can be followed by raw or vinegar-marinated "blue" or dark-skinned fish, such as the sardine relative known as gizzard shad (*kohada*), mackerel (*saba*), or horse mackerel (*aji*). Note, however, that the gizzard shad and mackerel are not raw—they have been lightly marinated in rice vinegar, because they do not keep fresh for long. Next would be stronger-flavored fish and shellfish, including fish eggs, thus: Atlantic blue-fin tuna (*maguro*), shellfish such as red clam (*akagai*), scallop, sea urchin (*uni*), and salmon roe (*ikura*). Items simmered in sauce, such as sea eel (*anago*) or clams (*hamaguri*), can come next. Omelet (*tamago yaki*) at this time is also fine. Finally, you eat the rolled items (*norimaki*): tuna roll (*tekka maki*), cucumber roll (*kappa maki*), gourd roll (*kanpyō maki*). Ordering the rolls is a signal to the chef that you are about to finish. In between types of fish, eat the pickled ginger to refresh your palate for the next items. Midway through or almost near the end, you can order miso or a clear soup (*osuimono*).

Nevertheless, according to the ninth-generation owner of a historical sushi restaurant, one should just eat whatever one fancies, without paying attention to any particular order. Additionally, this classic sushi restaurant does not allow a customer to order *omakase* (chef's choice). Sushi, he said, should reflect your personal choice, not anyone else's—not even the chef's, no matter how famous. Moreover, if this is your first time to order directly from the *itamae* (chef) of a specialist sushi restaurant, he has no idea what your preferences are, and by ordering *omakase* he may end up giving you items you may not care for.

CHAPTER TEN

# Food Issues and Dietary Concerns

## Introduction

The issues that affect Japanese food today are not so different from those that affect food and food culture worldwide. Food safety and food security top the list. Food safety is critically important to Japan because 60% of its food supplies are imported. Despite being banned, pesticides, antibiotics, and other toxic chemical additives in fresh and frozen foods are revealed by testing in 10% of all incoming food supplies, and the greatest number of violations in recent years have been found in shipments from China, which supplies 15% of Japan's food imports. Frozen spinach in 2002, and milk and other dairy products in 2016, are among the China-sourced products that have caused grave problems.

Another food safety concern is the impact of radioactivity on food products as a result of the Fukushima Daiichi Nuclear Power Plant accident in 2011. Radioactivity levels are under constant monitoring, and fruits and vegetables from agricultural production around the accident area have levels deemed safe. However, wild foods, such as game animals, mountain vegetables, wild herbs, and wild fungi sourced from the immediate area are not advisable for human consumption.

Within the umbrella of food safety are the environmental conditions under which foods are grown. Contamination of soil and water from chemical pollution as a byproduct of industrial processes, or from chemicals leached to nearby agricultural farms as a result of the maintenance of golf courses, are included as well. Measures to protect the consumer and allay public concern include legal measures, such as the Food Safety Basic Act and the establishment of the Consumer Affairs Agency and the Food Safety Commission.

Tied in to food safety is food security, because of Japan's low rate of food self-sufficiency. In 1960, Japan's self-sufficiency ratio stood at 79%, but it has been steadily declining since, and currently hovers between 37% and 39%. The New Basic Law on Food, Agriculture, and Rural Areas of 1999 had set a target rate of 45% self-sufficiency by 2010. Unfortunately this target ratio was not reached, and a New Basic Plan set a new target date to meet this ratio by 2015, which also was not reached. The current government is in the process of revising this law yet again.

Additionally, Japan has its own set of food concerns, which include the disappearance of traditional foods and foodways, declining self-sufficiency in food, massive amounts of food waste, the threat of extinction of major food species such as eel and maguro, and a set of food problems with its own unique epithet—the seven *koshoku* (food-related issues).

The seven *koshoku* are current problems concerning food and eating (*shoku*). The issues are all preceded by the syllable *ko*, but each is written with a different ideograph (*kanji*).

The first *koshoku* highlights individual eating: it refers to an all-too-common contemporary dining scenario where a family sits around the same table, but each member eats a different kind of food, according to his or her individual preference. The convenience of ready-prepared food that can be heated quickly in the microwave has made this kind of eating a usual occurrence not only in Japan, but also in other highly developed countries.

The second *koshoku* is eating on one's own, without company, due to family members' schedules not coinciding with meal times.

The third *koshoku* is flour-based foods, such as pizza, noodles, and bread, rather than the traditional staple of rice. Mainly as a result of the increasing Westernization of the Japanese contemporary diet, children and young adults (in common with their contemporaries the world over) tend to prefer pizza, pasta, and burgers. Japanese family-oriented restaurants overwhelmingly cater to this preference with their Japanized versions of these globally popular dishes.

The fourth *koshoku* is an unvaried, unchanging diet, based only on the foods that one likes. The risk of nutritional imbalance is high with this type of diet.

The fifth *koshoku* calls out small meals and undernourishment, due to conscious reduction of caloric intake, and this mainly affects the female population. Undernourishment also affects those who live below the poverty line, a hidden proportion of the Japanese population totaling around 20 million. Current statistics put this vulnerable group, which includes the homeless, the elderly, and single parents, at 1 in 6.

## Food Issues and Dietary Concerns

The sixth *koshoku*, relating to thick or rich food, refers to foods and dishes that are highly seasoned and complex, such that the flavors of the original ingredients are no longer discernible. It also includes foods of high caloric value, such as steaks, in particular those made from Japanese beef (*wagyū*), which are specifically bred to have marbled fat running throughout the flesh. This category of foods also includes a diet rich in dairy products, such as cheese and milk, as well as food products that contain high amounts of refined sugar, such as pastries, cakes, and ice cream (which has both high-fat cream and sugar). Middle-aged men in particular, and to a certain extent middle-aged women as well, are highly susceptible to metabolic diseases, such as diabetes and arteriosclerosis, from their high intake of these rich foods.

The seventh *koshoku* refers to children eating on their own. Either they prepare instant or microwaveable food by themselves, or they buy processed, ready-prepared food from convenience stores, due to both parents working long hours.

Recently, a further two *koshoku* have been cited. One is frequent dining out or eating ready-processed foods, and rarely having the opportunity to have a home-cooked meal. The other is hollow or empty food, referring to the habit of skipping breakfast before leaving home in the morning, due to lack of appetite or time.

These food-related problems have raised nationwide concerns, mainly because they not only affect individual and family eating, nutrition, and health, but also have wider and graver repercussions for Japanese society and Japanese food culture. Foremost is the erosion of the traditional Japanese meal, *washoku*, based on rice, miso soup, and two or three side dishes. The contributing factors are the increasing Westernization of Japanese meals, the increase in mothers working outside the home, the lack of time to cook meals (let alone the traditional *washoku* meal) at home, the convenience of ready-prepared foods and the variety and quality offered at department store food sections (*depa chika*), and frequent dining out.

Furthermore, when children eat on their own, they are not benefiting from the cultural and social opportunities for conversation and interaction with their parents. Additionally, they are missing opportunities for learning good manners: not only how to eat properly, but also the habitual use of the traditional table greetings exchanged between diners and the cook. The diner (whether a child or an adult) is expected, before partaking of food, to say *itadakimasu* ("I am eating/receiving"). When a diner has finished, the polite greeting is *gochisōsama deshita* ("that was a feast"). The response of the cook, or the parent sitting at the table, to the first greeting is *dōzō omeshiagari* ("please eat"). The post-meal response to *gochisosama deshita* is *iie, dō itashimashite* ("no, not at all"). When the person who has prepared the meal is not present, or the diner himself or herself is the one responsible for having prepared the food (even partially) or for having put the food on the table by buying it ready-prepared, it makes little sense to say these traditional greetings of gratitude. For older individuals eating on their own, the continued lack of social interaction also has a negative effect on well-being, and ultimately on health.

In 2005, the Basic Law on *Shokuiku* (Food and Nutrition Education) and in 2008, the School Health Law were passed, aimed to educate the younger generation and to provide a wider and deeper understanding, as well as appreciation, of where food comes from and the processes involved—farming, fishing, fermentation. Each participating region is encouraged to showcase local and regional specialties with the joint participation of parents and children. It is to counteract the threatened disappearance of traditional Japanese food and food culture, as well as the increasing Westernization of people's daily meals, that made Japan apply to UNESCO to recognize *washoku*, the traditional dietary cultures of the Japanese, as part of world cultural heritage. In 2016, the Third Basic Program for *Shokuiku* Promotion, a five-year program, was initiated. It is interesting that the first recommendation of the dietary guidelines of the program for food and dietary education is enjoyment and pleasure: to enjoy meals, to have pleasure during eating, and to delight in the different aspects of a meal; not only the taste or deliciousness of the foodstuffs themselves, but also all the peripheral elements, such as the atmosphere of the physical location of the meal, and the joy of being in company while eating the meal. The second to the seventh recommendations focus on health. Recommendation number 2 is to keep regular meal times and in so doing set a healthy rhythm to one's lifestyle. The third recommendation advises getting sufficient exercise and eating well-balanced meals to maintain a healthy weight. The fourth defines what a well-balanced meal is: a staple with a main dish and side dishes. The fifth elucidates that staples consist of grains such as rice and different cereals. The sixth further develops the theme of balancing one's diet with vegetables, fruits, dairy products, beans, and fish. It is interesting that meat is not mentioned, perhaps an acknowledgment that meat has become conspicuous and ubiquitous in contemporary Japanese diets. The seventh refers to balancing the elements of salt and fat in one's diet. The eighth recommendation addresses the issue of the current nature of the Japanese diet. With its increasing Westernization and exposure to foreign foods, it is losing touch with local traditional dishes and local food products. The ninth

*Food Issues and Dietary Concerns*

recommendation refers to food loss and food waste, and suggests conservation of food resources.

The final recommendation reinforces and sums up the previous ones, and advises developing an understanding of food and evaluating one's dietary life.

The novel coronavirus pandemic and the nationwide emergency measures to contain the spread of infection beginning in March 2020 have resulted in changes in contemporary dietary life. With people working from home and schoolchildren being home-schooled, there has been an increase in home cooking and baking, and opportunities for families to prepare and share meals together. A greater awareness of the role of food in maintaining health has been another positive outcome, as evidenced by the increased consumption since the beginning of the pandemic of *nattō*, a fermented soybean product, reputed to promote intestinal and general health.

## Food Self-Sufficiency and Food Safety

Japan relies on imports for much of its food ingredients. Its food self-sufficiency rate fluctuates between 37% and 39%, the lowest rate among the world's developed countries (the United States is at 124%, France at 111%, and Germany at 80%). Once the biggest fishing nation in the world, with its own fish production supplying 113% of its needs in 1964, its self-sufficiency rate for fish and seafood had decreased to 59% as of 2018. Its self-sufficiency rate for meat is at 51%, meaning that almost half of all the meat consumed in Japan, whether as fresh or frozen raw material or processed meat products, comes from other countries. The current government's goal is to increase the self-sufficiency rate to 45% by 2025. This low self-sufficiency rate is a matter of concern for reasons of food safety and food security.

In 2008, the fast-food chain Saezeriya found its pizza dough contaminated with the chemical melamine, traced to the use of powdered milk and other dairy products imported from China. Twenty other food manufacturers are known to have sourced dairy products from China that have been similarly contaminated with melamine. This scandal raised concerns about the safety of imported food ingredients—most recently poisoned chicken meat—from China.

Because of public disapproval, genetically modified (GM) crops are not planted in Japan (with the exception of the blue rose, developed by a Japanese-Australian joint venture). However, 238 foods and food additives derived from genetically modified materials have been tested and approved by the government for commercial use in Japan, making it a great importer (and the largest in East Asia) of genetically modified processed food and livestock feed. Among these are 8 types of potato, 15 types of soybean, and 198 types of corn. The Japan Consumers Cooperatives Union (JCCU) estimated the following percentages of genetically modified foods consumed by the Japanese: 68.7% of corn, 64.5% of soybean, 68.5% of canola (rapeseed), and 81.7% of cotton seed. GM corn is made into snack foods, cornstarch, popcorn, canned and bottled corn. GM soybeans are made into tofu and other tofu products, such as freeze-dried tofu (*kōya dōfu*), soy milk, soybean flour (*kinako*), and miso. GM potatoes are made into snack foods and potato starch. Many Japanese livestock farmers depend on GM crops such as alfalfa and corn to feed their animals.

The majority of Japanese consumers are unaware of just how much genetically modified content arrives at their dining table. The reason is because of the terms of the Japanese Food Labeling Act (FLA). A Japanese food manufacturer is permitted to label its processed foods "GM-free" despite those foods having GM ingredients, provided the GM component is not greater than 5% of the processed food item's total contents (in contrast to the United States' 0.9%), and provided it is not one of the major three ingredients. The high rate of GM-containing foods being consumed in Japan is a consequence of the country's low self-sufficiency in food, which fell to 37% in September 2018, thus requiring massive imports.

## Grass-Roots Food Cooperatives and Community-Supported Agriculture

Concerns about food safety are not a recent phenomenon. Since the late 1960s to early 1970s, small-scale, nonprofit mutually beneficial partnerships between consumers (*teikei*) and local food producers using organic methods of agriculture have been directly supplying families with vegetables, eggs, milk, meat, and condiments such as soy sauce and miso. The Teikei Movement comprises 650 groups throughout Japan, with 16 million members, and is said to have inspired community-supported agriculture in the United States and other countries. Consumers agree to support food producers by accepting a regularly delivered box, the contents of which depend on seasonally available produce. The boxes are delivered to a central collection point, and consumers pick up their boxes directly or take turns doing small group pick-ups. One of the basic principles of the Teikei Movement is personal interaction between producers and consumers.

Food Issues and Dietary Concerns

Most producers invite consumers to regular events, such as festivals, or hold cooking workshops (especially for the younger generation which has little experience of cooking). The Teikei Movement partners with the Japan Organic Agriculture Association.

Another active food cooperative is the Seikatsu Club, founded in 1965 (around the same time as the Teikei Movement) by women who wanted to offer safe food to their members at reasonable prices. Currently comprised of 340,000 members in 21 prefectures, the Seikatsu Club offers 1,700 food products ranging from rice, milk, and eggs, to fresh fruits and vegetables, meat, fish, and processed foodstuffs. It established its own milk cooperative, comprising 100 milk producers, to ensure a higher quality of milk—pasteurized, instead of the prevalent ultra-high-temperature sterilized milk. The Club also conducts research on food quality and how to reduce food waste and harmful chemicals. In its partnership with small-scale farmers and food producers, it supports their transition from conventional, chemically dependent agricultural production to sustainable systems. In an effort to help increase Japan's self-sufficiency ratio in grain (currently at 27%, including livestock feed), it persuaded the government to fund the cultivation of feed rice on 400,000 hectares of fallow farm land, a move calculated to increase the country's self-sufficiency ratio in grain by 5%. The Seikatsu Club recently signed an agreement with a major U.S. company to supply non-GM corn for livestock feed from 2023 onward. The Club received the Right Livelihood Award (also known as the alternative Nobel Prize) in 1989 for its pioneering work to provide an alternative to highly industrialized, chemically grown food.

*Anzen na Tabemono wo Tsukutte Taberu Kai* (Group for the Consumption and Production of Safe Foods) was founded in 1974 as a direct-marketing partnership (*teikei*) between producers and consumers in the small farming community of Miyoshi in Chiba Prefecture. The founding group, constituted of well-educated, middle-class women in their twenties and thirties who had read Rachel Carson's *Silent Spring*, formed a study group on the technical aspects of organic agriculture, as well as the international political aspects of food and agriculture. They managed to convince 19 farmers to switch to organic methods of production by guaranteeing that they would purchase whatever the farmers produced. The organization has since grown to 36 producers of more than 100 different crops and 1000 consumer members. The threat of a golf course being built near the farms, and exposing them to the carcinogenic "red water" (trihalomethane) produced during golf course maintenance, further mobilized the group into protecting the safety of the crops produced in adjoining fields. Using the tactic of Trees in Trust (*Tachiki Trust*), they convinced more than 3,000 people to buy trees that were on private lands bordering the planned golf course, which successfully halted the planned construction.

The Japan Consumers' Cooperatives Union (JCCU, *Nisseikyo*) and the Japan Organic Agriculture Association supported the anti-golf course campaign. The JCCU is the umbrella organization of consumers' cooperatives in Japan with a total membership of 60 million. Most of the member cooperatives are based on mutually beneficial partnerships between organic food producers and consumers. Annual gross sales in 2,668 JCCU-affiliated shops nationwide total 3.5 trillion yen (about US$30.5 billion). Altogether, almost half of the Japanese population depends on consumer cooperatives to supply their food and household needs.

## Emergency Food Stocks

That Japan imports more than 60% of its food supplies is a matter of grave concern, particularly in the event of natural disasters. Geographically, Japan is situated in the Ring of Fire, a region in the Pacific Ocean always at risk of earthquakes, volcanic eruptions, and tsunamis. Moreover, it is also on the path of frequent typhoons, whose destructiveness left thousands homeless in 2019 alone due to damage to homes and flooding from overflowing rivers. Through the Ministry of Agriculture, Forests, and Fisheries website and other media, the government is promoting the idea of having on hand at least one week's supply of food in the form of canned, freeze-dried, or microwaveable items, or those that only need boiling water to prepare. To get people accustomed to using and eating these emergency foods, it is suggested to incorporate them into the daily diet, so that the emergency food stocks are kept up to date. The general populace is reminded that it is not only disasters, but also unexpected illness and other unforeseen events for which these emergency food stocks can come in handy.

The Fukushima Daiichi Nuclear Power Plant meltdown as a result of tsunami damage has made foodstuffs grown in Fukushima highly suspect. However, constant monitoring of radiation levels since the 2011 meltdown has reassured the general populace that the majority of vegetables, meat, fish, and other seafood from Fukushima have been tested and found to contain acceptable levels of radiation. The exception is food sourced from the wild, such as wild game (boar, deer, birds), wild mushrooms, and mountain vegetables, whose radiation levels continue to fluctuate.

## Whaling and Depletion of Atlantic Blue-Fin Tuna and Japanese Eel

In July 2019, Japan opted out of the International Whaling Commission and resumed commercial whaling, despite global opprobrium, partly to provide employment in former traditional whaling regions and partly to provide an alternative source of protein. The whale catch cap is 227 this year (150 Bryde's whales, 25 sei whales, and 52 minke whales), which they say is less than the 333 that would have been caught under the agreement for research purposes with the IWC. Whaling will be within Japan's exclusive economic zone. In contrast to whale meat, which has ceased to be a regular foodstuff since the 1970s (except in traditional whaling communities), two commonly eaten marine species are at risk of extinction. On the endangered list is the Japanese freshwater eel (*Anguila japonica*), the main ingredient of a traditional dish eaten during the hottest days of summer as it is believed to provide stamina. The reasons for the eel's extinction include changes in ocean conditions, habitat loss, pollution, and overfishing. Japan is the world's highest consumer of eels, eating about two-thirds of the global eel catch. Another important ingredient in the Japanese diet, and now throughout the world, is the *maguro* (Atlantic blue-fin tuna, *Thunnus thynnus*), also threatened by extinction due to its popularity as an ingredient in sushi and sashimi.

Japan's traditional whaling communities are located in Wakayama, Shizuoka, Chiba, Northern Kyushu, Yamaguchi, and Hokkaido. The resumption of commercial whaling has been met with mixed feelings. On the one hand, Japanese whalers will only be fishing in Japanese territorial waters, and thus their catch is limited. On the other hand, they will not be receiving any of the government subsidies that they received during the whaling moratorium. Whalers risk not making any profit, because whale meat consumption has decreased to 1/50th of what it was in the 1960s when total annual consumption was at 200,000 tons. It remains to be seen whether whale fishing will continue as a viable industry.

About 1 million tons of frozen whale meat have been stockpiled for school lunches, although schoolchildren dislike it the most of all ingredients used in school lunches. The most common way of eating whale meat these days is as sashimi and deep-fried *tatsuta age*.

The two recipes that follow date from 1971, 18 years before commercial whaling ceased in 1988 [translated and adapted from *Osōzai 12 ka Getsu* (12 Months of Side Dishes)]. They are included here not to advocate the continued eating of whale meat, or to support the recent commercialization of whale fishing, but as information on traditional food culture.

## Grilled Whale Meat and Chinese Cabbage Salad in Mustard Dressing, *Kujira to Hakusai no Karashiae*

*Yield:* 4 servings

**Ingredients**
1 ¼ pounds red whale meat
2 tablespoons soy sauce
1 tablespoon mirin
1 tablespoon oil
1 ½ pounds Chinese cabbage
1 pinch salt

**Mustard dressing**
2 heaping tablespoons mustard powder
2 tablespoons hot water
3 tablespoons soy sauce
1 heaping tablespoon sugar
1 teaspoon *dashi* powder
1 teaspoon lemon juice, or more as needed
Finely sliced zest of 1 lemon, for garnish

**Procedure**
1. Slice the whale meat into large pieces about ¼-inch thick.
2. Marinate in the 2 tablespoons soy sauce, mirin, and oil for 5–8 minutes.
3. Grill the whale meat over charcoal until both sides are browned. Let cool to room temperature.
4. Wash the Chinese cabbage well, and cut in half lengthwise. Cut off and discard the core. Slice the Chinese cabbage into 1 ½ inch lengths.
5. In a large pan of boiling water, add a pinch of salt, and briefly parboil the Chinese cabbage slices. They should still be crisp.
6. Remove the Chinese cabbage slices from the pan and drain well. Press gently to extract as much excess water as possible.
7. In a mixing bowl, place the drained Chinese cabbage.
8. Slice the cooled grilled whale meat into bite-size pieces, and add to the cabbage in the bowl.
9. In a small bowl, mix the mustard dressing ingredients. Dissolve the mustard powder into the hot water. Add soy sauce, sugar, and *dashi* powder. Stir in the lemon juice.
10. Taste the dressing, and adjust the seasoning, adding more lemon juice or other ingredients to your taste.
11. Combine the dressing well with the Chinese cabbage and whale meat.

*To serve: Mound the salad into individual bowls. Garnish each serving with the finely sliced lemon zest.*

## Braised Whale Meat, *Kujira no Kakuni*

*Kakuni* is a dish most commonly made from belly pork. This recipe from 1971 is another traditional use of whale meat, when meat shortages made it an inexpensive source of protein. The recipe uses meat from the whale's tail, which, because it is streaked with fat, is suitable for braising. Marinating with fresh ginger neutralizes the characteristic smell of whale meat. [As with the preceding recipe, this is translated and adapted from *Osōzai 12 ka Getsu* (12 Months of Side Dishes)], and is included here only as an example of traditional dishes— not to support whale fishing.)

*Yield:* 8–10 servings

**Ingredients**
2 pounds fatty whale meat, cut from the tail end, frozen
1 teaspoon salt
3 tablespoons finely grated fresh ginger
1 cup *sake*
7 tablespoons sugar
6 tablespoons soy sauce
1 cucumber, peeled and sliced into small cubes

**Procedure**
1. Thaw the frozen whale meat, and slice into 2 or 3 large pieces.
2. Wash the whale meat well. In a large bowl, put the whale meat to soak in plenty of water with 1 teaspoon salt for 30 minutes to 1 hour.
3. Drain the whale meat, place in a large colander, and pour boiling water over all the meat's surfaces.
4. Place the whale meat in a heavy-bottomed pan, add 8 cups of water and 1 cup of *sake*, and bring to a rolling boil over high heat.
5. Reduce the heat, and let the whale meat simmer, uncovered. Skim all froth that rises to the surface.
6. When the water has been reduced by about half, add the grated ginger, and add 4 cups of water. Continue to simmer for about 2 hours.
7. Test for tenderness by sticking a chopstick through the whale meat. If it pierces through without any resistance, add the sugar. Once the sugar is thoroughly melted, stir in the soy sauce. Simmer for another 30 minutes.
8. The braising liquid should be thick but still fluid at the end of braising. Add a bit more water if needed to get it to the consistency of fluid sauce.

*To serve as* otsumami *(little bites to go with drinks): Thread on small bamboo skewers, alternating with small cubes of cucumber.*

## Food Waste and Food Loss

Notwithstanding Japan's low rate of food self-sufficiency, every year since 2012, between 5 million and 8 million tons of food are wasted. To put this amount of food loss into perspective, this is the equivalent of the amount of rice produced in Japan in one year. Half of the food loss is from households: about 20% of all household raw garbage consists of uneaten food products and foods thrown out before their expiration date. The other half of nationwide food loss is from food products that have remained unsold because their sell-by date has passed. The main reason is the Rule of Thirds in food distribution from manufacturers to retailers. A processed food item with a shelf-life of six months has to be delivered to retailers within two months (one-third of its shelf-life) of its manufacture. If not so delivered, retailers have the right to cancel the order or return the goods to the manufacturer, which then resells the goods to discount stores or flags them for quick sale, leading to massive profit loss for the manufacturer. Eventually, if unsold, the processed food items are thrown out even though they are still edible. Food loss in Japan is equal to the amount of food aid worldwide. In May 2019, the Japanese Parliament passed the Food Waste Reduction Law, which makes the national government and local authorities responsible for reducing food waste.

Second Harvest Japan, initiated in 2000, is a nongovernmental organization that addresses food waste, food loss, and food inequality through food banks and community-supported family dining rooms. The first food bank was set up in Tokyo in 2002. By 2017, there were 77 food banks; these collect products donated by large supermarkets and individuals, and distribute the products for free to welfare institutions, such as orphanages, after-school day care facilities for physically disadvantaged children, single-parent families, or homeless support groups. Despite the general affluence of Japanese society, between 15.6% of the total population and 16.3% of children under 18 live below the poverty line, defined as half the median amount of household disposable income of the total population. In the Kansai region, for instance, around 10,000 individuals in 100 institutions are fed monthly through food banks.

Community institutions partner with food banks to provide solutions to certain food-related issues. One such institution is *Kodomo Shokudō* (Children's Cafeteria), which provides supper to children for free or a low price, so that they do not have to eat alone or go hungry. In Fukushima, where many have not completely recovered from the aftermath of the nuclear reactor meltdown, an *Oyako Shokudō* (Parents and Children Cafeteria) program ensures that not only children, but entire families as well,

*Food Issues and Dietary Concerns*

whose lives and communities have been disrupted by the disaster, have an evening meal which participants prepare together. By hosting the meal and serving adults, children unlearn bad eating habits developed from eating on their own, and learn good manners and how to communicate with people other than their immediate family. The social interaction among different generations also provides opportunities for friendship and emotional comfort.

## Revitalizing Traditional Food Culture

The increasing Westernization of Japanese meals dismays the older generation, who note that while urban children are familiar with Western dishes such as "stew" and "salad," they are unfamiliar with the Japanese slow-cooked dish *nimono*, which is prepared similar to stew, or the Japanese dressed salad called *aemono*. The traditional New Year celebratory soup known as *ozōni* is also among the foods that young children are no longer acquainted with. Numerous factors have led to the loss of knowledge about traditional foods. First is the migration of young adults toward cosmopolitan areas, who then set up their own households there, cut off from their local or regional food cultures. Certain crops are highly specific to their locality and, for reasons of volume or lack of general demand, are not available for sale in city supermarkets, which are supplied by large-scale food suppliers. Vegetables typical of southern Japan, such as bitter melon (*niga uri*) and christophene or chayote (*hayato uri*), or the heirloom vegetables of Kyoto, rarely make it to neighborhood supermarkets in Tokyo. Without the familiar cycle of regional events such as festivals and local community activities, young families gradually take on a cosmopolitan, highly Westernized food culture.

---

### Kyoto Braised Taro and Salt Cod, *Imobō no Taitan*

This traditional dish is largely unknown to younger Kyotoites. *Imobō no taitan*, or *imobō* for short, is a braised dish (*taitan*), typical of home-style Kyoto dishes called *obanzai*. It is made of dried salted cod, a staple of the Kyoto kitchen since ancient times, when fresh sea fish was not to be had, because of Kyoto's distance from the sea. It is lightly salted, and is akin to the salted dried cod, much used in Spanish and Portuguese cooking, called *bacalao*. Substitute the more readily available *bacalao* from Mediterranean or Caribbean food shops. Kyoto salted dried cod was traditionally rehydrated in water that had been used to wash rice, but regular water is fine.

A special kind of taro, called *ebi imo* ("shrimp taro"), because its curved shape resembles cooked shrimp, is the traditional complement to salt cod in this dish. This type of taro is a specialty product of Kyoto, and is marketed as a branded vegetable, because its quality and flavor are unmatched. Production has now spread to other regions, with Shizuoka Prefecture producing 80% of the country's *ebi imo*. As well as being a well-loved everyday side dish, *imobō* is also a New Year dish in Kyoto. The braising process enables the flavor of the salt cod to seep into the taro, and the viscosity of the taro juices prevents the cod from disintegrating during cooking.

*Yield:* 4 servings

**Ingredients**
1 pound *ebi imo* (shrimp-shaped taro) or regular taro
⅔ pound dried salt cod (*bacalao*)
2 cups *dashi*
½ cup *sake*
2 tablespoons mirin
1 ½ tablespoons sugar
3 tablespoons soy sauce
3 tablespoons light soy sauce
½ *yuzu* zest, or lemon zest, very finely sliced, for garnish

**Procedure**
1. Peel the taro, slice into large chunks, and soak in plenty of cold water to cover for 30 minutes or longer to remove any irritants (*aku*).
2. Soak the dried salt cod to rehydrate in water that has been used to wash rice or regular tap water. Soak for 24 hours, and change water twice during that period. Once rehydrated, wash and rinse well.
3. Slice the rehydrated cod into large chunks, and place in a heavy-bottomed pan. Add the *dashi* and *sake*, and simmer all at low heat.
4. Add the taro slices to the pan to simmer until tender, about 30 minutes, or until a bamboo skewer can pierce it through without resistance.
5. Once the taro is tender, add the mirin, sugar, regular soy sauce and light soy sauce.
6. Let everything gently simmer until flavor has penetrated through to the taro and salted cod.
7. Remove the taro slices and cod, and set aside until needed.
8. Reduce the braising liquid left in the pan to about half.

*To serve: Place the taro slices and the cod in individual serving bowls, and pour the reduced braising liquid over them.*

*Garnish with finely sliced yuzu or lemon zest.*

*Food Issues and Dietary Concerns* 197

This worrying trend is, hopefully, being reversed. There are ongoing programs to entice young families to settle in underpopulated rural areas and to encourage the younger generation, especially young women, to take up land-based occupations such as farming. These regional revitalization programs offer training in how to raise vegetables and fruit organically, and additionally, how to process these into products that would appeal to cosmopolitan consumers, in the form of Westernized products such as jams, jellies, and fruit juices. One recent endeavor is a restaurant in Nara, opened in a renovated 250-year-old country house, which prepares traditional heirloom vegetables in innovative dishes. The vegetables are grown organically by local farmers, some of whom have newly taken up vegetable growing.

The central government's dietary education (*shokuiku*) promotion scheme has stimulated supportive regional events. In Yamaguchi Prefecture, traditional local dishes are being incorporated into school lunches. Parents and their children are invited to participate in workshops where they learn how to prepare regional specialties, such as *kenchō*, a side dish of braised seasonal vegetables.

## Yamaguchi Traditional Vegetable Stew, *Kenchō*

Regional dishes such as *kenchō* from Yamaguchi Prefecture are increasingly disappearing, overshadowed by global foods such as pizza, spaghetti, and hamburger among the younger generation. To showcase traditional dishes, one school district in Yamaguchi declared November 14 as regional food day and features *kenchō* in the school lunch menu for primary and middle school students. Another food education activity is demonstrating how food gets from the farm to the table. Vegetable beds are jointly planted and cared for by students and the school lunch staff. The harvested vegetables are then included in school meals.

The basic ingredients for *kenchō* are giant radish, carrots, and tofu—ingredients most often found in the Japanese kitchen. Seasonings are soy sauce and mirin. You may also add *shiitake* mushrooms or *aburaage* (pre-fried tofu), as well as *konnyaku* (devil's tongue root). A modern addition is chicken pieces, but purists insist that *kenchō* is a purely vegetable dish. Like all stewed dishes, *kenchō* tastes even better the following day, as the vegetables will have fully absorbed the seasonings and their flavors will have melded together.

*Yield:* 4 servings

**Ingredients**
1 block firm tofu (cotton-filtered *momen dōfu*)
2 pounds giant radish, peeled
1 large carrot, peeled
2 tablespoons oil
1 cup water
3 tablespoons soy sauce
1 teaspoon *dashi* powder
3 tablespoons mirin

**Procedure**
1. Place tofu between 2 cutting boards or plates, with a weight on top (such as canned food) to extract as much water as possible.
2. Cut the giant radish and carrot in half lengthwise, and slice into fine half-rings.
3. In a frying pan over medium heat, put the oil. Once it is hot, add the tofu and stir-fry it, at the same time mashing it with a wooden spoon into tiny pieces.
4. Add the giant radish and carrot slices, and continue to stir-fry them for about 10 minutes, or until the heat has penetrated them.
5. Stir in the water, soy sauce, *dashi* powder, and mirin, and turn the heat to low.
6. Let everything simmer until only a small amount of broth remains. Turn off the heat.

*To serve: Mound the* kenchō *in individual bowls and serve as a side dish.*

## Globalization of Japanese Food

The worldwide popularization of Japanese food has both positive and negative aspects. The number of restaurants outside Japan that serve Japanese food reached more than 117,000 in 2017, and an international survey of people's choices when dining out puts Japanese food in the top three. However, not all of these serve authentic Japanese dishes—a situation that led to an unsuccessful attempt by the Japanese government to certify Japanese restaurants abroad. Japanese food presentation and aesthetic styling; Japanese food preparation techniques, such as *tataki*, lactic acid and *kōji* (rice fungus) fermentation; and ingredients such as *panko*, miso, *shisō*, *shiitake*, *enokidake*, and *yuzu* are increasingly being applied to non-Japanese foods worldwide, sometimes leading to a harmonious fusion, but oftentimes puzzling local diners. This was the case recently in a small Valencian town with an innovative chef who had included salmon *tataki* on his menu without any explanation, leading locals to return the dish to the kitchen, complaining that it was not fully cooked.

In Spain, the Japanese demand for fish has created an offshore joint-venture company for raising blue-fin tuna in Catalonia, which now supplies European markets with *maguro*, as well as ready-to-eat packaged sushi and sashimi to Spanish supermarkets. Another Japanese company has set up an auxiliary plant in Vigo for processing fresh bonito into *katsuobushi* (bonito flakes for stock). In contrast, chefs of prominent Kyoto *ryōtei* are learning innovative non-Japanese food preparation techniques in a recently created food science laboratory and applying them to traditional Japanese dishes to streamline time-consuming traditional techniques. This trend of mutual borrowing from other food cultures into Japanese food culture, and vice versa, is likely to continue.

### Yellow-Fin Tuna in Ginger Sauce, *Kihada no Shōgayaki*

*Maguro*, the Atlantic blue-fin tuna, is one of the most popular fish for sashimi and sushi in Japan and the world over; hence its increasingly endangered status since 2010. Japan consumes 75% to 80% of the world's catch of blue-fin tuna. At the beginning of 2019, the record price of just over $3 million was bid by a Japanese sushi entrepreneur for a giant *maguro* weighing just over 600 pounds, translating to $5,000 per pound. Rather than the endangered *maguro*, yellow-fin tuna (*kihada*) or long-tail tuna, currently not at risk, is recommended for this dish.

*Yield:* 4 servings

**Ingredients**
2 pounds yellow-fin or long-tail tuna steaks
3 tablespoons oil
2 cups finely sliced giant radish for garnish

**Marinade**
1 ½ tablespoons soy sauce
1 tablespoon *sake*
1 tablespoon sugar

**Sauce**
2-inch piece fresh ginger
1 tablespoon soy sauce
2 tablespoons *sake*
1 tablespoon sugar

**Procedure**
1. Marinate the tuna steaks in 1 ½ tablespoons soy sauce, 1 tablespoon *sake*, and 1 tablespoon sugar for 15–20 minutes.
2. In a frying pan over medium heat, put the oil; when hot, sear the tuna steaks on both sides, then lower the heat and let the steaks continue cooking for 10 minutes. Turn off the heat, and leave the steaks in the pan, as the residual heat will continue to cook the fish. Do not overcook the tuna, as it tends to be rather dry.
3. Peel the ginger and slice into very fine julienne strips. Place it in a small saucepan over medium heat. Stir in the soy sauce, *sake*, and sugar, and simmer for 5–7 minutes. Taste and adjust the seasoning.

*To serve: Place the tuna steaks on individual serving plates and serve with the sauce.*

*Garnish each plate with the finely sliced giant radish.*

These borrowed elements eventually become embedded into the local food culture, such that they are no longer immediately recognizable as their original selves, as has happened before in the case of *rāmen*, *karē raisu*, tempura, and *castella*, which then astonishingly return to their originating food cultures, closing the loop. With digital communication today, what had previously taken years to evolve and become disseminated now takes place almost instantaneously. The global interest in developments in Japanese food and food culture, and their influence on international food and food culture, and vice versa, are sure to continue to engage the attention of many: those who love to eat and cook, as well as those who wish to know more and delve deeper into the background history and processes that have led to the current array of dishes prepared in the Japanese kitchen and served at the Japanese table.

## Food Ethics

A food issue whose importance is increasingly being felt in Japan is a philosophical one, and it concerns food ethics. A renowned Japanese food researcher summed it up thus: How can Japan, which has only 2% of the world's population, justify purchasing so much of the world's food exports? But the real tragedy is that Japan then wastes so much of this food, even while so many people in Japan itself and the rest of the world go hungry. The tenth recommendation of the food and dietary education program addresses this quite aptly. It is perhaps time for Japan as a society to consider a serious ethical evaluation of its dietary life.

# Glossary

**Aburaage**
Fried tofu with a pocket that can be filled.

**Aemono**
Salads of mixed raw and cooked ingredients with a thick dressing.

**Agemono**
Fried dishes.

**Amazake**
Literally, sweet *sake*; alcoholic and nonalcoholic versions are available.

**An**
Sweet bean paste, usually made of red beans (*azuki*) or white beans.

**Arare**
Rice cracker, smaller than *senbei* or *okaki* rice crackers.

**Atsuage**
Thick fried tofu.

**Awamori**
Okinawan alcoholic drink made from sugar cane.

**Ayu**
Sweetfish, *Plecoglossus altivelis*; a small, delicious river fish.

**Azuki**
A small red bean used for sweet bean paste (*an*); considered auspicious for its red color, and mixed with *mochi* rice for celebratory red rice (*sekihan*).

**Bancha**
Ordinary tea from tea leaves and tea stems, usually drunk in summer.

**Batterazushi**
Osaka-style sushi formed in a wooden mold.

**Bentō**
Box lunch, usually with rice and several side dishes; also *obentō*.

**Cha Kaiseki**
Multi-course meal at a tea ceremony.

**Chawanmushi**
A savory steamed custard soup with chicken or fish/seafood, mushrooms, and ginkgo nuts.

**Chirashizushi**
Sushi in which the toppings of vegetables and seafood are scattered over the rice; celebratory dish for Girls Day.

**Chirimenjako**
Sardine fry, in Osaka dialect.

**Chūka Soba**
Chinese noodles, usually served in soup; another name for *rāmen*.

**Daikon**
Giant white radish.

**Dashi**
Stock, commonly made of bonito flakes and kelp; vegetarian *dashi* is made of kelp or dried shiitake mushrooms.

**Depa Chika**
Short for *depāto no chika*, the basement floor of a department store; usually devoted to food ingredients and ready-prepared, cooked dishes.

**Doburoku**
Unfiltered, unpasteurized alcoholic drink made of similar ingredients as *sake*, but not by the same process; lower alcohol content and sweeter than *sake*.

**Donburi**
Rice in a bowl with toppings of various meat or seafood and vegetables.

**Ebi Furai**
Deep-fried, breadcrumb-coated shrimps, a popular main dish.

**Ebisen**
Rice crackers flavored with or pressed with dried shrimp.

**Edomaezushi**
Edo-style hand-shaped sushi; bite-size serving of vinegared rice with raw or cooked fish or seafood or other toppings.

**Ekiben**
Short for *eki bentō*; packed lunch from a train station.

## Glossary

**Enokidake**
White mushroom with thin, needle-like stalks.

**Fukuzai**
Side dish, to complement rice and a main dish.

**Furofuki Daikon**
Cylinders of giant radish (daikon) braised in a broth of *dashi*, soy sauce, and mirin, with miso topping.

**Ganmodoki**
Patty made of tofu mixed with assorted vegetables (literally "ersatz goose"), adapted from Portuguese fritters called *filhós*; see also *hiryōzu*.

**Gohan**
Cooked unflavored rice.

**Gosekku**
Five traditional seasonal celebrations.

**Gūzen Kashi**
Chinese-style sweets made as Buddhist temple offerings.

**Gyokurō**
Literally, "jade dew"; premium green tea.

**Gyūdon**
Beef and sliced leeks on rice in a bowl.

**Gyū Kushi**
Skewered barbecued beef.

**Gyūnabe**
Beef dish, precursor of sukiyaki.

**Hakusai**
Chinese cabbage.

**Hashi Arai**
Literally, chopstick rinse; light broth served during the tea ceremony.

**Hiryōzu**
Osaka term for *ganmodoki*, patty of tofu mixed with assorted vegetables, adapted from the Portuguese fritters *filhós*; also called *hirōsu*.

**Hishio**
Salty fermented seasonings, forerunners of soy sauce.

**Hitashi**
Parboiled green vegetables flavored with *dashi*; also called *ohitashi*.

**Hōchō**
Kitchen knife.

**Ichiban Dashi**
Primary stock, basic stock of seaweed and bonito flakes.

**Ichijū Sansai**
One soup, three side dishes format for a traditional Japanese meal.

**Imonoko Jiru**
Taro soup, an Akita specialty.

**Itamae**
A professional cook; chef of Japanese (usually haute) cuisine. Literally, "before the cutting board."

**Jūbako**
Stacked lacquer or ceramic boxes for New Year and picnic foods.

**Kabayaki**
Grilled eel, especially eaten on the hottest day of summer, to provide stamina and ward off illness.

**Kadomatsu**
New Year decor at entrance of houses and buildings, made of cut green bamboo, pine branches, and mandarin oranges or red berries bound in straw rope.

**Kaiseki Ryōri**
Multicourse banquet, haute cuisine of the Japanese kitchen.

**Kaiten Zushi**
Sushi restaurant where ready-made plates circulate on a conveyor belt.

**Kaki Furai**
Deep-fried, breadcrumb-coated oysters.

**Kamaboko**
Fish loaf; steamed white-fleshed fish paste molded into diverse shapes.

**Kanten**
Gelatin made from agar-agar for making desserts.

**Karaage**
Deep-fried or deep-frying.

**Karē Raisu**
Rice with thick curry-flavored sauce, adapted from British-type curry.

**Kaseita**
Kumamoto sweet pastry named after Portuguese sweet *caixa da marmelada*.

# Glossary

**Kasutera**
Castella sponge cake; a Nagasaki specialty, named after Castilla, an ancient name for Spain.

**Katsudon**
Deep-fried, breadcrumb-coated pork cutlet on rice, served in a bowl.

**Katsuo**
Bonito, *Katsuwonis japonicus*.

**Katsuobushi**
Preserved bonito flakes, used as basis for stock.

**Katsuobushi Kezuriki**
Shaving tool for dried bonito flakes.

**Katsuo Tataki**
Charred rare *katsuo* fillet.

**Kayu**
Rice gruel, also called *okayu*.

**Kazu**
Side dish, also called *okazu*.

**Kibidango**
Sweet balls made of *kibi* millet.

**Kinugoshi Dōfu**
Literally, "silk filter tofu"; fine, soft-textured tofu.

**Kishimen**
Flat wheat noodles, a Nagoya specialty.

**Kōcha**
Black tea, English-type tea.

**Kome**
Uncooked rice, also called *okome*.

**Konbini**
Convenience store or neighborhood store, usually part of a chain, that stocks ready-cooked dishes, groceries, and miscellaneous items.

**Konbu**
Giant kelp; various species of *Laminaria* seaweed for making stock.

**Konnyaku**
Devil's tongue jelly; calorie-free food prized for its texture.

**Konowata**
Condiment of small fish and their innards preserved in salt.

**Konpa**
Drinking party.

**Korokke**
Croquette, usually filled with mashed potato in bechamel sauce.

**Koshihikari**
Premium rice variety.

**Kōya Dōfu**
Freeze-dried tofu; must be reconstituted in water before use.

**Kuzu**
Kudzu vine, *Pueraria lobata*; its starch is used in traditional confectionery and for thickening.

**Makizushi**
Rolled sushi enclosed in nori.

**Manjū**
Steamed buns filled with sweet bean jam (*an*) or with savory fillings of meat and vegetables.

**Matcha**
Powdered green tea used in the tea ceremony.

**Matsuri**
Festival, usually celebrating a Shinto deity or a Buddhist holy day, or other local event.

**Matsutake**
Pine mushroom, prized for its aroma and flavor; an autumn delicacy.

**Meshi**
A meal; another word for cooked rice.

**Mirin**
Sweet rice wine for cooking.

**Miso Shiru**
Staple soup seasoned with salty fermented soybean paste (miso).

**Mitsuba**
Japanese trefoil.

**Mochi**
Glutinous rice cake traditionally eaten for New Year.

**Mochi Gome**
Glutinous or sticky rice variety.

**Momen Dōfu**
Literally, "cotton tofu"; firm tofu.

# Glossary

**Mukōzuke**
First course at a tea ceremony meal.

**Mushimono**
Steamed dishes.

**Myōga**
Pink flower buds (*Zingiber myoga*) pickled or used as garnish.

**Nabemono**
One-pot dish cooked at the table.

**Namban**
"Southern Barbarian"; refers to dishes adopted from Portuguese cooking, or to dishes made with leeks.

**Nameko**
A small viscous mushroom added to soups, *Pholiota nameko*.

**Nanakusa**
Seven herbs added to New Year rice gruel for health.

**Nappa**
Generic name for green leafy vegetables.

**Narezushi**
Forerunner of sushi; whole or sliced fresh fish packed in rice to undergo lactic acid fermentation as a preservative.

**Nattō**
Soybeans fermented in straw, with distinctive smell; breakfast delicacy from the Kantō region.

**Niban Dashi**
Secondary *dashi*, made from ingredients of the primary stock (*ichiban dashi*).

**Niboshi**
Small dried sardines or anchovies for stock.

**Nigirizushi**
Edo-style sushi; bite-size servings of vinegared rice topped with fresh raw or cooked fish, seafood or other ingredient.

**Nihon Shū**
*Sake*.

**Nimono**
Braised or stewed dishes.

**Noh**
Ancient, highly ritualized traditional theater.

**Nomiya**
A drinking place, pub, bar; also called *izakaya*.

**Nori**
Laver; various forms of *Porphyra* algae, dried and pressed into sheets for wrapping rice, sushi.

**Nukazuke**
Vegetables pickled in rice bran.

**Obanzai**
Kyoto home-style cooking.

**Obon**
Day of the Dead in midsummer, when the ancestors return to visit the living.

**Ochazuke**
Cooked rice mixed with tea and soup; popular hangover cure.

**Oden**
Braised vegetables and assorted *kamaboko* often served from a wheelbarrow at night; also available at convenience stores, pubs.

**Ofukuro no Aji**
The taste of mother's cooking; home cooking.

**Okashi**
Confectionery, both Japanese and Western style.

**Okazu**
Side dish in a meal, excluding soup and pickles.

**Okinawa Soba**
Okinawa-style wheat noodles.

**Okonomiyaki**
Large omelet or savory pancake of vegetables, meat/seafood.

**Omakase**
Chef's selection; table d'hôte.

**Omiotsuke**
A poetic name for miso soup.

**Omiyage**
Gift brought back from travel, often a famous local delicacy.

**Omotenashi**
Japanese art of gracious hospitality.

**Omuraisu**
Fried rice covered with plain egg omelet and a dab of ketchup; children's favorite.

# Glossary

**Onigiri**
Rice ball with savory fillings: salted plum, salted salmon.

**Orandani**
Literally, "Holland stew"; method of stewing vegetables or other ingredients by first frying, then simmering in flavored stock.

**Osechi**
Assorted cold dishes prepared for New Year, packed in tiered lacquer boxes called *jūbako*.

**Oshiruko**
Sweet bean soup with small *mochi* balls; a cold weather snack.

**Oshōgatsu**
New Year.

**Osōzai**
Side dish; also called *fukuzai, okazu*.

**Otsumami**
Snacks or appetizers to complement drinks.

**Oyatsu**
Snacks, sweet or salty, eaten between meals.

**Ozōni**
New Year's traditional soup with *mochi*, assorted vegetables; also called *ozōni*.

**Ponzu**
Dipping sauce of soy sauce and citrus juice.

**Rāmen**
Chinese-style noodles; also called *chūka soba*.

**Ramune**
Japanese lemonade in quaint glass bottle with glass stopper.

**Ryōtei**
Exclusive restaurant serving traditional haute cuisine.

**Saka Mai**
Rice variety bred for making *sake*.

*Sake*
Rice wine.

**Sake**
Pronounced "sha-ke," chum salmon.

**Sanbontō**
Artisanal sugar used in traditional confectionery; also called *wasanbon*.

**Sansai**
"Mountain" or wild greens.

**Sansankudō**
"Three-three nine times"; Japanese-style wedding toast with blessed *sake*.

**Sanshō**
Japanese pepper, roasted and ground seeds of *Zanthoxylum piperitum*, related to Sichuan pepper.

**Sashimi**
Thinly sliced raw fish and seafood.

**Sato Imo**
Taro, *Colocasia esculenta*.

**Satsuma Imo**
Sweet potato, *Ipomoea batata*.

**Sekihan**
Red rice, a celebratory food; rice cooked with red *azuki* beans.

**Senbei**
Rice cracker, in sweet and salty flavors.

**Sencha**
Green tea.

**Setsubun**
Ritual on February 2 to exorcise demons.

**Shichigosan**
Autumn ritual to ensure well-being for children aged 3 (*san*), 5 (*go*), and 7 (*shichi*).

**Shichimi Tōgarashi**
Literally, "seven-flavor chili pepper"; dry spice mix comprising *sanshō*, poppy seeds, hemp seeds, sesame seeds (black and/or white), ginger, *nori*, and hot chili; proportions of each spice differ according to the maker.

**Shiitake**
Brown mushroom, *Lentinus edodes*; most frequently used mushroom, fresh or dried, cultivated on logs of Japanese oak (*shii*).

**Shimeji**
Beige- or grey-beige capped mushroom, *Lyophillum* species; commonly used in cooking.

**Shiokara**
Condiment of preserved salted squid.

**Shiozuke**
Salt pickle.

# Glossary

**Shirasu**
Sardine fry (see also *chirimenjako*).

**Shisō**
Aromatic leaves of beefsteak plant, *Perilla frutescens*, used as flavoring, edible garnish; flower stalks (*hōjisō*) similarly used.

**Shōchū**
Liquor distilled from sweet potatoes and other grains.

**Shōgatsu**
New Year.

**Shōjin Ryōri**
Vegetarian cuisine; Buddhist temple cooking.

**Shottsuru**
Fish sauce from northeastern Japan.

**Shōyu**
Soy sauce.

**Shun**
Best time or the season to consume a particular food; usually used in reference to marine foods, vegetables, fruits.

**Shushoku**
Main food, staple.

**Shuzai**
Main side dish.

**Soba**
Japanese buckwheat noodles.

**Sobaya**
Noodle restaurant.

**Sōmen**
Thin wheat noodles, usually eaten cold in summer.

**Sōsu**
Japanese-style Worcestershire sauce; sweeter and thicker than original, also called *osōsu*.

**Suimono**
Generic name for soup and broth.

**Sukiyaki**
Dish of finely sliced meat and vegetables quickly cooked in an iron pan at the table.

**Sunomono**
Foods dressed with vinegar.

**Surimi**
Mock crab and crustaceans made by shredding, compressing, and dyeing fish paste.

**Surume**
Dried squid usually eaten as *otsumami* (drinking snack).

**Sushi**
Vinegar-flavored rice topped with raw or cooked fish and seafood.

**Taiyaki**
Fish-shaped waffle filled with bean jam.

**Takikomi gohan**
Flavored rice cooked with vegetables or meat.

**Takuan**
Pickled giant white radish; commonly eaten pickle.

**Tamari**
Premium grade of soy sauce; preferred for dipping sushi and sashimi.

**Teishoku**
A set meal; table d'hôte.

**Temaki**
Literally, "hand-wrapped"; sushi wrapped in a rolled cone of *nori*.

**Tempura**
Deep-fried, lightly battered small fish, seafood, and vegetables, adapted from 17th-century Portuguese cooking; from Portuguese *temporas*, fish and seafood meals on (Catholic) meatless days.

**Teppanyaki**
Cooking on an iron griddle; usually meat with vegetables.

**Tofu**
Bean curd formed in blocks, made from soybean milk.

**Tonkatsu**
Deep-fried breaded pork cutlet.

**Tororo**
Mountain yam finely grated to a viscous foam, often used as sauce.

**Tsukemono**
Generic term for pickled vegetables.

**Tsukudani**
Foods preserved in soy sauce; long braising in soy sauce and mirin or *sake*.

## Glossary

**Udon**
Thick wheat noodles.

**Umeboshi**
Salted, dried Japanese plum, *Prunus mume*; common pickle.

**Umeshū**
Sweet liqueur of *ume* (Japanese plums), macerated in sugar and alcohol.

**Umi no Sachi**
Literally, "delights of the seas"; food ingredients from the sea.

**U no Hana**
Lees from *tofu* making; used as dressing for *aemono* (salads), for sprinkling over foods as edible garnish.

**Uruchimai**
Regular rice for daily meals; also called *uruchigome*.

**Ustāsōsu**
Japanese-style Worcestershire sauce; also called *sōsu, osōsu*.

**Wabi Cha**
Literally, "impoverished" or "imperfect tea"; tea ceremony school promoted by Sen no Rikyū.

**Wagashi**
Traditional Japanese confectionery.

**Wakame**
*Undaria pinnatifida*, kelp type used in salads, added to soups.

**Wasabi**
Japanese horseradish, *Wasabia japonica*.

**Washoku**
Traditional cuisine and food cultures of Japan.

**Yakimono**
Grilled, roasted, or pan-fried foods.

**Yakiniku**
Grilled or barbecued meat.

**Yakisoba**
Stir-fried Chinese-style noodles.

**Yakitori**
Charcoal-grilled chicken pieces on bamboo skewers.

**Yama imo**
True yams (not sweet potatoes), *Dioscorea* species; also called *Yamato imo*.

**Yama no Sachi**
Literally, "delights of the mountains"; wild or hunted food ingredients.

**Yanakawafū**
Yanakawa style of cooking, originally for eel, with sauce containing burdock, leek, trefoil, and beaten egg.

**Yatai**
Food cart, barrow.

**Yōkan**
Sweet jelly made from agar-agar and sweet bean paste.

**Yuba**
Fresh or dried tofu sheet.

**Yuzu**
Small citrus fruit with prized scent, *Citrus junos*.

**Zaru Soba**
Buckwheat noodles served drained on a flat bamboo colander (*zaru*), eaten with a dipping sauce; preferred style of eating 100% buckwheat noodles by connoisseurs.

# Bibliography

Anderson, Jennifer L. 1991. *Introduction to Japanese Tea Ritual*. Albany: State University of New York Press.
Ashkenazi, Michael, and Jeanne Jacob. 2000. *The Essence of Japanese Cuisine: An Essay on Food and Culture*. Richmond, VA: Curzon Press.
Ashkenazi, Michael, and Jeanne Jacob. 2003. *Food Culture in Japan*. Westport, CT: Greenwood Press.
Assmann, Stephanie. 2010. "Food Action Nippon and Slow Food Japan: The Role of Two Citizen Movements in the Rediscovery of Local Foodways." In *Globalization, Food and Social Identities in the Pacific Region*, edited by James Farrer. Tokyo: Sophia University Institute of Comparative Culture. Republished in *Critical Readings on Food in Asia*, edited by Katarzyna J. Cwiertka, 977–993. Leiden: Brill.
Assmann, Stephanie. 2015. "The Remaking of a National Cuisine: The Food Education Campaign in Japan." In *Globalization and Asian Cuisines: Transnational Networks and Contact Zones*, edited by James Farrer, 165–185. Basingstoke, England: Palgrave Macmillan.
Beatty, Theresa M. 1999. *Food and Recipes of Japan* (Kids in the Kitchen Series). New York: PowerKids Press.
Belleme, John, and Jan Belleme. 1993. *Culinary Treasures of Japan: The Art of Making and Using Traditional Japanese Foods*. Garden City, NY: Avery.
Bestor, Theodore C. 2000. "How Sushi Went Global." *Foreign Policy* (November/December): 54–63.
Bestor, Theodore C. 2001. "Supply Side Sushi: Commodity, Market and the Global City." *American Anthropologist* 103: 76–95.
Bestor, Theodore C. 2004. *Tsukiji: The Fish Market at the Center of the World*. Berkeley: University of California Press.
Booth, Shirley. 1999. *Food of Japan*. London: Grub Street.
Buckley, Sandra, ed. 2002. *Encyclopedia of Contemporary Japanese Culture*. London: Routledge.

Cwiertka, Katarzyna. 1995. "Minekichi Akabori and His Role in the Development of Modem Japanese Cuisine." In *Cooks & Other People: Proceedings of the Oxford Symposium on Food and Cookery*, edited by Harlan Walker, 68–80. Totnes, England: Prospect Books.

Cwiertka, Katarzyna. 1998. "How Cooking Became a Hobby: Changes in Attitude Toward Cooking in Early Twentieth-Century Japan." In *The Culture of Japan as Seen Through Its Leisure*, edited by Sepp Linhart and Sabine Frühstück, 41–58. Albany: State University of New York Press.

Cwiertka, Katarzyna. 1999. *The Making of Modern Culinary Tradition in Japan*. PhD dissertation. University of Leiden.

Cwiertka, Katarzyna. 2003. "Eating the World: Restaurant Culture in Early Twentieth Century Japan." *European Journal of East Asian Studies* 2(1): 89–116.

Cwiertka, Katarzyna. 2004. "Western Food and the Making of the Japanese Nation-State." In *The Politics of Food*, edited by Marianne Lien and Brigitte Nerlich, 121–39. Oxford: Berg Publishers.

Cwiertka, Katarzyna. 2015. *Modern Japanese Cuisine: Food, Power and National Identity*. London: Reaktion Books.

Detrick, Mia, and Kathryn Kleinman. 1983. *Sushi*. San Francisco: Chronicle Books.

Dwyer, Eric, and Ide Risako. 2004. "Japan." In *Teen Life in Asia*, edited by Judith J. Slater, 87–111. Westport, CT: Greenwood Press.

Emi, Kazuko. 2003. *The Japanese Kitchen: A Cook's Guide to Japanese Ingredients*. New York: Southwater.

Harper, Philip. 1998. *The Insider's Guide to Sake*. Tokyo: Kodansha.

Hendry, Joy. 2005. "Japan's Global Village: A View from the World of Leisure." In *A Companion to the Anthropology of Japan*, edited by Jennifer Robertson, 231–43. Malden, MA: Blackwell.

Hosking, Richard. 1996. *A Dictionary of Japanese Food: Ingredients and Culture*. Devon, UK: Prospect Books.

Inglis, David, and Debra Gimlin, eds. 2010. *The Globalization of Food*. Oxford: Berg Publishers.

Ishige, Naomichi. 2001. *The History and Culture of Japanese Food*. London: Kegan Paul.

Jacob, Jeanne, and Michael Ashkenazi. 2014. *The World Cookbook: The Greatest Recipes from around the Globe*. Santa Barbara, CA: Greenwood Press.

Judson, D. H., and Raymond A. Jussame, Jr. 1991. "Household Composition and the Consumption of Fruits and Vegetables in the U.S. and Japan." *Journal of International Consumer Marketing* 3: 73–97.

Kijima, Naomi. 2001. *Bento Boxes: Japanese Meals on the Go*. Translated by Laura Driussi. San Francisco: Japan Publications Trading.

Kimura, Aya Hirata. 2011. "Nationalism, Patriarchy, and Moralism: The Government-Led Food Reform in Contemporary Japan." *Food and Foodways: Explorations in the History and Culture of Human Nourishment* 19(3): 201–27.

# Bibliography

Kinski, Michael. 2010. "How to Eat the Ten Thousand Things: Table Manners in the Edo Period." In *Japanese Foodways: Past and Present*, edited by Eric C. Rath and Stephanie Assmann, 42–67. Urbana: University of Illinois Press.

Konishi, K. 1990. *Entertaining with a Japanese Flavor*. Tokyo: Kodansha International.

Kosaki, Takayuki, and Walter Wagner. 2017. *The Food of Japan: 96 Authentic Recipes from the Land of the Rising Sun*. Tokyo: Tuttle.

Koyama, S. 1981. "A Quantitative Study of Wild Food Resources: An Example from Hida." In *Affluent Foragers: Pacific Coasts East and West. Senri Ethnological Studies 9*, edited by S. Koyama & D. H. Thomas, 91–115. Osaka: National Museum of Ethnology.

Krouse, Carolyn R. 1995. *A Guide to Food Buying in Japan*. Tokyo: Tuttle.

Kushner, Barak. 2012. *Slurp! A Social and Culinary History of Ramen: Japan's Favorite Noodle Soup*. Leiden: Brill.

Matsuyama, T. 1981. Nut-Gathering and Processing Methods in Traditional Japanese Villages. In *Affluent Foragers: Pacific Coasts East and West. Senri Ethnological Studies 9*, edited by S. Koyama & D. H. Thomas, 117–39. Osaka: National Museum of Ethnology.

Mouritsen, Ole G. 2009. *Sushi: Food for the Eye, the Body and the Soul*. New York: Springer Verlag USA.

Nagashima, Yukikazu. 2014 (February 5). UNESCO Japanese Food: Intangible Cultural Heritage. http://www.discovernikkei.org/en/journal/2014/2/5/unesco-washoku

Ogawa, Seiko. 2003. *Easy Japanese Pickling in Five Minutes to One Day*. Tokyo: Graph-Sha.

Ohnuki-Tierney, Emiko. 1994. "Rice as Metaphor of the Japanese Self." In *Paths Toward the Past*, edited by Robert W. Harms, Jan Vansina, and David S. Newbury, 455–72. Atlanta, GA: African Studies Association Press.

Ohnuki-Tierney, Emiko. 1997. "McDonald's in Japan: Changing Manners and Etiquette." In *Golden Arches East: McDonald's in East Asia*, edited by James Watson, 161–82. Stanford, CA: Stanford University Press.

Ohnuki-Tierney, Emiko. 1999. "We Eat Each Other's Food to Nourish Our Body: The Global and the Local as Mutually Constituent Forces." In *Food in Global History*, edited by Raymond Grew, 240–72. Boulder, CO: Westview Press.

Omae, Kinjiro, and Yuzuru Tachibana. 1981. *The Book of Sushi*. Tokyo: Kodansha.

Onabe, Tomoko. 2010. "Bento." In *Japanese Foodways: Past and Present*, edited by Eric C. Rath and Stephanie Assmann, 201–218. Urbana: University of Illinois Press.

Rath, Eric. 2010. *Food and Fantasy in Early Modern Japan*. Oakland: University of California Press.

Rath, Eric. 2010. "Honzen Dining: The Poetry of Formal Meals in Late Medieval and Early Modern Japan." In *Japanese Foodways: Past and Present*, edited by Eric Rath and Stephanie Assmann, 19–41. Urbana: University of Illinois Press.

Redfern, Mary. 2014. "Getting to Grips with Knives, Forks and Spoons: Guides to Western-Style Dining for Japanese Audiences, c. 1800–1875." *Food and Foodways: Explorations in the History and Culture of Human Nourishment* 22(3): 143–174.

Rodriguez del Alisal, Maria Dolores. 2000. "Japanese Lunch Boxes: From Convenient Snack to the Convenience Store." In *Consumption and Material Culture in Contemporary Japan,* edited by Michael Ashkenazi and John Clammer, 40–80. London: Kegan Paul International.

Sakamoto, Rumi, and Matthew Allen. 2011. "There's Something Fishy about That Sushi: How Japan Interprets the Global Sushi Boom." *Japan Forum* 23(1): 99–121.

Salyers, C. 2008. *Face Food: The Visual Creativity of Japanese Bento Boxes*. New York: Mark Batty.

Sansom, George B. 1986. *Japan: A Short Cultural History*. Stanford, CA: Stanford University Press.

Shibusawa, Keizo, ed. 1958. *Japanese Life and Culture in the Meiji Era*. Translated by Charles S. Terry. Tokyo: Obunsha.

Shurtleff, William, and Akiko Aoyagi. 1976. *The Book of Miso*. Hayama-shi, Japan: Autumn Press.

Shurtleff, William, and Akiko Aoyagi. 1979. *The Book of Tofu, Food for Mankind* (vol. 1). New York: Ballantine Books.

Shurtleff, William, and Akiko Aoyagi. 2013. *History of Tofu and Tofu Products (965 CE to 2013)*. Lafayette, CA: Soyinfo Center.

Smith, Stephen R. 1992. "Drinking Etiquette in a Changing Beverage Market." In *Re-made in Japan: Everyday Life and Consumer Taste in a Changing Society*, edited by Joseph Tobin, 143–58. New Haven, CT: Yale University Press.

Sosnoski, Daniel, and Narumi Yasuda. 1996. *Introduction to Japanese Culture*. Tokyo: Tuttle.

Sternsdorff Cisterna, Nicolas. 2014. "On Food and Safety: What Is the Meaning of Safety in Post-Fukushima Japan?" In *To See Once More the Stars. Living in a Post-Fukushima World*, edited by Daisuke Naito, Ryan Syre, Heather Swanson, and Satsuki Takahashi, 74–75. Santa Cruz, CA: New Pacific Press.

Takeda, Hiroko. 2008. "Delicious Food in a Beautiful Country: Nationhood and Nationalism in Discourses on Food in Contemporary Japan." *SEN: Studies in Ethnicity and Nationalism* 8(1): 5–29.

Takeda, Wakako, Cathy Banwell, and Jane Dixon. 2016. "Advancing Food Sovereignty or Nostalgia: The Construction of Japanese Diets in the National Shokuiku Policy." *Anthropological Forum* 26(3): 276–88.

Tamotsu, Aoki. 2001. "The Domestication of Chinese Foodways in Contemporary Japan: Ramen and Peking Duck." In *Changing Chinese Foodways*, edited by David Y. H. Wu and Tan Chee-Beng, 219–36. Hong Kong: The Chinese University Press.

Tanaka, N., and M. Miyoshi. 2012. "School Lunch Program for Health Promotion Among Children in Japan." *Asia Pacific Journal of Clinical Nutrition*, 21(1): 155–58.

Tanaka, Senō, and Sendō Tanaka. 1973. *The Tea Ceremony*. Tokyo: Kodansha International.
Tobin, Joseph. 1992. "Introduction." In *Re-made in Japan: Everyday Life and Consumer Taste in a Changing Society*, edited by Joseph Tobin. New Haven, CT: Yale University Press.
Tokoyama, H., and F. Egaitsu. 1994. "Major Categories of Changes in Food Consumption Patterns in Japan 1963–1991." *Oxford Agrarian Studies* 22: 191–202.
Traphagan, John W., and Keith L. Brown. 2002. "Fast Food and Intergenerational Commensality in Japan: New Styles and Old Patterns." *Ethnology* 41: 119–35.
Tsuji, Kaichi. 1972. *Kaiseki: Zen Tastes in Japanese Cooking*. Kyoto: Kodansha International.
Tsuji, Shizuo. 1980. *Japanese Cooking: A Simple Art*. Tokyo: Kodansha International.
Udesky, James. 1995. *The Book of Soba*. Tokyo: Kodansha.
Varley, H. Paul, and George Elison. 1981. "The Culture of Tea: From Its Origins to Sen no Rikyu." In *Warlords, Artists and Commoners: Japan in the Sixteenth Century*, edited by George Elison and Bardwell Smith, 187–222. Honolulu: University of Hawaii Press.
Varley, H. Paul, and Isao Kumakura, eds. 1989. *Tea in Japan—Essays on the History of Chanoyu*. Honolulu: University of Hawaii Press.
Walraven, Boudewijn. 2002. "Warm Mushroom Sushi? An Afterword." In *Asian Food: The Global and the Local*, edited by Katarzyna Cwiertka and Boudewijn Walraven, 167–73. Richmond, UK: Curzon.
Webb, Lois Sinaiko, Lindsay Grace Cardella, and Jeanne Jacob. 2018. *International Cookbook of Life-Cycle Celebrations*. Santa Barbara, CA: Greenwood.
*The Whale and the Japanese: Traditions of Diet*. Tokyo: Japan Whaling Association.
White, Merry I. 2002. "Ladies Who Lunch: Young Women and the Domestic Fallacy in Japan." In *Asian Food: The Global and the Local*, edited by Katarzyna Cwiertka and Boudewijn Walraven, 63–75. Richmond, UK: Curzon.
Yoneda, Soei. 1982. *Good Food from a Japanese Temple*. Tokyo: Kodansha International.

## Japanese-Language References

Baba, Ichiro. 1976. *Dishes of Japanese Culture*. The Sun Special Issue. Tokyo: Heibonsha.
Fukuda, Hiroshi. 1991. *Edo Ryōri o Tsukuru* [Creating Edo Cuisine]. Tokyo: Kyōiku Sha.
Harada, Nobuo. 2005. *Washoku to Nihon Bunka: Nihon Ryōri no Shakaishi* [Japanese Cuisine and Japanese Culture: A Social History of Cooking]. Tokyo: Shōgakkan.
Kagawa, Aya. 1988. *Uo Gaidobukku* [Fish Guidebook]. Tokyo: Joshi Eiyo Daigaku Shuppanbu.

Kitaoji, Rosanjin, and Masaaki Hirano. 1995. *Rosanjin Midō* [The Taste of Rosanjin]. Tokyo: Chūōkōron Shinsha.
Kojima, Nobuhira. 1971. *Osōzai 12 Kagetsu* [12 Months of Side Dishes]. Tokyo: Kurashi no Techō Sha.
Matsuda, Michiko. 1996. *Shiawase no Gohan* [The Joyful Table]. Tokyo: Bunka Shuppan Kyoku.
Sen, Sōshitsu. 1985. *Shōgo no Chaji, Chanoyu Jissen Kōza* [Midday Tea Ceremony: Practical Course for the Tea Ceremony]. Kyoto: Tankōsha.
Shufunotomosha, ed. 1996. *Ryōri Shokuzai Daijiten* [The Encyclopedia of Cooking and Food]. Tokyo: Shufunotomo.
Suzuki, Tsutomu. 1974. *Chakaiseki to Kyōto Ryōri* [Tea Ceremony Kaiseki and Kyoto Cuisine]. Tokyo: Sekai Bunkasha.
Tanaka, Tsuneo. 1976.,*Hōchō Nyūmon* [Introduction to the Kitchen Knife]. Shibata Shoten.
Tsuchiya, Mamoru. 1981. *Katei Ryōri no Jiten* [Dictionary of Home Cooking]. Tokyo: Sekai Bunka Sha.
Tsuji, Isao. 1982. *Nihon no Aji to Bunka* [Japanese Taste and Culture]. Tokyo: Sankei Shuppan.
Yoshida, Yoshio. 1979. *Edo no Osōzai* [Edo Side Dishes]. Tokyo: Chuo.

## Online References

Heritage of Japan. https://heritageofjapan.wordpress.com
Japan Ministry of Agriculture Forestry and Fisheries. http://www.maff.go.jp/e/japan_food/washoku
Kankokeizai Shimbun. 2020. November 8. *Korona de Henkashita Shokuseikatsu to Shoku ni Kansuru Ishiki Chōsa*. [Survey on Dietary Changes and Food Awareness during the Coronavirus (Pandemic)]. https://www.kankokeizai.com
Kumakura, Isao. *The Globalization of Japanese Food Culture*. https://www.kikkoman.co.jp/kiifc/foodculture/pdf_01/e_006_007.pdf
Promotion of Shokuiku (Food and Nutrition Education). http://www.maff.go.jp/e/policies/tech_res/shokuiku.html
Rogers, Krista. 2015. January 14. "A Brief History of the Evolution of Japanese School Lunches." *Japan Today*. https://japantoday.com/category/features/food/a-brief-history-of-the-evolution-of-japanese-school-lunches
Sake World. https://sake-world.com

## Videography

https://artsandculture.google.com/exhibit/the-world-of-food-through-manga/tgICs0osPCDZJQ

*Bibliography*

https://artsandculture.google.com/exhibit/rosanjin-kitaoji-a-chef-a-pottery-artist-and-a-lover-of-japanese-food/GwISABprjz3tIA
https://artsandculture.google.com/exhibit/why-washoku-is-part-of-japanese-culture/4QIS5aIke-piIQ
https://artsandculture.google.com/project/japanese-food
https://artsandculture.google.com/project/japanese-food-history

# Index

*Aburaage*, 27–28, 37, 57, 68, 197
Aesthetic
 allusions in *wagashi*, 104
 Buddhism and, 6
 experiences in everyday life, xii
 food presentation and styling, 198
 formal table arrangement, xii
 ideals, and Kūkai, xix
 presentation of sushi, 178
 principles of tea masters and the arts, 111
 quality of formal cuisine, xii
 restrained, in art and food, xix
 Rikyū's taste in tableware, 115
 sensibilities of tea connoisseurs and *wagashi*, 99
 sensitivity, xi
 significance of rice fields, 1
Agar-agar (*kanten*), 100, 102–103, 109
*Age ichiban*, 158. *See also Senbei,* rice cracker
*Agedashi*, 17
*Ame, mizu ame*, 97
*An, anko* (sweet bean paste), 97, 99, 100–101, 104, 106, 107, 148. *See also Tsubushi-an*
Anpan, xxi, 19
*Ao kinako*, 100
Appetizers, 57–74. *See also Otsumami*
 *gyōza*, 168–170
 *gyū kushi*, 156
 *yakitori*, 172–173
*Arare* (rice cracker), 157–158; *hina arare*, 137
Artisanal sugar (*awasanbon*), 97
As You Like It Crepes, *Okonomiyaki*, 153–155
Autumn equinox festival (*higan*), 102, 141, 143, 144
*Awamori* (Okinawa distilled alcoholic beverage), 90, 91
Azuki (red beans), xviii, 5, 6, 7, 37, 95, 99–104, 106–108, 110, 129–134, 147; *azuki* jelly (*yōkan*), 99, 102, 103. *See also An, anko*

Baking, xix, 13, 105; at home, 21, 54, 167–168, 187
Bamboo shoots (*takenoko*), 27, 36, 64–65, 142
Banana Yogurt Amazake Smoothie, 123
*Bancha* (ordinary tea), 81–82, 116, 117
Barley tea (*mugi cha*), 117, 157
*Baumkuchen*, ix, 105
Beef Skewers, *Gyū Kushi*, 156
*Bentō* (boxed lunch), xxii, 19, 82
Bitter melon (*niga uri, gōya*), xiii, 38, 70, 195
 Stir-Fried Bitter Melon, *Gōya Itame*, 43–44

Black tea (*kōcha*), 116
Blanched dishes (*hitashimono, hitashi, ohitashi*), 35, 38, 58
   Blanched Chinese Cabbage, *Hakusai no Hitashi*, 63–64
   Blanched Trefoil, *Mitsuba no Ohitashi*, 40
   Spinach Nori Rolls, *Horensō no Norimaki*, 61–63
*Bota mochi*, 103
Boys' Festival, *Tango no Sekku*, 139
Braised dishes (*nimono*)
   Braised Carp, *Koikoku*, 139–140
   Braised Giant Radish, *Furofuki Daikon*, 71–72
   Braised Squash, *Kabochani*, 42–43
   Braised Wakame, Bamboo Shoots, and Sugar Pea Pods, *Take no Ko to Wakame to Saya Ingen no Takiawase*, 64–65
   Braised Whale Meat, *Kujira no Kakuni*, 193
   *cha kaiseki* main course, 113
   Dutch-Style Braised Eggplant, *Nasu no Orandani*, 16–18
   *itokoni*, 131; Cousins Stew, *Kabocha to Azuki no Itokoni*, 132–133
   Kagoshima Braised Pork, *Kakuni*, 92
   Kinpira-Style Burdock Root, *Kinpira Gōbō*, 72–73
   Kyoto Braised Taro and Salt Cod, *Imobō no Taitan*, 195–196
   Okinawa Braised Pork, *Rafute*, 90–91
   placement in *osechi* tiered box, 136
   *tsukudani*, xiii, 48, 69–71, 77; Chicken Tsukudani, *Toriniku no Tsukudani*, 94; Green Beans Tsukudani, *Ingen no Tsukudani*, 70–71
   Yamaguchi Traditional Vegetable Stew, *Kenchō*, 197–198

Breakfast, ix, 7, 26, 36, 37, 45, 46, 57, 71, 76, 77–82
   coffee with, 77, 118–119
   green tea with, 116
   salted fish, 45, 46, 76–78
   skipping, as food-related problem (*koshoku*), 185
   traditional, 57, 76, 77; Crisp-Fried Baby Anchovies, *Karikari Shirasu*, 78; Grilled Overnight-Dried Salmon, *Sake Hitoyaboshi Shioyaki*, 77–78; Rikyū Tea-Flavored Rice, *Rikyū Meshi*, 81–82; Rolled Omelet, *Dashimaki Tamago*, 80–81
   Western-style, 26; morning service, 77; Poached Egg and Ham Salad, *Pōchito Eggu to Hamu no Sarada*, 79–80
Brown (unrefined) sugar, xix, 6, 97; in *shōchū*, 124
*Bûche de Noël*, 106
Buckwheat, xvii, xviii, 3, 26
   noodles (*soba*), 13, 36, 83; Cold Buckwheat Noodles, *Zaru Soba*, 84–85
   in *shōchū*, 124
Buddhism
   Chinese script and, 6
   cuisine, 6, 9, 131
   development of sweets (*okashi*), 6
   food practices, xix, 1, 6, 7
   introduced to Japan, xviii, 6
   Jōd sect, 131
   Shingon sect, xix
   sociocultural, political, philosophical, aesthetic aspects, 1, 6
   tea and, 11, 96
   temple cooking styles, xix
   temple offerings, 6, 131
   vegetarian cuisine (*shōjin ryōri*), xii, xv, xix, 7, 131
   Zen, 96

# Index

Buffet-style, all-you-can-eat (*tabehōdai*), 95, 166, 168
Burdock (*gobō*), xviii, 3, 27, 36, 58, 131, 136, 140, 144–145
  Kinpira-Style Burdock Root, *Kinpira Gobō*, 72–74
  Yanakawa-Style Pork Cutlet in a Bowl, *Yanakawafū Katsudon*, 85–88
Butterbur (*fuki no tō*), 38

*Caixa de marmelada, queijada*, 104; Squash-Filled Hand Pies, *Kesaina Mochi*, 13–14
*Caixa de marmelos*, 15; *queijada de marmelos*, 16; Quince Sweet, *Kaseita*, 15–16
Calpico (brand name of Calpis in the USA). See Calpis
Calpis, fermented milk drink, xxii, 19, 51, 119, 120, 163; Calpis Strawberry Soda, 119–120
Candy floss (*wata gashi*), 147
Carp, 2, 8, 9
  Braised Carp, *Koikoku*, 139–140
  celebration and, 133
  Children's Day and, 139
  symbolism, 133, 139
Cereal grains other than rice, 98, 99, 110. *See also* Buckwheat; Wheat
  barley, xvii, 3, 5, 25, 57, 98, 99; barley tea (*mugi cha*), 117, 157; in *hishio*, 8; in miso, 10; mixed with rice, 25; in *shōchū*, 124; in whisky, 126
  barnyard millet (*hie*), 3, 26
  broomcorn, common, regular, or proso millet (*kibi*), xvii, 3, 26, 98
  foxtail millet (*awa*), xvii, 3, 26, 98
  millet, xvii, xviii, 3, 5, 25, 26, 57, 98, 99
  mixed with rice, 25, 26, 57
  sweets, 98, 99
*Cha kaiseki*, xii, xix, 10, 58, 111–115
  basic principles, 112–113
  *shōgo kaiseki* (midday tea ceremony banquet), 113–115
  structure, 113–115
Chestnut, xvii, xviii, 3, 4, 5, 7, 53, 66, 67, 95, 96, 100, 136, 163
  Chestnut Rice, *Kurumi Gohan*, 4–5
  Jōmon Burgers, *Jōmon Bāgā*, 4
  sweet chestnut paste (*kinton*) for New Year, 136
Chinese and Korean eating customs, 7
Chinese cabbage (*hakusai*), 35, 63, 89, 168–170, 171, 172
  Blanched Chinese Cabbage, *Hakusai no Hitashi*, 63–64
  Grilled Whale Meat and Chinese Cabbage Salad in Mustard Dressing, *Kujira to Hakusai no Karashiae*, 192
  in *kimchi*, 170
Chinese sweets (*kara kashi, kara kudamono, tōgashi*), 8, 96, 98
Chinese-style
  cooking, dishes (*chūka ryōri*), xii, 34
  noodles: cold (*hiyashi chūka*), 84; fried (*yakisoba*), 83; in soup (*rāmen*), 26, 33, 83, 96, 167, 168, 200
  restaurants (*chūka ryōriya*), 83, 168
Chrysanthemum greens (*shungiku*), 35, 40, 142, 153, 176
Chunky-Style Azuki Paste, *Tsubushi-An*, 100–101
Cider (*saidā*, classic soft drink), 119
Cilantro (*pakuchi*), 33, 76, 89
Cinnamon, 8, 9, 98, 128, 135
Citrus fruits, 8, 102, 115, 126. *See also* Yuzu
  *daidai*, 34, 52
  *kabosu*, 34, 52
  *natsu mikan* (summer mandarin), 52
  *ponkan*, 52
  *shikwasa*, 51, 52, 120, 125
  *sudachi*, 163
  *tankan*, 51, 52

Coffee shops (*kissaten*), 118
Coming of Age day (*Seijin no Hi*), 141
Community-supported, agriculture, 188; family dining rooms, 194
Confectionery, 3, 22, 26, 53, 95, 96, 104–110
 first Japanese cookbook on, xx, 13, 107–108
 magazine, *Cafe Sweets*, 108
 Morinaga Confectionery Company, xxii
 Portuguese-style (*namban* gashi), 104–105
 traditional Japanese (*wagashi*), 98–100, 108
 Western-style (*yōgashi*), 95, 96, 105
Consumer Affairs Agency, 183
Cookbooks, Japanese
 *Edo Ryōri o Tsukuru* (Creating Edo Cuisine), 16
 *Kokon Meibutsu Gozengashi Hidenshō* (Secrets of Past and Present Famous Sweets), xx, 13, 107–108
 *Manpo Ryōri Himitsu Bako* (Secret Chest of Myriad Cooking Treasures), xx
 *Osōzai 12 ka Getsu* (12 Months of Side Dishes), 191, 193
 *Ryōri Monogatari* (The Story of Cooking), xx
 *Seiyō Ryōrishinan* (Guide to Western Food), xxi, 18
 *Seiyō Ryōritsu* (Western Food Connoisseur), xxi, 18
Cooking methods, 20, 54, 114
Coronavirus pandemic, xxiv, 21, 37, 187
 changes in dietary life, 187
 and impact on dining out, 167
 innovative food business alternatives, 167
 *nattō* consumption during, 22, 37, 187
 preparing food at home, 21, 22, 167–168, 187
 and role of food in maintaining health, 187
 unemployment in food industry, 167
Court dishes, 8
Craft sake (*jizake*), ix, xvi, 121, 122
Cucumber (*kyūri*), 38, 59, 84, 157, 176, 177, 181, 193

*Daikon oroshi* (grated giant radish), xvi, 33, 35, 60, 61, 77, 78, 143, 144
*Dashi*, xvi, 8, 10, 17, 18, 29–31, 40, 41, 42, 43, 44, 58, 61, 62, 65
 *dashi* powder, 28, 63, 64, 65, 80, 192, 198; *hondashi* powder (granules), 151, 152, 155
 instant, 30, 63, 150
 *konbu* (kelp-based *dashi*), 30, 64, 68, 132
 primary dashi (*ichiban dashi*), 31, 113
 secondary dashi (*niban dashi*), 31, 113
Devil's tongue jelly or root (*konnyaku*), xxiii, 11, 131, 197
Dioscorea or mountain yam (*yama imo*), xviii, 3, 36, 58, 144, 145
Disposable chopsticks invented, 13
*Doburoku*, 124, 171
Dōgen, *Instructions for the Cook*, 10
Donburi, 82
*Donko shiitake*, 28
Dressed dishes (*aemono*), 36, 37, 38, 39, 48, 49, 58–59, 195
 Bamboo Shoot Taro in Shirazu Dressing, *Takenoko Imo no Shirazu Ae*, 41–42
 Squid and Vegetables in Mayonnaise and Sesame Miso Dressing, *Ika to Yasai no Mayonēzu Goma Miso Ae*, 59–60

Eating out preferences, 49, 76, 82, 88, 168
*Ebi imo* (shrimp-shaped taro), 36, 196; Kyoto Braised Taro and Salt Cod, *Imobō no Taitan*, 195, 196
*Ebisen, ebi senbei* (shrimp-flavored rice cracker), 163
*Edamame*, 36
  Green Soybean (*Edamame*) Paste, Zunda, 101–102
  Green Soybean Jelly, *Zunda Yōkan*, 103
  paste (*zunda*), 36, 37
*Edo Meibutsu Shuhan Tebikigusa*, xx, 13
*Edomaezushi* (Edo-style sushi), xiv
Eggplant (*nasu*), xiii, xiv, 8, 38, 54, 58
  Dutch-Style Braised Eggplant, *Nasu no Orandani*, 16–18
  Fried Eggplants in Tempura Sauce, *Agenasu ni Tentsuyu*, 60–61
Emergency food stocks, 21, 190

Fast foods, 83
  sushi and tempura, 13, 179
Fermented milk products, xxii, 19, 51, 119, 163
*Filhós* (*hiryōzu*), 104, 105, 141, 144
Fish, ix, x, xi, xiv, xvi, xvii, xxii, 1, 6, 7, 8, 9, 13, 20, 44–48, 57, 69, 75, 76. *See also* Dashi
  *aji* (Japanese horse mackerel), 45, 77, 181
  *akōdai* (red rockfish), 45
  *anago* (sea eel) sushi, 181
  Atlantic blue-fin tuna (*see maguro*)
  Braised Carp, *Koikoku*, 139–140
  *buri* (yellowtail), 45, 133, 144, 180; Hokuriku region New Year food, 136
  celebratory/festive fish, 47, 133, 134, 139
  *chirimenjako*, 42, 77, 78. *See also shirasu*
  commonly eaten species, 45–47
  decreased consumption, 44, 49
  *dōjō*, loach, 85
  eel (*unagi*), 13, 33; endangered, xxiii, 21, 191
  fish loaf (*kamaboko*), 81, 132, 136
  fish sauce, Japanese (*shottsuru*), 6; Thai (*nampla*), 76, 89
  grouper, xx, 8
  *hamachi*, 45, 180
  herring roe (*kazunoko*), 136
  *hirame* (flounder), 181; *engawa*, 180
  *karei* (plaice), 181; *engawa*, 180
  *katsuo* (bonito), 8, 29, 46; *bushi* (flakes), 17, 18, 30, 35, 46, 58, 163; Spanish production of, 199; *tataki*, 46. *See also* Dashi
  *koikoku*, 139
  mackerel (*saba*), 46; flakes, 84; pickled, 8; salted and marinated (*shimesaba*), 46; in sushi, 181
  *madai* (sea bream), 47; Savory Custard Soup with Sea Bream, *Madai no Chawan Mushi*, 66–67. *See also* Sea bream (*tai*)
  *maguro*, Atlantic blue-fin tuna, 21, 46, 180, 181; threatened by extinction, 184, 191; Spanish production of, 199
  *niboshi*, 2
  *nodoguro* (rockfish), 180
  pickled: *narezushi*, 7; *izushi*, xiv, 174
  salmon (*sake*), 2, 20, 46, 93; Grilled Overnight-Dried Salmon, *Sake Hitoyaboshi Shioyaki*, 77–78; Hokkaido cuisine, xiii, xiv, 136; jerky, 163; Namban-Style Salmon, *Sake no Nambanyaki*, 93; roe (*sujiko, ikura*), 46, 136, 180, 181; smoked, 174; Smoked Salmon Scattered Sushi, *Smōku Sāmon no Chirashizushi*, 137–138; sushi, 180; *tataki* in Spain, xv, 198

sea bream (*tai*), xvii, 7, 47; celebratory fish, 47, 133, 135; Salt-Grilled Sea Bream, *Tai no Shioyaki*, 133–134; Savory Custard Soup with Sea Bream, *Madai no Chawan Mushi*, 66–67; sushi, 181. *See also Madai*
seasoning (*hishio*), 6, 7, 8, 9, 112
*shirako* (milt), 180
*shirasu*, 42; Crisp-Fried Baby Anchovies, *Karikari Shirasu*, 78. *See also chirimenjako*
*suzuki* (Japanese sea bass), 47; in sushi, 181
sweetfish (*ayu*), 7, 8, 34, 45; in *narezushi*, 174
*toro*, 46, 179, 180
trout, 2, 8, 66
whale, xiv, xvii, 2, 20, 57, 191; Braised Whale Meat, *Kujira no Kakuni*, 193–194; Grilled Whale Meat and Chinese Cabbage Salad in Mustard Dressing, *Kujira to Hakusai no Karashiae*, 192; jerky, 163
Yellow-Fin Tuna in Ginger Sauce, *Kihada no Shōgayaki*, 199
Five-based elements of a meal, 114
Food
 banks, 194
 cooperatives: *teikei* movement, 188; *Anzen na Tabemono wo Tsukutte Taberu Kai* (Group for the Consumption and Production of Safe Foods), 189; Japan Consumers' Cooperatives Union (*Nisseikyo*), 190; *Seikatsu* Club, 189
 ethics, 200
 and health: *azuki* (red beans), 131; *azuki* and squash, 132; bitter melon, 38; bitter melon and longevity, xiii; decreased salt consumption, 20; five fruits daily, 119; freedom from nutritional diseases, 21; functional foods, 21; green tea, 108, 116; health drinks, 120; increase in average height, 21; *itokoni*, 132; metabolic diseases, 21, 185; miso, 10–11; mixed grains with rice, 25; *nattō* and coronavirus pandemic, 22, 37, 187; nutritional minerals and vitamins in yams, 36; *toso*, 135
 loss, 187, 194; No Food Loss Project, xxiii
 safety, 20, 183, 187, 188; Food Safety Basic Act, 183; Food Safety Commission, 183
 security, 20, 183, 187
 self-sufficiency, 2, 21, 183, 187, 194
 trucks, 21, 167
 waste, xxiii, 112, 184, 187, 189, 194; Food Waste Reduction Law, 194
Fried dishes (*agemono*)
 As You Like It Crepes, *Okonomiyaki*, 153–155
 Fried Eggplants in Tempura Sauce, *Agenasu ni Tentsuyu*, 60
 Fried Noodles, *Yakisoba*, 149–150
 frying, xix, 13, 20, 54, 105, 114
 Glazed Sweet Potatoes, *Daigaku Imo*, 160–161
 *gūzen gashi* (temple offerings), 6, 98
 *hiryōzu* (Portuguese *filhós*), 104–105, 141; Tofu Fritters, *Ganmodoki, Hiryōzu*, 144–145.
 *karintō*, 95, 158; Glazed Fritters, *Karintō*, 159–160
 Pan-Fried Dumplings, *Gyōza*, 168–170
 Sweet Bean-Filled Cakes, *Dorayaki*, 147–149
 Vegetarian Tempura, *Shōjin Age*, 141–144

# Index

Fruits, 3, 5, 8, 51–53, 96–98, 100, 102, 108, 123–127, 163, 186, 189. *See also* Citrus fruits
Fuji apple, 51, 119
Grape, 51, 52, 125; *Koshu*, 125; *Kyohō*, 52; Muscat Bailey A, 125; wild, xiv, xviii, 3
haskap berry, 52–53, 120
introduced, xviii, 7
Japanese apricot or plum (*ume*), 51, 53; flavoring, 119, 162; juice, 120; liqueur (*umeshū*), 53, 126–128; pickle, 8, 33, 34, 53; in *shōchū*, 125
mountain fruits, xiv
nuts, 53–54
persimmon, 53
quince, Western (*Cydonia oblonga*), 13, 15–16, 51, 53, 105; Japanese (*karin, Chaenomeles japonica*), 16, 105; Quince Sweet, *Kaseita*, 15–16. Squash-Filled Hand Pies, *Kesaina Mochi*, 13–14

*Ganmodoki* (tofu fritters). *See Hiryōzu, hirōsu*
Garlic, 33, 168, 170; contemporary use of, 34
Garlic chives (*nira*), 34, 89, 168
Genetically modified food, 187–188
Ghost or cloud kitchens, 21, 167
Giant kelp (*konbu*), 29, 30–31, 69, 141, 143, 175
auspicious for New Year, 136
Giant radish (*daikon*), 33, 35–36, 57, 58
Braised Giant Radish, *Furofuki Daikon*, 71–72
condiment, 33, 35, 61, 77, 78
*takuan* pickles, 36
Ginger (*shōga*), xiv, xvi, xviii, 33
dipping sauce, 35, 60, 61, 143, 144
flavoring for rice crackers, 162
garnish, 91, 114
palate refresher, 181
pickled, 83, 149, 150, 154, 155, 177, 178, 180
smell neutralizer, 193
Ginkgo nuts, xviii, 53, 66, 67
Glutamine, naturally occurring, 30
*Gobō* (burdock), 36, 58, 72–73
Gohyakumangoku, *sake* rice variety, 122
*Gosekku* (five seasonal festivals), 136
Grilled Overnight-Dried Salmon, *Sake Hitoyaboshi Shioyaki*, 77–78
Grilled Skewered Chicken, *Yakitori*, 172–173
Grilled Whale Meat and Chinese Cabbage Salad in Mustard Dressing, *Kujira to Hakusai no Karashiae*, 192
Guide to Edo's Famous Restaurants, *Edo Meibutsu Shuhan Tebikigusa*, xx, 13
*Gūzen gashi* (edible temple offerings), 6, 98
*Gyōza*, 34, 168–170
*Gyū kushi*, 147, 156
*Gyūnabe*, xxi, 18

Hakata *tonkotsu rāmen*, 83
*Hama nattō* (dry fermented soybeans), 37
*Hanafubuki*, *sake* rice variety, 122
Hangzhou *dongpo* pork, 90
*Hashi arai*, 115
*Hassun*, 115
*Hatchō miso*, 32
*Hatsumiyamōde*, 140
*Hayashi raisu* (hashed beef and rice), xxi, 18
*Hayato uri*, 38, 195
Highball (*mizuwari*), 126
*Hime ii*, 7
*Hina Matsuri*, Doll Festival, 123, 137
*Hinomaru bentō* (rising sun lunch box), xxii, 19

Hiroshima
  *otsumami: senjigara*, 163
  As You Like It Crepes, *Okonomiyaki*, 153–155
*Hiryōzu, hirōsu* (Portuguese *filhós*), 104, 105, 141; Tofu Fritters, *Ganmodoki, Hiryōzu*, 144–145
Hishio (fermented seasonings), 6, 7–8, 9, 112; *koku bishio*, 8; *kusa bishio*, 8; *shishi bishio*, 8
*Hiyashi chūka* (chilled Chinese noodles), 84
*Hōjicha* (chilled summer tea), 117
Hokkaido food culture
  buckwheat, 26
  crab and other seafood, xiii, 48, 83
  dairy products, 51
  haskap berry, 52–53
  *izushi*, xiv, 174
  *konbu*, 29
  nuts, 53, 54
  *rāmen*, xiii, 83
  salmon jerky, 163
  *sekihan*, 129
  *tōji nankin*, 132
  wheat, 26
  wine production, 125
  Yumepirika rice, xiii, 25
  *zōni*, xiv, 136
*Honzen ryōri* (banquet cuisine), xii, xv
Horned turban shell, turbo shell (*sazae*), 8, 48

*Ichiban dashi*, 29
*Imobō no taitan*, Kyoto New Year dish, 195–196
*Izakaya* (gastro-pubs), ix, 89, 165, 168
*Izushi*, Hokkaido New Year dish, xiv, 174

Jamaican Blue Mountain coffee, 118
Japan Consumers Cooperatives Union, 188, 190
Japanese cuisine, beginning of genuine, 11
Japanese Food Labeling Act, 188
Japanese food processing companies in Spain, xv, 199
Japanese gin, 126
Japanese hazelnut, xvii, 53
Japanese miso, development of, 10
Japanese whisky, 126; from rice, 126
Japanese-style mayonnaise, 151–152
Jerky, meat and fish, 163
Jōmon Burgers, *Jōmon Bāgā*, 3, 4
Jōmon cookies, 3

*Kabosu*, 34, 52
*Kagami mochi*, 157
Kagoshima Braised Pork, *Kakuni*, 92
*Kaki no tane*, 162
Kansai food culture
  *batterazushi*, xiv
  *hiryōzu*, 105, 144
  miso, xiv, 32
  New Year dish, *tataki gobō*, 136
  *shichimi*, 35
  soy sauce, 32
  *zōni*, 136
*Kanten* (agar-agar, agar), 100, 102, 103, 109
Kanto food culture
  *ganmodoki*, 105, 144
  miso, xiv
  *nattō*, 37
  *nigirizushi*, xiv
  *shichimi*, 35
  *shiokara*, 6
  soy sauce, 32
  *zōni*, 136
Kanto vs. Kansai food culture, xiv, 32, 35, 37, 42, 66, 105, 136, 144
*Kara gashi, kara kashi, kara kudamono, tōgashi* (Chinese sweets), 8, 98
*Karē raisu*, xxi, 18, 19, 95, 200
*Karintō* (traditional glazed fritters), 95, 158–160
*Kaseita* (Portuguese *Caixa de Marmelada*), 15–16

# Index

Kashi, *okashi* (sweets), 96. *See also Gūzen gashi*; *Kara gashi*; *Shinsen gashi*
  *dagashi*, 158
  *hoshi gashi*, dry sweets, 99, 102
  *namban gashi* (Portuguese-style), 104–105; *kesaina*, 13–15, *kaseita*, 15–16
  *wagashi* (traditional Japanese), 95, 98–100, 102–104
  *yōgashi* (Western-style), 95, 105–108
*Kasutera, kasuteira*, xix, 104
*Kibi*, 26, 98
*Kinako*, 37, 100, 108, 188
Kinpira-Style Burdock Root, *Kinpira Gōbō*, 72–73
*Kishimen* noodles, 26, 83
Kitchen equipment, 55; *hōchō* (kitchen knife), 55; *katsuobushi kezuriki*, 29, 30
Knife ritual (*shiki bōchō*), 9
*Kodomo Shokudō*, Children's Cafeteria, 194
*Kōji* (*Aspergillus oryzae*), 122, 123, 147, 198
*Kokon Meibutsu Gozen Kashi Hidenshō*, Secrets of Past and Present Famous Sweets, xx, 13, 107–108
*Komatsuna*, 35
*Kome, okome*, 25. *See also* Rice
*Konbu* (laver)
  auspicious, 136
  *mizukashi*, 96
  stock (*konbu dashi*), 5, 29, 30–31, 68, 141, 143
  varieties, 29
*Konnyaku* (devil's tongue root), xxiii, 11–12, 131, 197
*Konowata*, 6, 8
*Konpeito*, Portuguese *confeito*, 104
Korean seasoning, *gochujang*, 76
*Korokke*, croquettes, xxi, 18, 19
*Koshihikari* rice variety, xiii, 25
*Koshoku*, contemporary food-related issues, 184–185

*Kudamono*, sweet course in imperial banquets, 8, 98
*Kukicha*, 117
*Kuzu*, xviii, 3, 97, 99, 104, 108
*Kyōna*, 35
Kyoto food culture, xiv, xv, 9, 166. *See also* Kansai food culture
  New Year traditions, 135, 196;
  Kyoto Braised Taro and Salt Cod, *Imobō no Taitan*, 195–196
  Tanba chestnut, 53
  traditional food preparation techniques, streamlining, 199
  Uji *matcha*, 118
  vegetables, 36, 41, 195
  *wagashi*, 99

Lacquer ware, xix, 7, 114, 115;
  boxes (*jūbako*) for New Year celebratory foods, 134, 135, 136
Laghman-Style Udon Noodles, *Raguman-fū Udon*, 89–90
Leaching (*aku nuki*), 3, 54
Leek, xviii, 33, 85–88, 156, 169, 172, 173; as garnish, 140
Light soy sauce (*usukuchi shōyu*), 31–32, 66, 93, 158, 196
Lily bulbs, 2, 3
Lotus root, 39, 40, 70, 72, 73, 137, 138, 139, 142
  auspicious, 39, 54
  Lotus Root with Walnut Miso Dressing, *Renkon no Kurumi Miso Ae*, 39–40
Lunch, 57, 71, 76, 77, 82–88
  *donburi*, 82, 88

*Manjū*, dumplings, 99
*Matcha*, 95, 108–110, 118, 163
  in Kit Kat, 163
  latte, 117
  milk jelly, 108–110
*Matsutake*, pine mushroom, 27, 38

Mayonnaise, 59, 60, 149, 150; as flavoring for rice crackers, 158, 162; Japanese-style, 151–152
Meat, wild, 2, 3, 4
　ban: on wild animals for food, xix, 6; lifted on meat-eating, 18
　beef, xxi, 18, 20, 48–50; cattle breeding initiated, 19; *gyū kushi*, 147, 156; *gyūdon*, 83; *Gyūnabe*, xxi, 18; *Hayashi raisu*, hashed beef and rice, xxi, 18; Korean-Style Grilled Meat, *Kankoku-Fū Yakiniku*, 170–172; *tanindon*, 82; *wagyu*, 49–50, 185
　chicken, 20, 48–50, 66; Chicken Tsukudani, *Toriniku no Tsukudani*, 94; Grilled Skewered Chicken, *Yakitori*, 172–173; *kara age*, 83, 88; *oyakodon*, 82; poisoned, 187; sushi, 174
　consumption, 20, 44, 48
　jerky, meat and fish, 163
　Jōmon Burgers, *Jōmon Bāgā*, 3, 4
　main side dishes, 57, 76
　pork, xiii, 20, 48–50; *butaniku no shōga yaki*, 76; Gifu Mizunami Bono, 50; Hakata *tonkotsu rāmen*, 83; Kagoshima Braised Pork, *Kakuni*, 92; *katsudon*, 82; *kurobuta*, 50; Okinawa *Agubuta*, 50; Okinawa Braised Pork, *Rafute*, 90; *tonkatsu*, xxi, 18, 19, 83, 85; Yanakawa-Style Pork Cutlet in a Bowl, *Yanakawafū Katsudon*, 85–88
　preference, 49, 50
Metabolic diseases, 21, 185
Mibuna, 35
Michelin: guide, 13; starred restaurants, 21, 83, 165
Microwave, 55, 80, 81, 184
Milk: candies, 19; caramel, xxii; dairy products, 51; health food, 50; introduced, xix; melamine contamination in, xxiii

*Mirin*, 32
Miso, ix, x, xiii, xv, xvi, 6, 8, 37, 85, 115, 183
　battlefield meal, 11
　development as everyday seasoning, 10
　GM soybeans in, 188
　health and, 10
　in ice cream, 108
　Lotus Root with Walnut Miso Dressing, *Renkon no Kurumi Miso Ae*, 39–40
　*rāmen*, 83
　regional miso (dark, red, light/white), xiv, 10, 32
　rice and wheat in, 26
　soup, ix, 10, 57, 75, 76, 77, 83, 166, 167; in *cha kaiseki*, 113
*Mitsuba* (trefoil), 28, 29, 34, 35, 40, 66, 67, 85, 86, 142, 153
*Mizore jiru*, sleet soup, 35
*Mizu yōkan*, 99, 102
*Mizukashi, mizugashi*, 96, 97
*Mizuna*, 35
Mochi
　celebratory food, 25, 129–131, 136–137, 139
　frozen pastry in Europe, xv, 110
　*kagami mochi*, 157
　New Year *zōni*, 136
　rice, 25
　seasonal sweets, 103
　snacks (rice crackers), 95, 157, 158, 163
　*wagashi*, 99
*Mogusa* leaf, 100
Morning service, 77, 119
*Mōsō* bamboo, 36
Mountain vegetables (*sansai*): butterbur (*fuki no tō*), 38; horsetail (*tsukushi*), 38; *kogomi* (ostrich fern), 38; *warabi* (bracken shoots), 38, 100; *yama*

# Index

imo, 36, 58; *zenmai* (Asian royal fern, *Osmunda japonica*), 38
Mukokuseki, ix, 13, 75
Mukōzuke, *cha kaiseki* course, 113, 114
Mushrooms
    enokidake, xv, 38, 79, 198
    maidake, 38
    matsutake, 38
    nameko, 58
    shimeji, 28, 38
    shiitake, 28, 38, 198; *donko*, 28
    Shiitake and Carrot Rice, *Shiitake to Ninjin no Takikomi Gohan*, 27–29

*Namazake*, unpasteurized *sake*, 124
*Namban gashi*. See Portuguese-style, confectionery
Name-giving ceremony (*oshichiya*), 133
Nanohana, 35
Naorai, traditional food-sharing ritual, 122, 136
*Narezushi*, 7, 174
*Natsu mikan*, summer mandarin, 52
Nattō, 22, 37, 158, 187
    health and, 37, 187
    pandemic and, 22
New ways of food preparation and dining from China, 6
New Year
    dishes: Kyoto *imobō*, 196; *osechi*, 134, 135, 136; seven-herb gruel, 136; *toshikoshi soba*, 135; *toso, otoso*, 135; *zōni, ozōni*, xiv, 136, 195
    festive ingredients: burdock, 36; *buri*, 45; *kagami mochi*, 157; lotus root, 39, 54; *mochi*, 25; shrimp, 47; water chestnut, 54
    gift-giving, 52
    *jūbako*, 136
*Nigirizushi*, hand-shaped sushi, xiv, 178
*Niinamesai*, rice harvesting festival, 1

Noodles
    Cold Buckwheat Noodles, *Zaru Soba*, 84–85
    eating out and, 166–167
    fried (*yakisoba*), 83, 147, 152, 154–155; Fried Noodles, Yakisoba, 149–150
    *kishimen*, 26, 83
    *koshoku* (flour-based food issue) and, 184
    *rāmen*, xiii, xv, xvi, 26, 33, 96; regional variants, 83
    rice, 26
    *soba* (buckwheat), 3, 13, 26, 36, 83, 141, 167; Cold Buckwheat Noodles, Zaru Soba, 84–85
    *sōmen*, 26, 84
    *toshikoshi soba*, 135
    *udon*, 13, 26, 83, 84; Laghman-Style Udon Noodles; *Raguman-fū Udon*, 89–90
*Nukazuke*, rice bran pickles, 26, 36

*Obanzai*, Kyoto home-style dishes, xiv, 195
*Oden*, hodgepodge stew, ix, 30, 152, 166
Ogura ice cream, 106–107
*Ohagi*, 104, 141
*Okaki*, rice cracker, 157–158
Okinawa
    Braised Pork, *Rafute*, 90–91
    branded pig, *Agubuta*, 50
    food culture, xiii
    fruits: papaya, pineapple, *tankan*, 51; shikwasa, 51, 53, 120, 125
    *rāmen* (Okinawa *soba*), 83
    Stir-Fried Bitter Melon, *Gōya Itame*, 43
    sugar cane, 126
Okonomiyaki, 147, 153–154
Okowa, 7, 129
*Omakase*, chef's choice, 179, 182
*Omiki*, blessed sake, 122

*Omotenashi*, hospitality, xii, 113, 166
One soup-three dishes (*ichijū sansai*), 11, 112, 115
One-pot dishes (*nabemono*), ix, 30, 34, 35, 46, 47
Oolong tea, 116
*Orandani*, 13, 16–17
*Oshiki, shiki*, food tray, xix, 114
*Otsumami*, 162–163, 168, 181, 193
*Oyako Shokudō* (Parents and Children Cafeteria) program, Fukushima, 194

Pan-Fried Dumplings, *Gyōza*, 168–170
Pancakes with sweet red bean paste (*dorayaki*), 147–149
Pickles (*tsukemono*), x, xiii, xiv, xvi, 8, 26, 34, 57, 83
 in *cha kaiseki*, 115
 Hakata mustard leaf, 83
 *kimchi*, 172
 *nukazuke*, 36
 with set lunch, 166
 *takuan*, 36
 teatime snacks, 157
 traditional meal format, 75, 77
 *umeboshi*, 34, 53
Plum liqueur, 53; Japanese Plum Liqueur, *Umeshū*, 126–127
Poached Egg and Ham Salad, *Pōchito Eggu to Hamu no Sarada*, 79–80
Poppy seeds (*keshi no mi*), 35, 100, 144, 145
Population living below poverty line, 184
Portuguese-style
 baking, xix, 13
 confectionery (*namban gashi*), 104; *caixa de marmelada*, 104; *kaseita* (*queijada, caixa de marmelos*), 15; *kesaina*, 13; *Queijada, queijada de marmelos*, 13, 16

deep-frying method, 13
 tempura, original recipe, xvi, 142
*Potapota yaki*, 158
Puréed *edamame* (*zunda*), 36, 37, 101–103

Radioactivity and food products, 183
*Rāmen*, xv, xvi, 26
 eating out, 167, 200
 regional, xiii, 83
 spices and herbs in, 33
*Ramune*, lemonade-flavored soft drink, 19, 119, 147
Recipes for Western-style dishes, 18
Restaurants, 165–166, 168
 coronavirus lockdown and, 167
 exclusive (*ryōtei*), 166
 family-style and fast-food, 20, 83
 first established, Edo, xx
 first guide to, *Edo Meibutsu Shuhan Tebikigusa*, xx, 13, 167
 first Western-style for local diners, 18
 Japanese, outside Japan, xv
 Michelin-starred, 21, 83, 165
 *yatai*, 179
Rice, ix, x, xiii, xvii, xviii, xxi, xxii, 1, 7, 8, 25, 26. *See also* Mochi; Sake
 basic recipe, 27
 bran (*nuka*), 26, 36
 cakes, 37, 95, 96, 97, 116, 137, 139, 140, 141, 158
 crackers, 26, 116, 137, 157, 162
 cultivation in irrigated fields, 5, 7
 decreased consumption, 20, 26
 *hinomaru bento*, 19
 mixed cereal grains with rice, 3, 6, 25, 26, 57
 noodles, 26
 recipes: Chestnut Rice, *Kuri Gohan*, 4–5; Crab Sushi Rolls, *Kani Hosomaki*, 176–178; Red Rice, *Sekihan*, 130–131; Rikyū Tea-Flavored Rice, *Rikyū Meshi*,

# Index

81–82; Shiitake and Carrot Rice, *Shiitake to Ninjin no Takikomi Gohan*, 27–29; Smoked Salmon Scattered Sushi, *Smōku Sāmon no Chirashizushi*, 137–139; Sushi Rice, *Sushi Meshi*, 175–176
 red (*sekihan*), 129, 130–131
 ritual planting, 1
 polish percentages, 26
 in *sake*, 26; in *shōchū*, 124; in whisky, 126
 sticky (glutinous), 7, 8, 25
 *takikomi gohan*, 4
 varieties, xiii, 25; for *sake*-making, 122
Rikyū. *See* Sen no Rikyū
Roasted or grilled dishes (*yakimono*)
 Beef Skewers, *gyū kushi*, 156
 in *cha kaiseki*, 115
 Grilled Skewered Chicken, *Yakitori*, 172–173
 Korean-Style Grilled Meat, *Kankoku-Fū Yakiniku*, 170–171
 New Year *osechi*, 136
 roasted pheasant, 8
 Salt-Grilled Sea Bream, *Tai no Shioyaki*, 133–134
 sweet potatoes, 160
 *yakitori*, ix, 33, 38, 147, 152, 168
Rolled Omelet, *Dashimaki Tamago*, 80
Rule of Thirds in food distribution, 194

*Saidā* (cider), classic soft drink, 119
Sake (rice wine), 121–124
 *ama kuchi*, 122
 festivals and, 152; for Girls' Day, 123, 137; sweet (*amazake*), non-alcoholic, 147; white (*shirozake*), for mothers on Girls' Day, 123, 137
 *kara kuchi*, 122
 lees (*okara*), xiii, 37, 58, 59, 157
 in light soy sauce, 32
 *nigori zake*, 171

regional sake, craft sake, xvi, 122
 rice varieties for: Gohyakumangoku, Hanafubuki, Yamadanishiki, 122
 spiced, for New Year (*toso*), 135
 as seasoning, 8, 9, 32
 unpasteurized (*namazake*), 124
 vinegar for traditional sushi, 179
 wedding ritual, *sansankudō*, 122
*Sakura mochi*, 103
*Sasami* (inner fillet of chicken breast), 49
*Sato imo* (taro), 36, 41, 58
Savory Custard with Wakame Seaweed, *Wakame no Chawan Mushi*, 68
School Health Law, 186
Seafood, 44
 *amaebi*, 47
 crab, xiii, 44, 47, 48, 83, 134, 153
 Crab Sushi Rolls, *Kani Hosomaki*, 176
 dried cuttlefish, 8, 48
 *ebi* (shrimp), 44, 47
 *ika* (squid, cuttlefish), 7, 44, 48, 59
 *Ise ebi*, 47
 *kuruma ebi*, 47
 mantis shrimp (*shako*), 47
 octopus, 7, 44, 48; balls (*tako yaki*), 147, 152; dried, 8
 self-sufficiency in, 187
Seasonings. *See also* Mirin; Sake
 contemporary, 76
 *hishio*, 6
 *konowata*, 6
 *shiokara*, 6
 *shottsuru*, 6
 soybean-based, xv, 5, 6, 8, 10, 31–32, 37
Second Harvest Japan, 194
Secondary dashi (*niban dashi*), 30, 31, 113
Sekihan, 37, 129, 134; Red Rice, *Sekihan*, 130–131

Semi-fresh sweets (*hannama gashi*), 99
Sen no Rikyū
  aesthetics, 111
  genuine Japanese cuisine, 11
  *okashi* and, 96
  one soup-three side dishes meal format, 11, 112
  principles of *cha kaiseki*, xix, 112–113
  Rikyū-Style Konjac, *Konyakku Rikyū Yaki*, 11–12
  Rikyū Tea-Flavored Rice, *Rikyū Meshi*, 81–82
  tea ceremony, xix, 11, 111
  *wabi cha*, 11
  way of cooking, 81
*Senbei*, rice cracker, 116, 157, 158, 162, 163
  *age ichiban*, 158
  *ebisen*, shrimp-flavored rice cracker, 163
  *potapota yaki*, 158
  *yuki no shuku*, 158
Sesame oil, xviii, 6, 8, 9, 62, 73, 74, 98, 143, 168–170, 171
Sesame seed, 26, 62, 70, 100, 158, 162
  garnish, 58, 63, 71, 72, 109, 110, 160, 161
  Kinpira-Style Burdock Root, *Kinpira Gobō*, 73–74
  in Korean-style grilled meat, 170–172
  paste (*neri goma*), 12, 58, 59
  in *sekihan*, 130–131
  Sen no Rikyū and, 11–12, 81–82
  *shichimi tōgarashi*, 35
  Squid and Vegetables in Mayonnaise and Sesame Miso Dressing, *Ika to Yasai no Mayonezu Goma Miso Ae*, 59–60
*Setsubun* and roasted *azuki* (red beans), 131, 141
Seven-herb gruel for New Year, 136

Shellfish, 44, 142, 174; in sushi, 180–181
  *akagai* (blood shellfish), 48, 181
  *aoyagi* (surf clam), 48
  *asari* (short-neck clam), 48
  *awabi* (abalone), 7, 8, 180
  *hamaguri* (hard clam, Venus clam), 48, 181
  *hotate*, scallop, 162, 174, 180, 181
  *kase* clam, 8
  *ou*, *aoyagi* (surf clam), 8, 48
  *sazae* (horned turban shell or turbo clam), 8, 48
  *shijimi* (freshwater clam), 48
  *taira gai* (pen shell), 48
  *torigai* (Japanese cockle), 48
  *uni*, sea urchin, 162, 180, 181
*Shibugaki*, 53
*Shichimi tōgarashi*, 33, 34–35
*Shiki*, xix, 7; *oshiki*, 114
*Shinsen gashi* (Shinto shrine offering), 98
*Shiokara*, salted squid, 6, 48
*Shippoku* cuisine, 13
*Shirataki* (*konyakku* noodles), 11
*Shirozake* (white *sake*), 123, 137
*Shishitōgarashi*, 38, 70
*Shisō*, xii, xviii, 2, 4, 33, 34, 35, 89, 142, 153, 198
  flavoring: for *shōchū*, 125; for *kaki no tane* rice crackers, 162
  flower stalks (*hōjisō*), in dipping sauce, 34, 178
  garnish, 178
  red, in umeboshi pickles, 33, 34
  *shichimi tōgarashi*, 35
*Shōchū*, 119, 124–125, 126, 127, 163, 166
*Shōjin ryōri*, xii, xv, xix, 7, 131, Vegetarian Tempura, *Shōjin Age*, 141–144
*Shokuiku*, food and nutrition education, 186
  Basic Law on *Shokuiku*, 186

# Index

*Shottsuru*, 6
Shrine offerings, edible (*shinsen gashi*), 98, 129. *See also* Temple offerings, edible
Side dish (*okazu, osōzai*), 57, 58
   blanched dishes, *hitashimono*, 61–64
   braised dishes, nimono, 64–65, 69–73
   dressed dishes, *aemono*, 58–60
   fried dishes, agemono, 60–61
   *fukuzai*, 57
   *Osōzai 12 ka Getsu*, 12 Months of Side Dishes, 191, 193
   *shuzai*, 57
   steamed dishes, mushimono, 66–69
Slicing methods, 9, 54, 138, 174
   chamfering (*mentori*), 54, 72
   *kakushi bōchō*, 54, 72
   *kazari kiri*, 54
   *rangiri*, 54, 161
   *shiki bōchō*, 9
Snacks (*oyatsu*), 157–163
   *arare, okaki*, 157
   Chinese *tenshin*, 9
   Glazed Fritters, *Karintō*, 159–160
   Glazed Sweet Potatoes, *Daigaku Imo*, 160–161
   *hina arare*, for Doll Festival, 137
   *kaki no tane*, 162
   *otsumami*, 162–163
   *senbei*, 116, 158
   Western-style, 163
Soufflé cheesecake, 22–23
Soy sauce, xv, 6, 8, 10, 13, 37
   dark vs. light, 31–32
   *saishikomi* (double-fermented), 32
   tamari, 32
   white (*shiro*), 32
Soybean, xv, xviii, xix, 5, 9, 10, 11, 32, 36–37, 188. *See also* Tofu
   curd (*tōfu*), xv, 9, 37; sheets (*yuba*), 9, 37
   *edamame*, 37
   as fermented seasoning (*hishio*), 6, 10. *See also* Miso; Soy sauce, tamari
   flour (*kinako*), 37, 100; *ao kinako*, 37, 100
   GM (genetically modified), 188
   *nattō*, 22, 37, 158, 187; *hama nattō*, 37
   soy milk, 36, 188
   *zunda*, 100; Green Soybean (Edamame) Paste, *Zunda*, 101–102; Green Soybean Jelly, *Zunda Yōkan*, 103
Spain
   Japanese cooking methods in, xv
   Japanese food ingredients in supermarkets, xv
   production of Japanese food ingredients, 199
   use of *mochi* as pastry shell for ice cream, 110
Spices and herbs, 33–35. *See also* Ginger; *Mitsuba; Shisō*
   Chinese spices, 6
   cinnamon (*keishin*), 8, 9, 98, 128, 135
   cloves, 98
   contemporary use of, 33
   coriander, 89
   cumin, 89
   *myōga*, 33, 82
   *naga negi*, 33
   *nira*, 34, 168
   *sanshō*, Japanese pepper, also Japanese mountain pepper, xviii, 2, 33, 135, 156, 172; bark, *kara kawa*, 33; flowers (*hanazanshō*), 33; garnish, 72, 114; in gin, 126; leaves (*kinome*), 33
   *seri*, 34
   *shichimi tōgarashi*, 34–35
   *tade*, 34
   *toso* spices, 135
Spring equinox festival (*higan*), 102, 141, 143, 144

Squash-Filled Hand Pies, *Kesaina Mochi*, 13–15
Squid preserves (*ika no shiokara*), 6, 48
Staple (*shushoku*), 57; *Koshoku*, flour-based staples, 184; sweet potatoes as, 20
Steamed dishes (*mushimono*), 65–69
　Savory Custard Soup with Sea Bream, *Madai no Chawan Mushi*, 66–67
　Savory Custard with Wakame Seaweed, *Wakame no Chawan Mushi*, 68–69
　Steamed glutinous rice, 8
Stewed or braised dishes (*nimono*), 69–74
*Stollen*, 106
Strawberry jam industrially produced, xxi, 19
Strawberry Tomato Amazake Smoothie, 124
Sugar, artisanal (*awasanbon, sanbontō*), 97
Sukiyaki, xxi, 18
*Sunomono* (vinegared dishes), 48, 115, 136
Sushi, ix, xiv, xv, 8, 13, 20, 21, 32, 34, 137, 173–180
　how to eat, 180–182
　*izushi*, xiv, 174
　*kaiten zushi*, 180
　most popular food, 167, 168
　*narezushi*, 7, 174
　origin of, 174
　Smoked Salmon Scattered Sushi, *Smōku Sāmon no Chirashizushi*, 137–139
　Sushi Rice, *Sushi Meshi*, 175–177
　tea and, 116
　toppings, 45–48, 80, 180–181
　*toro*, 46, 179; origin of name, 179, 180
　traditional Edo-style, 174, 179, 180

Sweet Bean-Filled Cakes, *Dorayaki*, 147–149
Sweet chestnut paste (*kinton*), 136
Sweet potato, xxii, 20, 131, 142, 163; Glazed Sweet Potato, *Daigaku Imo*, 160–161; in *shōchū*, 124
Sweets, xx, 19, 25, 95–99, 102–106, 108–110, 141, 147, 158. *See also Kashi, okashi; Tenshin; Wagashi*
　Buddhist, 6, 96
　Chinese, 8, 9, 96
　dairy-based, 51
　fresh sweets (*nama gashi*), 99, 115, 158
　history of, 96–99
　*hoshi gashi*, dry sweets, 99, 102
　Japanese ingredients in Western-style sweets, 108, 110, 163
　*namban gashi* (Portuguese-style), 13, 16, 96, 104–105
　semi-fresh sweets (*hannama gashi*), 99
　sugar, introduction of, 97; *awasanbon*, 97
　tea ceremony and, 115
　*yōgashi* (Western-style), xxi, 19, 96, 105–108

*Tabehōdai*, 95, 166, 168
Tableware, xii, xix, 6, 9, 11, 55, 115, 118, 135; spoons, xix, 6, 7
*Tade*, water pepper, 34
*Takesha*, also *chikutō*, bamboo sugar, 97. *See also* Artisanal sugar
*Takikomi gohan*, 4, 27–29, 76
*Tako* (octopus), 7, 8, 44, 48, 147, 152
*Tama negi* (onion), 34
*Tamari*, xv, 6, 8, 10, 11, 32, 37
Tanba chestnut, 53
Taro, xviii, 3, 4, 7, 36, 58, 131, 136; Bamboo Shoot Taro in Shirazu Dressing, *Takenoko Imo no Shirazu Ae*, 41–42; Kyoto Braised Taro and Salt Cod, *Imobō no Taitan*, 195–196

# Index

Tea
  ceremony, xix, 10, 11; as art form (*sado*), 111
  *cha kaiseki*, xii, xix, 10, 11, 111; basic principles, 112–113; *ichijū sansai* (one soup, three side dishes) meal format, 11; order of courses, 113–115
  elite drink, xix, 9
  grades (*bancha*, *sencha*, *gyokurō*), 116
  green, 116
  *hōjicha*, 117
  *kōcha* (English, black tea), 116
  *kukicha*, 117
  *matcha*, 118
  *mugicha* (wheat tea), 117
  Oolong, 116
  plant, 116
  seeds brought from China, xviii
Teikei movement, 188, 189
Temple offerings, edible (*gūzen gashi*), 6, 98, 131. See also Shrine offerings
Tempura, ix, xv, xvi, xix, xx, 13, 38, 83
  dipping sauce, 60–61; giant radish in, 35; ginger in, 33
  as fast food, 13, 179
  original recipe, 142
  Vegetarian Tempura, *Shōjin Age*, 141–142
*Tenshin* (sweet snacks), 9, 97
*Tenzo Kyōkun*, Instructions for the Cook, 10
Third Basic Program for Shokuiku Promotion, 186, 197
Tofu, xv, 9, 10, 37
  *aburaage*, 27–28, 37, 57, 68, 197
  *atsuage*, 37, 57
  fritters, 104, 105, 141; Tofu Fritters, *Ganmodoki*, *Hiryōzu*, 144–145
  *kinugoshi dōfu*, 37, 41
  *kōya dōfu*, 37, 57, 188
  *momen dōfu*, 37, 140, 144, 196
  *yuba*, 37

*Tonkatsu*, xxi, 18, 19, 83, 85
*Toshikoshi soba*, 135
*Toso, otoso*, 135
Toyosu market (replaced Tsukiji), 44
Traditional
  breakfast, 77
  confectionery, *wagashi*, 95, 98–100, 102–104, 106, 108, 110, 158
  cuisine, styles of, xii
  food culture, revitalizing, 195, 197. See also Washoku
  meal, x, 57, 167, 185
*Tsubushi-an* (chunky-style sweet azuki paste), 100, 107
*Tsukudani*, xiii, 48, 69–71, 77; Chicken Tsukudani, *Toriniku no Tsukudani*, 94; Green Beans Tsukudani, *Ingen no Tsukudani*, 70–71; insect larvae as *tsukudani*, xiii
Tuna production in Spain, xv, 199

*Ubumeshi* ("birth rice"), 139
*Udon* (wheat noodles), 13, 26, 83, 84, 89
*Umeshū*, 53, 126
  Japanese Plum Liqueur, *Umeshū*, 127
  Sparkling Drink, 127
  *Umeshū* Warmer, 128
Undernourishment, 184
UNESCO list of world's intangible cultural heritage, xv, 186

Vegetables, 35–44. See also Konbu; Mushrooms; Soybean; Wild plants
  bitter melon *niga uri*, *gōya*, xiii, 38, 43–44, 70, 195
  burdock, xviii, 3, 27, 36, 58, 72–74, 85–88, 131, 136, 140, 144–145
  Chinese cabbage (*hakusai*), 35, 40, 58, 63–64, 89, 168–170, 171, 172, 192

devil's tongue jelly or root (*konnyaku*), xxiii, 11–12, 131, 197
*ebi imo* (shrimp-shaped taro), 36, 196
giant radish (*daikon*), 33, 35–36, 57, 58, 71–72, 81. *See also* Daikon oroshi
*hayato uri*, 38, 195
*mitsuba*, 34, 35, 40–41, 66, 67, 85, 86, 142, 153
*mōsō* bamboo, 36
*nappa* (green vegetables), 58, 63; *komatsuna, kyōna, mibuna, mizuna*, 35; *nata ingen* (sword bean), 38
*nukazuke* (rice bran pickles), 26, 36
*shishitōgarashi*, 38, 70
spinach (*horensō*), 35, 39, 40, 58, 61–63, 176; frozen, in food safety violation, 183
squash (*kabocha*), xiv, 13–15, 38, 42–43, 131, 132–133
taro, xviii, 3, 4, 7, 36, 41–42, 58, 131, 138, 195–196
water chestnuts (*kuwai*), xviii, 39, 54
water dropwort (*seri*), 34
Western, xxi, 18, 19
Vinegar, 8, 9, 26, 34; red (*sake*) vinegar, 174, 179; in *sunomono*, 115, 136; in sushi, 174, 175, 179
Virtual kitchens, 21, 22, 167

Wabi cha, 11, 111
*Wafū makaron, wakaron* (Japanese-style macaron), 163
Wagashi, 95–96, 98–99, 102–105, 107–110; Matcha Milk Jelly, 108–110; Ogura Ice Cream, 106–107
Wagyū, 49–50, 185
*Wan purēto* (one-plate) style, 76
Washoku, xv, xxiii, 185, 186

Western-style
biscuits and pastries, xxi, 19
confectionery (*yōgashi*), 105; Fujiya strawberry shortcake, 105
cookbooks, xxi, 18
cooking, foods (*yōshoku*), xii, 19
distillery, xxii, 19
food (*yōshoku*), xii, 19
fusion pastry, first (*anpan*), 19
restaurants, xx, xxi, 18, 168
sweets, xxi, 19, 105
Whale, xvii, 2, 20, 57, 191
bacon and sausages, 20
Braised Whale Meat, *Kujira no Kakuni*, 193
Grilled Whale Meat and Chinese Cabbage Salad in Mustard Dressing, *Kujira to Hakusai no Karashiae*, 192
jerky, 163
minke whale back fat in *zōni*, xiv
school lunches and, 20, 191
Whaling: commercial whaling, 191; communities, xiv, 191
Wheat. *See also* Noodles
bread, confectionery, 26
Buddhist temple ritual offerings, 98
buns with sweet red bean paste (*anpan*), xxi, 19
confectionery (Portuguese-style), xix, 13–15, 104–105
flour, xxii, 20
Hokkaido, xiii
pastries fried in sesame oil (*kakko, tensei*), 8
in soy sauce and miso, 8, 10, 26
sprouted wheat and rice syrup (*ame, mizu ame*), 97
tea (*mugi cha*), 116
Whisky, 19, 126
from rice, 126
Wild animals, xvii, 2, 3, 5, 7; ban on eating of, xix, 6; Fukushima radioactivity level and, 183, 190;

# Index

in *hishio*, 6, 8; Jōmon Burgers, *Jōmon Bāgā*, 4
Wild plants, xii, xiii, xiv, xvii, xviii, xxii, 1, 2, 3, 5, 8, 20, 27, 38, 57, 100; radioactivity and, 183, 190
Wine, from grapes, xxi, 19, 52, 125

*Yakimono*, 115, 136
*Yakisoba*, 83, 147, 149–150, 152
*Yakitori*, ix, 33, 38, 147, 152, 168; Grilled Skewered Chicken, *Yakitori*, 172–173
*Yama imo*, xviii, 3, 36, 58, 144
Yanakawa-Style Pork Cutlet in a Bowl, *Yanakawafū Katsudon*, 85–88
Year-end noodles (*toshikoshi soba*), 135

*Yōkan* (sweet bean jelly), 99, 102, 104; Green Soybean Jelly, *Zunda Yōkan*, 103–104
Yumepirika rice variety, xiii, 25
*Yuzu*, 34, 52, 102, 104, 110, 114, 115, 120, 163; globalization, xxiii, 52, 198; winter solstice bath and health, 132; *Yuzu* Avocado Yogurt Smoothie, 121; *Yuzu Shōchū* Cocktail, 125

*Zaru soba*, 36, 84–85
*Zensai* (appetizers), 58
*Zenzai* (sweet red bean soup), 147
*Zōni*, *ozōni*, xiv, 136, 157, 195
*Zunda*, 36, 37, 100, 101–102, 103, 107

## ABOUT THE AUTHOR

**Jeanne Jacob**, BA, MSM, MSc, is a researcher and writer on international food culture and food crops, specializing in Japanese food and food culture. Born and raised in the Philippines, and educated at the International School of Manila, her friendship with Japanese classmates stimulated her early interest in Japan. Following undergraduate studies in linguistics and Japanese studies in Tokyo as a Japanese Ministry of Education (Mombusho) scholar, she was a technical translator and scientific editor at a major Japanese petrochemical construction company in Tokyo, and at universities in the United States, Canada, Israel, UK, and Germany. After business school, she worked in business development and international marketing for the electronics industry and a horticulture research organization. A personal interest in neglected food crops led to further graduate studies and research in natural resource management and agroforestry at the University of Bonn, Germany. She is developing an olive grove in Valencia, Spain into an organic permaculture farm to produce extra premium organic virgin olive oil, subtropical fruits, and Japanese herbs and vegetables. Her publications include *The Essence of Japanese Cuisine: An Essay on Food and Culture*; *Food Culture in Japan*; *The World Cookbook for Students*; *The World Cookbook: The Greatest Recipes from around the Globe*; and *International Cookbook of Life-Cycle Celebrations*.